Fostering a Relational Pedagogy

T0394727

Fostering a Relational Pedagogy

Self-Study as Transformative Praxis

Edited by

Ellyn Lyle

BRILL

SENSE

LEIDEN | BOSTON

All chapters in this book have undergone peer review.

The Library of Congress Cataloging-in-Publication Data is available online at http://catalog.loc.gov

Typeface for the Latin, Greek, and Cyrillic scripts: "Brill". See and download: brill.com/brill-typeface.

ISBN 978-90-04-38871-0 (paperback)
ISBN 978-90-04-38885-7 (hardback)
ISBN 978-90-04-38886-4 (e-book)

Contents

Foreword: Searching Ruminations

Carl Leggo

1

Alan Doyle (2017), formerly the frontman of Great Big Sea, and now more simply Alan Doyle, extraordinary musician, writer, and Newfoundland ambassador, concluded his recent memoir with the resonant testimony: "I am a Canadian from Newfoundland" and "I am a Newfoundlander in Canada" (p. 240). Me, too! In chronicling his initiation into the music scene of Canada, Doyle notes that "for every pat on the back, there's ten boots in the arse" (p. 56). I like Doyle's rough, homespun humor, resonant with the voices of many Newfoundlanders, but now that I have read *Fostering a Relational Pedagogy: Self-Study Transformative Praxis*, edited by Ellyn Lyle, I am going to offer only pats on the back! In *Educated: A Memoir*, Tara Westover (2018) notes how "we are all more complicated than the roles we are assigned in stories" (p. 334). Last year I wrote an article about the death of my brother who was diagnosed with cancer in early summer and died before the end of August. One peer reviewer commented that the article was "sentimental and self-indulgent." My first thoughts were simple: How can you write about a brother's death without being sentimental? Why is writing about a brother's death self-indulgent? In *Poetry* David Constantine (2013) promotes "the power of particularities" (p. 14), and he reminds us that the personal is paradigmatic. He explains that "out of the interplay, or it may be the fighting, of the personal and the exemplary comes a unique self-identity" (p. 26). *Fostering a Relational Pedagogy* is a collection of nineteen lively narratives and ruminations on lived and living experiences, on the art and heart of learning to live well in words and the world. Constantine is eager to ask about "what it is like being human *now*; what the truth of our condition is, what responsibilities that truth entails" (p. 95). Because "most people most of the time live in a state much closer to total *un*consciousness than to any degree of consciousness even half ways adequate to our real situation" (p. 96), Constantine is keen "to quicken us to the condition of being human" (p. 99).

2

Twenty-six Synonyms

autobiography
blog

confession
drama
epic
Facebook
gag
history
Instagram
journal
knowledge
letter
memoir
narrative
obituary
photograph
question
record
story
tale
ululation
vita
wit
X-ray
yearbook
zodiac

3

In *Place, being, resonance: A critical ecohermeneutic approach to education* Michael W. Derby (2015) notes that "ambiguity is the world's condition" (p. 36), and he invites all teachers and learners to "think intensely and beautifully" (p. 55), especially because "attentiveness is an active, conscious and intentional discipline" (p. 38). Instead of experiencing school as "fundamentally prosaic" and "characterized by fragmentation" (p. 25), Derby recommends that we find ways to invite students to challenge and change the current experience of "mass distraction" (p. 27). Derby understands that education is "storytelling: where chatter, laughter, conversations, stories, songs and dreams are as continuous as breathing" (p. 14). In a like-minded way, bell hooks (2013) reminds us that "we must dare to love" (p. 194). For hooks, love is necessary for "ending domination" (p. 1) as we commit ourselves to "the development of critical thinking and critical consciousness" (p. 18) because "decolonizing the mind lays a groundwork for healthy self-actualization" (p. 23). The spirit of hooks is infused throughout the chapters in *Fostering a Relational Pedagogy*: "Diversity is the reality of all our lives. It is the very essence of our planetary survival. Organically, human survival as a species relies on the interdependence of all life" (p. 26).

4

Abecedarian
(*one among many*)

Aoki
Bochner
Cole
Denzin
Ellis
Freire
Gadamer
hooks
Irving
Jardine
Kohl
Lincoln
Makaiau
Noddings
Oliver
Pinar
Quinn
Richardson
Snyder
Tsong-kha-pa
Unwin
van Manen
Wang
Xavier
Yolen
Zeichner

5

Sensational Sentences
(*found poem*)

Ellyn Lyle

Sometimes we face uncomfortable renderings of self that leave us feeling fractured, our identities in crisis.

David W. Jardine

Language is something I and others find ourselves in, not something we find in us and at our beck and call.

Kathleen Pithouse-Morgan

I offer my professional learning story and my poetic research practice as an invitation to other teacher educators and teachers who wish to never fall asleep.

Jennifer Markides

I navigate both settler and Indigenous lineages, and bring my complex identity into the classroom, wondering how I will be received.

Timothy M. Sibbald

The transformation of my praxis began in earnest when some students arrived to class very upset that their patterns did not work.

Cher Hill & Laura Piersol

As with diffractive reading, when listening for subtle energies, the goal is not to ascertain *Truth* but rather to uncover one of the many potential existing realities within the human and more-than-human entanglement that create openings and allow for something new to occur.

Elizabeth Kenyon

The challenge of whiteness is that it is so present, persistent, and pervasive.

Sepideh Mahani

It is essential for educators to create a learning environment in which students are inspired to make sense of new ideas and form their own understandings by using their personal experiences.

Sherry Martens

We have been exposed to a variety of teachers, philosophies, and school experiences that have helped shape not only who we are as individuals, but also who we may be as teachers.

Chinwe H. Ikpeze

Self-study opened a way for me to interrogate, construct, and reconstruct my identity to align with the realities of my new cultural context, thereby transforming my practice.

Kate McCabe

Life, like the cherry blossom, is fleeting and precarious. Impermanent. Beautiful.

Deborah Graham

Undoubtedly, in teacher education programs, there must be room for stories.

Vy Dao & Yue Bian

These pedagogical strategies combined the traits of student autonomy and freedom of expression – which we had learned to value in the U.S. – and the attentiveness and caring that we had each acquired from our home country cultures.

Sara K. Sterner, Amanda C. Shopa, Lee C. Fisher, & Abby Boehm-Turner

Collective memory work draws on the knowledge and experiences of its members, and the line between the personal and the professional is erased.

Teresa Anne Fowler & Willow S. Allen

We do not have the answers, but we continue to ask the questions.

Aaron Zimmerman

Relationships in the teacher education classroom create moments of vulnerability and frustration as well as moments of affirmation and fulfilment.

Charity Becker

Through writing, I have come to view the world differently. I am more attentive to details, to colours, to patterns. I see beauty in brokenness and decay, in transitions and juxtapositions.

Diane Burt

I intend to develop a collaborative learning group or community of practice with colleagues who are also interested in exploring the potential of looking in and leading out.

Jodi Latremouille

Each time I return to a story, I am changed, too, and thus the work is never completely, neatly bound up and finished.

6

In her searing memoir *Gently to Nagasaki* Joy Kogawa (2016) writes about how she sees "the world as an open book embedded with stories. We hear them if we have ears to hear" (p. 149). May we hear the stories of *Fostering a Relational Pedagogy*!

7

Teasing Titles
(*found poem*)
Engaging Self-Study
(Lyle)

Too Late
(Jardine)

Became a Gift
(Pithouse-Morgan)

Impossible and Imperative
(Markides)

Transform
(Sibbald)

Becomings
(Hill & Piersol)

Negotiating
(Kenyon)

Culturally Relevant
(Mahani)

Seeing Ourselves
(Martens)

Relational Pedagogy
(Ikpeze)

Opening
(McCabe)

Navigating
(Graham)

Transitional Sel(ves)
(Dao & Bian)

Finding Layers
(Sterner, Shopa, Fisher, & Boehm-Turner)
Eavesdropping
(Fowler & Allen)

Illuminating
(Zimmerman)

Always
(Becker)

Looking
(Burt)

Cultivating Not-Knowing
(Latremouille)

References

Constantine, D. (2013). *Poetry.* Oxford: Oxford University Press.

Derby, M. W. (2015). *Place, being, resonance: A critical ecohermeneutic approach to education.* New York, NY: Peter Lang.

Doyle, A. (2017). *A Newfoundlander in Canada.* Toronto: Doubleday Canada.

hooks, b. (2013). *Writing beyond race: Living theory and practice.* New York, NY: Routledge.

Kogawa, J. (2016). *Gently to Nagasaki.* Half Moon Bay, CA: Caitlin Press.

Westover, T. (2018). *Educated: A memoir.* Toronto: HarperCollins Publishers.

Illustrations

Figures

Table

Notes on Contributors

Willow Samara Allen
holds a PhD in the Languages, Cultures and Literacies Program in the Faculty of Education at Simon Fraser University (2017). Her doctoral work investigates the lives of ten white Euro-Canadian women in transracial/cultural families with black African immigrant partners in the Canadian socio-political context. Her research interests are: diversity, migration and multiculturalism; multiracial families, antiracism education, Indigenous education, whiteness and white femininity, and feminisms.

Charity Becker
is an English language arts and creative writing teacher at Charlottetown Rural High School, a PhD in Educational Studies student at the University of Prince Edward Island, and a writer. She primarily writes poetry but also dabbles in short fiction and creative nonfiction and has a couple of novels in draft, and is an active participant in the local literary community. Charity lives in Charlottetown with her partner, Jason, and their dog, Romero.

Yue Bian
is a doctoral candidate in Curriculum, Instruction, and Teacher Education at Michigan State University. Her research is in teachers' identities, pedagogical practices in teacher education, English as it is taught as the Second Language, and new teacher development. Her research mainly draws on (auto) ethnography. Yue is an instructor of the *Immigrant Languages and Teacher Education* course in the teacher preparation program.

Abby Boehm-Turner
is a doctoral student in literacy education with a focus on critical literacy. She taught 7–12 English in a large public urban school district for 17 years and currently works with future English teachers, experiences which inspire her interest in revolutionary pedagogies and racial identity work in teacher education.

Diane Burt
is both an educator and educational leader. She has experience in the non-profit, for-profit, and public sectors, but has spent most of her career in post-secondary education. She is currently the Director of Applied Research and Innovation at NBCC and she teaches part-time in the MEd in Educational

Leadership program at Yorkville University. She holds a BA in English, BEd in Secondary Education, MEd in Adult Education, and EdD in Educational Leadership. Her areas of interest are teaching and learning, leadership, change management, and organizational development.

Vy Dao

is a doctoral candidate in Curriculum, Instruction, and Teacher Education at Michigan State University. Her research lies in the intersections between teacher educators' identities, multiculturalism, pedagogy of teacher education, and novice teacher educator development. Vy employs auto-inquiries (self-studies), critical qualitative ethnography, and comparative research (with focus on the nexus between East-West cultures) as her methodological lenses. Vy is an instructor of the *Human Diversity and Social Justice in Education* course in the teacher preparation program.

Lee C. Fisher

is a doctoral student in literacy education with a focus on language and culture. His interest in narrative as spaces for learning and identity negotiation is informed by his experience as a high school English and Theater teacher and now as a teacher educator.

Teresa Anne Fowler

is a doctoral candidate at the University of Calgary Werklund School of Education, Curriculum and Learning. Her study, *Taking a Bourdieusian turn on the "boy crisis": A depiction of disengagement* is a photovoice project looking at boys experiences in school. Her academic interests are in Masculinities Studies, Sociology of Education, Anti-Racist Education, and Critical Youth Studies.

Deborah Graham

is an Associate Professor at St. Francis Xavier University where she teaches courses in principles and practices of teaching and literacy in the B.Ed. program, and principles of learning and various other courses at the M.Ed. level. Prior to joining the faculty at St. F.X., she was a public school teacher and regional administrator for 32 years. Her research interests include teacher identity and the power of stories to reconceptualise practice.

Cher Hill

is Assistant Professor of Professional Practice and an in-service teacher educator in the Faculty of Education at Simon Fraser University. She supports teachers in studying their own practice as educators through the use of self-study and practitioner inquiry methodologies. Her current research utilizes new materialist theories to make visible the complex relations between human and more-than-human entities within educational contexts.

Chinwe Ikpeze
is an Assistant Professor of Literacy at St. John Fisher College, Rochester, NY. Her research interest includes literacy teaching and learning in K-12 and teacher education, urban education, teacher learning, self-study, and cultural studies. Chinwe has published in several referred journals. She is the author of the book, *Teaching across Cultures: Building Pedagogical Relationships in Diverse Contexts* (2015), and a co-editor of the book, *Reprocessing Race, Language and Ability: African Born Educators in Transnational America* (2013).

David W. Jardine
is a retired Professor of Education whose latest books include *In Praise of Radiant Beings: A Retrospective Path through Education, Buddhism and Ecology* (2016) and, with Jackie Seidel, *The Ecological Heart of Teaching: Radical Tales of Refuge and Renewal for Classrooms and Communities* (2016).

Elizabeth Kenyon
is an assistant professor of social studies education at Kent State University. She focuses on global citizenship education, teaching against racism, and citizenship education in her teaching and research. Currently she teaches early childhood and middle childhood social studies methods courses as well as graduate courses. When not working, she enjoys spending time with her two young children, being outside, and dancing in the kitchen.

Jodi Latremouille
is a doctoral candidate in Educational Research at the Werklund School of Education, University of Calgary, and a sessional instructor in the Master of Education program at Thompson Rivers University. Her research interests include hermeneutics, ecological and feminist pedagogy, social and environmental justice, life writing, and poetic inquiry.

Carl Leggo
is a poet and professor in the Faculty of Education at the University of British Columbia. He has published nineteen books of poetry and scholarship, including: *Sailing in a Concrete Boat* (2012); *Arts-based and Contemplative Practices in Research and Teaching: Honoring Presence* (2016, co-edited with Susan Walsh and Barbara Bickel); and *Poetic Inquiry: Enchantment of Place* (2018, co-edited with Pauline Sameshima, Alexandra Fidyk, and Kedrick James). He daily seeks to know the heart of living poetically.

Ellyn Lyle

has a longstanding background in innovative education practices, ranging from traditional classrooms to workplace and community partnerships, and technologically supported learning. In all these contexts, she has remained intensely interested in supporting the development of students and teachers as they contribute to socially equitable and sustainable programs. Ellyn holds a PhD in Education and has been teaching in university since 2010. She is currently Dean of the Faculty of Education. The use of critical methodologies shape explorations within the following areas: praxis; teaching and learning as lived experience; issues of identity; reflexive inquiry; narrative inquiry; and education for social justice.

Sepideh Mahani

is Associate Dean and Chair of Education Leadership in the Master of Education program at Yorkville University. She holds degrees in Education Leadership (PhD and MEd), Political Science (BA), and Teaching English to Foreign Learners (TEFL). Sepideh has over 15 years of experience teaching at tertiary and K-12 levels in both traditional and online settings, as well as being a consultant to various government agencies. Her research interests span a wide range of issues including education leadership and public policy, diversity in education, first-generation students, gender equality in education, and culturally relevant and responsive pedagogy.

Jennifer Markides

is an educator, graduate student, writer, photographer, curler, and proud member of the Métis Nation. She lives in High River, Alberta, with her husband, Derek, and their two sons. Her work explores the stories of youth living through the 2013 Alberta Floods. She values relationships built on care, reciprocity, honesty, and trust. Concerned with the experiences of vulnerable populations, she sees storytelling as an emancipatory act: giving audience; raising consciousness; and exposing themes. She is completing her PhD at the Werklund School of Education, University of Calgary.

Sherry Martens

was a teacher, curriculum specialist, and school-based administrator in Alberta for 29 years. She completed her PhD in Interpretive Studies in Education at the University of Calgary in 2012. Her dissertation, "Visual Displays in Elementary Schools: more than just a pretty picture," combined her interests in curriculum with visual methodology, historic school spaces, arts-based research, and hermeneutics. Currently, Sherry is the Associate Dean of Education/Assistant Professor at Ambrose University in Calgary, Alberta.

Kate McCabe

teaches preschool age children in the morning, elementary school-aged children in the afternoon, and adults in the evening. This weave is made more beautiful by in between forest and ocean wanderings. Kate studies at Simon Fraser University where she is a doctoral candidate. She continues to be inspired by mentors far and near who help her explore hermeneutics, that is, they help her develop the awareness of reading and being read back by the world.

Laura Piersol

is a Faculty Associate and an in-service teacher educator in the Faculty of Education at Simon Fraser University. She has worked as an ecological educator for 20 years throughout Canada and the U.S. She has helped to start two public elementary schools, the Maple Ridge Environmental School and NEST (Nature Education for Sustainable Todays and Tomorrows), where she has worked as an educational researcher.

Kathleen Pithouse-Morgan

is an associate professor in teacher development studies at the University of KwaZulu-Natal, South Africa. Her work has contributed to scholarship on professional learning through self-reflexive methodologies of self-study, narrative inquiry, and autoethnography. Recent book publications include *Polyvocal Professional Learning through Self-Study Research* (2015, with Samaras). Kathleen is convenor of the Self-Reflexive Methodologies Special Interest Group of the South African Educational Research Association, and chair-elect of the Self-Study of Teacher Education Practices Special Interest Group of the American Educational Research Association.

Amanda C. Shopa

is a doctoral student in culture and teaching with a focus on education for social justice. She taught elementary school for 13 years in the United States and South Korea, and she is interested in teacher education and teacher identity formation.

Timothy Sibbald

is an associate professor at the Schulich School of Education, Nipissing University. His research focus is classroom instructional issues, content development and delivery, as well as teacher development in mathematics education. He has also researched teacher movement within school boards and the tenure process in higher education. His interest in self-study began early in graduate school and has been supported by a series of publications and conference presentations since that time.

Sara K. Sterner

is a doctoral candidate in literacy education with a specialization in children's and adolescent literature and white teacher identity studies. Her scholarship stems from a passion for teaching, 14 years as an upper elementary school teacher, and her role as a social justice oriented teacher educator.

Aaron Zimmerman

is an Assistant Professor of Curriculum and Instruction in the College of Education at Texas Tech University. He earned his Ph.D. in Curriculum, Instruction, and Teacher Education from Michigan State University. He is interested in the study of teachers' classroom thinking as well as the beliefs and identities of teacher educators.

CHAPTER 1

Engaging Self-Study to Untangle Issues of Identity

Ellyn Lyle

I don't recall worrying much in my youth about who I was; I just assumed I knew until I realized I did not. The first time I grappled with issues of identity was in the early 90s. I was pursuing a Bachelor of Education degree and, growing increasingly disenchanted with its dehumanized studies, I began to question if I belonged in the education system at all. Because I had planned on being a teacher from a very young age, I could not imagine myself differently. This myopia fueled a crippling crisis of identity and, ill-equipped at the time to make sense of it, I just ran for my life. It was several years before I circled back to the source and site of my rupture. When I did, my re-entry point was through a Master of Education program that allowed me to theorize my previous experience. Using personal journal entries recorded during the years when I had broken up with schooling, I drew on writing as a way of knowing (see Richardson, 2000) and autoethnography (see Ellis & Bochner, 2000) to explore my disengagement with Education as a field of study and a profession. Because a primary concern of autoethnography involved how the personal and cultural informed each other, I conceptualized the field of Education as a micro culture and then proceeded to look inward at the *vulnerable self* in relation to its cultural context while also looking outward to consider the social and cultural aspects of my lived experience (Ellis & Bochner, 2000). At the time, autoethnography would support me within one of three possible approaches: *interpretive autoethnography* invited scholars to consider the more nuanced understandings of engagement with human participants; *analytic autoethnography* focused heavily on coding and reporting by adhering to traditionally rigid academic conventions; and *critical autoethnography* sought to remedy social inequity. While none of these was a perfect fit, I settled on critical autoethnography because I had neither participants apart from myself, nor the appetite to be further hamstrung by rigid convention. Looking back, either evocative ethnography or self-study methodology would have been more appropriate frameworks but neither had, at that point, been fulsomely developed. Some 25 years later, when I detected the disquieting rumblings of personal/professional incongruence once more, I embraced self-study to interrogate issues of identity.

Self-Study Methodology

It has long been established that teaching and learning are autobiographical endeavours (Bochner, 1997; Bochner & Ellis, 2016; Feldman, 2005), so it follows that self-study is central to sound practice. Despite historic criticisms, self-study is neither narcissistic nor egocentric. Being critically conscious of the embodied wholeness we bring to the classroom benefits both students and teachers (James, 2007; Palmer, 2017). As a framework, self-study allows researchers to use their experiences to problematize *self-in-practice* with the aim of personal and professional growth (Feldman, 2002, 2005; Samaras & Freese, 2009). Said another way, self-study focuses on the development of both the personal and professional. In so doing, it makes transparent personal processes of inquiry by offering them up for public critique (Samaras & Freese, 2009). This type of public inquiry of the personal happens in at least two ways: first, through the inclusion of *critical friends*, or trusted Others who can provide alternative perspectives on our closely held discourses (LaBoskey, 2004; Loughran, 2007); and, second, through making our research publicly available so that others might learn from our inquiries. Self-study, then, requires openness to vulnerability as we attempt to reconceptualize ourselves as teachers. Approaching inquiry from this perspective supports the development of critical reflexivity where impressions of self can be understood in terms of our social contexts (Hickey, 2016). Aware that self-study researchers are sometimes criticized for lack of rigour, I turned to reflexive inquiry to pre-emptively address this concern.

Reflexive Inquiry

While self-study historically grew out of practitioner research and reflective inquiry, it seems to me that the inclusion of a reflexive stance is helpful. Like self-study, reflexive inquiry (RI) encourages critical introspection of self in relationship with social context (Creswell, 2006; Hara, 2010; Hickey, 2016; Langer, 2016; Roebuck, 2007; Zinn, Adam, Kurup, & du Plessis, 2016). It also has as its aim heightened consciousness. Apart from these similar touch points, though, RI is unique in demanding that we take responsibility for our choices and actions within a relational system (Oliver, 2004). In making this accountability central, reflexive inquiry interrogates agency while probing philosophical notions about the nature of knowledge. By its very design, then, RI disrupts normalized assumptions about how I come to knowledge and presents essential questions about my capacity to account for my ever-evolving understanding of lived experience (Cunliffe, 2003; Lyle, 2017a). Increasingly, reflexive inquiry is thus positioned as the responsibility of every conscious researcher (Doyle, 2013) and is often employed as a complementary methodology with the explicit aim of augmenting critical consciousness and research rigour. As such, it nicely supports self-study to examine crises of identity.

Self-Study in Crises of Identity

The first time I faced an identity crisis, I was consumed by implications for my budding career. Having sought direction in research, I found a community of scholars that continue to exemplify congruent ways of teaching, learning, and being. The second time I grappled with issues of identity I was nearly 40 and, apart from drawing on personal journal entries, I approached it very differently. Having long since been engaged in daily dialogue with the scholarship, I embraced my familiarity with it to interrogate the disequilibrium within myself. As I have suggested in previous research, "examining personal identity as it affects professional practice is messy and vulnerable work" (Lyle, 2016, p. 34). James (2007) reminds me, though, that interrogating the space between what I claim to value and how I act out those values can expose important opportunities for growth. This became evident when I married a soldier.

As a critical qualitative scholar, I thought I was living my values: I care about the students, the subject areas I teach, the process, and their multiple points of intersection; I intentionally but compassionately work to expose assumptions (mine and others) while nurturing multiple perspectives; and I am conscious of power and encourage its interrogation as we move in solidarity toward more just practices. When I married into the Canadian Armed Forces (CAF), it didn't occur to me that this new association would lead me to question my integrity as teacher, scholar, even wife. Propelled by the euphoric naïveté reserved for new love, I simply assumed we would move through our conjoined future, if not always with ease, with fortitude.

7 March 2014
I don't know how this has all gone so horribly wrong. When he was home from work last weekend, we giggled and laughed our way through planning our elopement: we chose the location, set the date, and conspiratorially kissed each other goodbye until we could meet again this weekend to finalize our plans. When he got home Friday, though, he was nervous and preoccupied. He paced around the living room for a few minutes before he turned to me and said he was being deployed. How the hell is he being deployed? He swore up and down when we talked about getting married that, barring global

catastrophe, there'd be no surprise tours. I cannot do this. I am not wired to endure daily the fear of the phone call.

Facing a year apart when we'd not yet made it down the aisle had a sobering affect. I began to unravel in the wake of discovering our future was not our own to determine. As he worked toward readiness, I dug in my heels and clung to the hope that he'd find a way to stay. The selfishness of my hopes was not lost on me. How could I possibly identify as a critical scholar if I was unable to support my husband's service as he works to improve conditions for others? As I wrestled with this question, I began to fear that I was a hypocrite.

5 April 2014
Just a month ago I discovered that our future is determined by people wholly unconnected to me. I fought this point until I realised I could not win without losing him. In that realisation, it occurred to me that I also faced losing a piece of myself – the moral authority to teach, research, and advocate for social equity. Wanting to lose neither him nor myself, I am newly determined to live my values more consistently. Even in this single-mindedness, though, I have no idea how to balance my fears and disappointments with the necessity of supporting his service.

Wanting to prove that I was deserving of both my partner and my profession, I set out to examine self closely in terms of how I live (or fail to live) my ideals. From reading hooks (2010), I knew that thinking critically about personal perceptions, assumptions, and actions was central to being a good educator. I assumed it would also support being a good partner. In the few months we had left before his deployment, we spent as much time together as possible. We anticipated voids and tried to fill them pre-emptively. We laughed, cried, dreamed, lamented and, when there was neither time nor choice left, we said goodbye.

7 August 2014
We've spent the last month getting ready for the next year. I dropped him at the airport today knowing that the loss and fear I feel right now is nothing compared with what's ahead. I don't know how to do this –

As we tried to settle into our new together-alone contexts, we worked to find the balance between leaning and supporting. On any given day that balance would shift depending on events half a world away.

25 September 2014

He's been gone almost two months now, and I feel as though I'm treading water and catching bricks. I go through the motions everyday but fear and anxiety have taken up residence where joy used to live. I am never without my phone for fear of missing a call. I can't sleep, and food is unpalatable. In my desperation to be present for him, self-care has become impossible. Somewhere in a more reasoned part of myself, I recognise that this is unsustainable. Worse, I worry that I'm a burden to him. I have no idea what he's going through. How am I to support him if I don't know his reality?

I hoped that the ebb and flow of leaning and supporting would move us closer together but it seemed to have the opposite effect. As the days turned into weeks, our conversations sought safety in the superfluous and we left unacknowledged that widening gap between us. Then, entering the fourth month of his tour, I found the lump.

5 October 2014

I awoke this morning before sunrise and, under the now familiar weight of anxiety, I pressed my hands into my sternum so I could draw a deeper breath. I felt the hot flush of panic in the same instant that I felt the lump. I pulled my hands away as though scalded and then checked again. Still there. As I tried to quiet the mounting panic, I began to collect reasons this was surely nothing: I am in my thirties; there is no family history of breast cancer; I have an active, healthy lifestyle ... I am stressed and underweight and maybe it was a rib ... check again. Dammit – okay. I need to see my physician and find out what's going on.

In the wake of discovering what I feared was a tumour, my focus shifted once again. The ground that I fought myself to gain was slipping away as I acknowledged the unvarnished reality of how I was feeling.

1 November 2014

I continue to schedule tests around work and my son's activities so as to avoid unnecessary worry for him. I try to limit discussions related to my health when I talk to my husband because he doesn't need the additional stress, but sometimes I'm not sure if I'm more scared or angry.

Weeks passed in the blur of teaching, protecting, testing, and worrying. Then, on 24 November, on my way to campus, I was called to my physician's office and informed that I had invasive ductal carcinoma. Breast Cancer. I left her clinic in a daze and headed to the university to teach. I sent a message to my husband and asked him to call me when he got a chance. When we were able to connect, I told him that I'd been diagnosed with breast cancer and that my margins were not clear so I needed to see the surgeon to determine how to proceed. It was obvious in his incredulity that this was not the news he expected. After the initial shock passed, he provided me with a fax number where I was to send a copy of my diagnosis. He was granted compassionate leave the next day.

> 26 November 2014
> *I picked him up from the airport today. I don't know what I expected but it was not hostility. I appreciate that he's been thrust into family trauma fresh from prolonged exposure to a trauma I can't even begin to imagine, but he's not the one facing a crisis right now. I am.*

During the next year, we grew increasingly frustrated with each other as we continued to pass judgment more than seek understanding. Each of us perceived the other in ways in which we, ourselves, could not identify. I came to understand these competing perceptions as counter-narratives and, curious how they impacted identity, I returned to scholarship once.

Identity as a Narrative Construct

Rolling (2010) and Sachs (2005) claim that narrative is integral to the construction of identity because it allows us to story who we are, what has informed our development, and what is important to us. Kraehe (2015) reminds me that the narrative construction of identity is often the result of interactions with others. Understood this way, identity is both personal and a situated activity (Hofmann-Kipp, 2008; Lyle, 2016). It follows that identity emerges from critical personal narratives as well as counter narratives held by others. Drawing from Denzin (2017), I came to understand counter-narratives as conceptualizations that disturb closely held discourse; when interrogated openly, these become a valuable source of reflexive self-consciousness.

Like Stets and Burke (2012), I understand this "reflexivity as central to the process of negotiating selfhood, and selfhood as central to identity" (Lyle, 2017b, p. 2). Considered in the context of social constructions we negotiate identity based on our interactions with others, so it follows that we must be conscious of both self and self-in-relation. This cognizance suggests we are continually renegotiating self-understanding by interpreting our inter/actions.

As an outflow of this process, identity becomes a fleeting, transitory phenomena created and re-created in response to experience (Jones, 2013). Epson (2013) reminds me that this process of re/negotiation positions identity as

> an expression of the meaning that each of us attaches to ourselves and a reflection of the meaning that others attach to us. We are therefore engaged in an ongoing struggle to create a coherent sense of self within this shifting context as we construct, repair, maintain, and review our identities. (p. 231)

Thoughts as We Part Company

Returning to the context in which I came to question my moral authority as teacher, even my integrity as wife and scholar, I have no tidy resolution to offer. Sometimes we face uncomfortable renderings of self that leave us feeling fractured, our identities in crisis. In these times of disequilibrium, whether the battlefields are literal or metaphorical, we must face disquieting forces before we can reclaim peace. Now, three years after chemotherapy and radiation, three and a half years since my soldier/husband came home, I have stopped waiting for our lost idealism to return and accepted what Aoki (1993) calls *our continual emergence*. Learning to recognize our identities as composites of personal and relational knowledge helps me to embrace our complexity. Although I still struggle to make sense of the hypocrisy I uncovered within myself, it helps me understand the soldier who struggled at home. I am more forgiving of us both as I work to understand the spirit's limitations.

References

Aoki, T. (1993). Legitimating lived curriculum: Towards a curricular landscape of multiplicity. *Journal of Curriculum and Supervision, 8*(3), 255–268.

Bochner, A. (1997). It's about time: Narrative and the divided self. *Qualitative Inquiry, 3*(4), 418–438.

Bochner, A., & Ellis, C. (2016). *Evocative autoethnography: Writing life and telling stories.* New York, NY: Taylor & Francis.

Creswell, J. W. (2006). *Qualitative inquiry and research design: Choosing among five approaches.* Thousand Oaks, CA: Sage Publications.

Cunliffe, A. L. (2003). Reflexive inquiry in organizational research: Questions and possibilities. *Human Relations, 56*(8), 983–1003.

Denzin, N. K. (2017). Critical qualitative inquiry. *Qualitative Inquiry, 23*(1), 8–16.

Ellis, C., Adams, T. E., & Bochner, A. P. (2010). Autoethnography: An overview. *Forum Qualitative Sozialforschung/Forum: Qualitative Social Research, 12*(1), Article 10. Retrieved from http://nbn-resolving.de/urn:nbn:de:0114-fqs1101108

Ellis, C., & Bochner, A. (2000). Autoethnography, personal narrative, reflexivity: Researcher as subject. In N. Denzin & Y. Lincoln (Eds.), *The handbook of qualitative research* (2nd ed., pp. 733–768). Thousand Oaks, CA: Sage Publications.

Epson, L. (2013). My affair with the "other": Identity journeys across the research–practice divide. *Journal of Management Inquiry, 22*(2), 229–248.

Feldman, A. (2002). Bec(o/a)ming a teacher educator. In C. Kosnik, A. R. Freese, & A. P. Samaras (Eds.), *Making a difference in teacher education through self-study: Proceedings of the fourth international conference on self-study of teacher education practices, Herstmonceux Castle, East Sussex, England* (Vol. 1, pp. 66–70). Toronto, OISE, University of Toronto.

Feldman, P. (2005). Self-study dilemmas and delights of professional learning: A narrative perspective. *English Teaching, 4*(2), 46.

Hara, B. (2010). *Reflexive pedagogy.* Retrieved from http://www.chronicle.com/blogs/profhacker/reflexive-pedagogy/22939

Hickey, A. (2016). The critical aesthetic: Living a critical ethnography of the everyday. In S. Steinberg & G. Cannella (Eds.), *Critical qualitative research reader* (pp. 166–181). New York, NY: Peter Lang.

Hoffman-Kipp, P. (2008). Actualizing democracy: The praxis of teacher identity construction. *Teacher Education Quarterly, 35*(5), 151–164.

hooks, b. (2010). *Teaching critical thinking: Practical wisdom.* New York, NY: Routledge.

James, J. (2007). Autobiographical inquiry, teacher education, and (the possibility of) social justice. *Journal of Curriculum and Pedagogy, 4*(2), 161–175.

Jones, M. (2013). Traversing no man's land in search of an (other) identity: An autoethnographic account. *Journal of Contemporary Ethnography, 42*(6), 745–768.

Kraehe, A. (2015). Sounds of silence: Race and emergent counter-narratives of art teacher identity. *Studies in Art Education, 56*(3), 199–213.

LaBoskey, V. K. (2004). The methodology of self-study and its theoretical underpinnings. In J. J. Loughran, M. L. Hamilton, V. K. LaBoskey, & T. Russell (Eds.), *International handbook of self-study of teaching and teacher education practices* (Vol. 1, pp. 817–869). Dordrecht: Kluwer.

Langer, P. (2016). The research vignette: Reflexive writing as interpretative representation of qualitative inquiry—a methodological proposition. *Qualitative Inquiry, 22*(9), 735–744.

Loughran, J. (2007). Researching teacher education practices: Responding to the challenges, demands, and expectations of self-study. *Journal of Teacher Education, 58*(1), 12–20.

Lyle, E. (2016). The role of counter narratives in the re/negotiation of identity: A curricular perspective. *Journal of the Canadian Association for Curriculum Studies, 14*(2), 33–42.

Lyle, E. (2017a). *Of books, barns, and boardrooms: Exploring praxis through reflexive inquiry* (2nd ed.). Rotterdam, The Netherlands: Sense Publishers.

Lyle, E. (2017b). Autoethnographic approaches to an identity-conscious curriculum. In E. Lyle (Ed.), *At the intersection of selves and subject: Exploring the curricular landscape of identity* (pp. 1–8). Rotterdam, The Netherlands: Sense Publishers.

Oliver, C. (2004). Reflexive inquiry and the strange loop tool. *Journal of Systemic Consultation and Management, 15*(2), 127–140.

Palmer, P. (2017). *The courage to teach.* San Francisco, CA: Jossey-Bass.

Richardson, L. (2000). *Writing: A method of inquiry.* In N. K. Denzin & Y. S. Lincoln (Eds.), *Handbook of qualitative research* (2nd ed., pp. 923–948). Thousand Oaks, CA: Sage Publications.

Roebuck, J. (2007). Reflexive practice: To enhance student learning. *Journal of Learning Design, 2*(1), 77–91.

Rolling, J. (2010). Art education at the turn of the tide: The utility of narrative in curriculum-making and education research. *Art Education, 63*(3), 6–12.

Sachs, J. (2005). Teacher education and the development of professional identity: Learning to be a teacher. In P. Denicolo & M. Kompf (Eds.), *Connecting policy and practice: Challenges for teaching and learning in schools and universities* (pp. 5–21). Oxford: Routledge.

Samaras, A., & Freese, A. (2009). Looking back and looking forward: An historical overview of the self-study school. In C. Lassonde, S. Galman, & C. Kosnik (Eds.), *Self-study research methodologies for teacher educators* (pp. 20–36). Rotterdam, The Netherlands: Sense Publishers.

Stets, J. E., & Burke, P. J. (2012). A sociological approach to self and identity. M. Leary & J. P. Tingley (Eds.), *Handbook of self and identity.* New York, NY: Guilford Press.

Zinn, D., Adam, K., Kurup, R., & du Plessis, A. (2016). Returning to the source: Reflexivity and transformation in understanding a humanising pedagogy. *Educational Research for Social Change, 5*(1), 70–93.

CHAPTER 2

"We Arrive, as It Were, Too Late"

David W. Jardine

Preamble

Understanding is not ... hold[ing] [my]self back and refus[ing] to take a stand with respect to the claim made on [me]. The ... self-possession necessary for one to withhold oneself in this way is not given here. Someone who understands is always already drawn into an event. When we understand a text, what is meaningful in it captivates us, just as the beautiful captivates us. It has asserted itself and captivated us before we can come to ourselves and be in a position to test the claim ... that it makes. In understanding we are drawn into an event ... and arrive, as it were, too late, if we want to know what we are supposed to [now] believe. (Gadamer, 1989, p. 490)

Much of my work has been centered on hermeneutics as a theory and practice of human and more-than-human encounter. I have been involved in not only exploring how hermeneutics can provide a research methodology for exploring classroom practice, but also how *classroom practice itself* can be understood as a hermeneutic, interpretive act of encounter and mutual formation.

What follows is an exploration of features of this coincidence. In particular, I am interested in Gadamer's characterization of understanding and questioning as "more a passion than an action," and how, therefore, understanding ourselves and studying our shared and contested circumstances – including the great topics entrusted to teachers and students in schools – sometimes "presses itself on us" (Gadamer, 1989, p. 366), captivates us, and compels us into studiousness before we are able to have a hand in gathering what we may from such often-unexpected moments. This is as simple and as mysterious as being charmed by an idea, a comment, an image, an event, and being drawn towards it and outside of our zones of real or presumed comfort. Something *happens*. Something *befalls* me. "We can no longer avoid it and persist in our accustomed opinion" (p. 366) – a telling statement about teaching and learning as well as the conduct of interpretive inquiry *into* teaching and learning.

Identity Theft

"Hermes is cunning … a trickster, a robber. So, it is not surprising that he is also the patron of interpreters" (Kermode, 1979, p. 1). Disturbing the peace, the pacification, the sleepy assurances of familiarity and self-possession, this little god of gateways, borders, and boundaries is bent on their opening, their passages, crossing and double-crossing.

Here, now, right at the cusp of where we attempt to hold fast, Hermes pulls a fast one, fleet. Right there comes the trick. There is a hint here of how self-study, at its most effective and telling, does not exactly issue from my self.

Hermes. Thief. In the midst of so much contemporary talk of such matters, most of all, *identity theft*:

> When Hermes is at work … one feels that one's story has been stolen and turned into something else. The [person] tells his tale, and suddenly its plot has been transformed. He resists, as one would try to stop a thief … "this is not what I meant at all, not at all." But too late. Hermes has caught the tale, turned its feet around, made black into white, given it wings. (Hillman, 1983, p. 31)

I know full well as an author that others have been able to read what I've written better than I am able. Others can sometimes find clues and traces to which I am blind no matter how much I study myself and my own intimate work. I can even attest that sometimes what I *intended* is clearer to others than to myself. The reason for this is simple, hermeneutically understood. Language is something I and others find ourselves *in*, not something we find *in us* and at our beck and call. It is not an internal possession. It is an eco-poetic habitat in which we live – contested, multivocal, obscured and obscuring, clarifying, articulate, foolish. We live in its implicated folds, often contradictory histories, allusions, precedents, images, prejudices, presumptions, bloodlines, allusions, mixed histories, relations, agencies. We *find ourselves* in it, such that self-study is not exactly self studying the self. Not exactly. We often can get *found out*.

This Solace

"Understanding begins when something addresses us" (Gadamer, 1989, p. 299) and if my pretense to self-study doesn't allow me to be addressed by things beyond my self – by the topics I am exploring, the texts I am reading, the voices I hear – self-study risks having the self caught in and by its own confines.

This is the great risk that this work involves: "Understanding is an adventure and, like any adventure, it always involves some risk" (Gadamer, 1983, p. 141). Understanding begins when something addresses me, but it only begins there. What also begins there is the sometimes-arduous trek of exploring *what it is that is being asked of me* in this moment of finding my ears pricked. I have to risk venturing towards precisely those moments that interrupt my self-narration, my categories or themes, my expectations, my self-reflections:

> It is truly a tremendous task which faces every human moment. His prejudices – his being saturated with wishes, drives, hopes, and interests – must be held under control to such an extent that the other is not made invisible or does not remain invisible. It is not easy to acknowledge that the other could be right, that oneself and one's own interests could be wrong. This solace ... is in truth a basic constant that shapes our whole human experience. We must learn to respect others and otherness. This implies that we must learn that we could be wrong. We must learn how to lose the game – that begins with the age of two or may be even earlier. He, who has not learned this early, will not be able to completely handle the greater tasks of adult life. (Gadamer, 1992, p. 233)

"Yes, It Could Turn out Like This"

Every experience worthy of the name thwarts an expectation. (Gadamer, 1989, p. 356)

To begin a story, someone in some way must break a certain silence. (Wiebe & Johnson, 1999, p. 3)

Something awakens our interest. That is what comes first. (Gadamer, 2001, p. 50)

Thus, the agency of self-study is outside the self. "It would not deserve the interest [I] take in it if it did not have something to teach [me] that [I] could not know by [my]sel[f]" (Gadamer, 1989, p. xxxv). Thus, the locale of inquiring into myself is outside my own self.

In my former life before retirement, I would often announce to a large class of pre-service teachers (a couple of hundred in one of those classrooms where you are, so to speak, teaching uphill) – that, first and foremost, you stand up in front of your students as an example of how life just might turn out. I would then gesture towards myself and say, "Yes, it could turn out like this."

The inevitable ensuing laughter betrayed more than I'll ever know and, I suppose, helped blunt some of the sting that can come with realizing that, despite any and all concerted confidence and effort at identifying myself and my teacher identity, I'm also, always and already (too late!) out in the open, spotted, considered, ignored, presumed upon – sometimes benignly, sometimes otherwise. Like any fabric of the world (Latin, *textus*) I am readable "beyond [my] wanting and doing" (Gadamer, 1989, p. xxviii; see Jardine, 2006). I am legible and illegible in ways I cannot imagine all by myself. I must wait, sometimes, for the yellow-eyed side-glances of Ravens.

Whatever story I might tell about myself and my experiences, including this one, and whatever comfort I find within the confines of these layers of my self-narration and self-identification, those very same students will read back to me my own most heartfelt gestures in ways that just might be different than I meant, more than I hoped, or far less. More telling is the fact that I may be required to recognize that their readings of what I have said or done are not just sometimes quite *different than my own*. They are, sometimes, *better than my own*. However studious my study of myself might be, their readings may be more insightful, more hale and healing, more honest, more timely, less self-deceptive, more helpful and sound – one whose truth I might have to concede. This is no different than the arcs of smoke this past summer from the British Columbia interior, and the wild-eyed storms setting records to the south, reading back to me my own very intimate self in ways that are sometimes more intimate than I can bear. I become the object of *their* parsing, *known* as much as knower.

In such encounters, I sometimes get hurt or humiliated and retreat to an afflicted locale of self-possessive self-protection, ashamed of the complicities now outed. Sometimes, however, I am *relieved of myself* and the burdensome constrictions of my own self-possession:

> I don't want to "tell my story." I want to be relieved of it by going to a place (ecos-, topos-/topica-) where I can meet others who can read me back to myself from beyond my own failings and limits and delusions, beyond the story I've presumed. (Jardine, 2016a, p. xvi)

This is what it is like *to have an identity*, teacher or otherwise. It is precisely this susceptibility that makes this odd thing, *identity*, a living matter. As teachers, we deliberately and repeatedly seek out these interstices of mutual formation, not only with the students we encounter each year, but also with the topics entrusted to us in schools (or in research) and with the ancestral voices that lend us their consideration. These topics, too, must lend themselves to the upcoming encounters, the upcoming queries and questions. All over again, they must show themselves to be worthy of attention and devotion, and students and teachers alike must likewise demonstrate their "readiness ... to be 'all ears' [*ganz Ohr zu sein*]" (Gadamer, 2007, p. 189; see Jardine, in press).

This gives self-study a truly pedagogical heart. This strange pleasure spot is exactly the job of teaching: each September, to place our fragile identity, again and again and again, out in the open fray of arrival, out into "a sort of opening, play, indetermination, signifying hospitality for what is to come [*avenir*]" (Derrida, with Ferraris, 2001, p. 31). And when I consider those right-angled triangles inscribed in circles in a Grade 4 mathematics classroom, or commiserate with a colleague over a student's woes, it is as if my self is not just studying but *being studied*. I am caught in *its* measure as much as it is in mine – spotted, tested, taught.

These encounters have archaic shapes. The young meet the old. The new meets the established. The familiar meets the strange. The case meets the rule. The story meets the moment of its tell. The elder tells the tale to *this* child just *thus* (the child thus summoning the rightness of the tell). The dead meet the living – not meant occultly, because, see, there? Derrida (1930–2004) and Gadamer (1900–2002) have just now arrived, and Pythagoras as well.

And all this is true far beyond the human orbit of encounter. That Cross Fox that trotted by a few days ago, or that Coyote pair that set the dogs howling, or the Chinook wind that took two trees a month back, can also serve to startle, to interrupt my self-absorption and somnolence.

"*The true locus of hermeneutics is this in-between*" (Gadamer, 1989, p. 295), this *event* of encounter. My own self-enclosed self-narrations must, shall we say, give way in order for my own narration to become, again, a living one, alert, aware, un-self-possessed.

"It Always Involves an Escape"

My story of my living is consistently and persistently read back to me in ways different than I might have been able to read it by myself and from my own point of view. And sticking to my story just might involve layers and layers of pathology – fears of having my voiced robbed and violated and silenced – sticking to my own story as a defense against such matters, self-delusion, self-denial, self-aggrandizement, defensiveness. My own inner and outer narrative is often the confine of my safety, my self-definition. This is why hermeneutics relies upon a phenomenological source in lived-experience, but then enters considerations of such reliance with an eye to the possibility of false consciousness. The face-value of experience can sometimes be just a façade, no matter how heartfelt and immediate.

It is thus the *interruption of narrative continuity*, the *event* of the arrival of insight beyond what my self-narration and self-studying might have heretofore allowed, that is the centerpiece of hermeneutic work:

> Insight is more than the knowledge of this or that situation. It always involves an escape from something [Latin *fugere*] that had deceived us and held us captive. Thus, insight always involves an element of self-knowledge and constitutes a necessary side of what we called experience in the proper sense. Insight is something we come to. It too is ultimately part of the vocation of man – i.e., to be discerning and insightful. (Gadamer, 1989, p. 356)

The droning repetition of the same old story is not remedied by counter posing it with another story doomed to the very same droning fate. The silencing of voices is not overcome by simply having a turn at being the one who can now speak without interruption. It is remedied, instead, by seeking out, in each other's presence, insight and escape itself, where the refuge is found in remaining fugitive. That is to say, "You have your story, I have mine" is potentially the site of great ecological disaster, ripe with the odor of the very sort of "possessive individualism" (MacPherson, 2010) that the burgeoning voices of "others" outside the Eurocentric orbit are wont to interrupt. It is not just that *they* have *their* story, *too*:

> Our specific human identities constructed through tribe, race or religion can never be ultimately secured, not only because they are always open onto the horizons of others but also, more important, because they are always already everywhere inhabited by the Other in the context of the fully real. (Smith, 2006b, p. xxiv)

Remaining fugitive in each other's presence: *that* is where self-study can live a wild life, between – porous, always-already-implicated, finite, vulnerable, susceptible, dependently co-arising, ecologically re.

"Hermeneutic Experience"

The whole value of hermeneutical experience ... seemed to consist in the fact that here we are not simply filing things in pigeonholes but that what we

encounter ... says something to us. Understanding ... is a genuine experience.
(Gadamer, 1989, p. 489)

In *Truth and Method*, a great deal of attention is given to the difference between the two German terms for "experience": *Erlebnis* (Gadamer, 1989, pp. 60–80) and *Erfahrung* (pp. 346–361). *Erlebnis* is etymologically linked to the intimacies of one's personal and inner life ([from] *Leben*, to live). *Erfahrung* contains the roots both of a journey (*Fahren*) and of ancestry (*Vorfahren*, those who have journeyed [*Fahren*] before [*Vor-*]). [W]e are drawn out of ourselves, our constructions, our methods, [our established narratives] and invited into something of a worldly sojourn, an experience (*Erfahrung*) that does not issue from myself. (Jardine, 2012, p. 107)

Hermeneutic experience describes moments of the encounter of my own self-narrative with that which calls it out, calls it to account, calls it to become less finalized and fixated and self-maintaining, more generous and pliable and true to the dependent co-arising nature of being hun.

A Proposal on What Self-Study Is for

Like Dogen, the Zen master, said, "We study the self to forget the self. And when you forget the self, you become one with all things." (Snyder, 1980, p. 65)

Self-study can lead to coming to understand "the self in its original countenance" (Nishitani, 1982, p. 91), as delicately and multiply interwoven in this earthly fabric in which we find woven all things. "One sees one's own self in all things, in living things, in hills and rivers, towns and hamlets, tiles and stones, and loves these things 'as oneself'" (Nishitani, 1982, pp. 280–281).

Imagine. Eyeing those Ravens eyeing me as self-study, *providing* I let my self come to in such a moment of recognition – of them, of me, of the arriving spring sun, of our mutually held, conspiratorial breathing. One way or another, we form ourselves – we lose and re-gain ourselves, we forget ourselves or worry over ourselves in concert with the subterranean, often hidden or occluded, roils of the world. These under-roils can be palpably sensed; their workings can be felt and suffered. "The self that we are does not possess itself; one could say that it happens (Gadamer, 1977, p. 55). Without the endless effort to explore these underpinnings and to maintain alertness, we miss a deep experience of who we *are* – dependently co-arising, earthly beings whose selves are mixed in air and water and fire and earth, the mix of image and idea, of ancestry and "the fact of natality" (Arendt, 1989, p. 196), of arising and perishing, of living and dying.

Self-study is not mandatory. And study clearly poses its own suffering – facing the sore fleshy mortality of our living *on purpose* and *repeatedly* – that one must become willing, hopefully more *able*, to bear. I'm reminded, here, first, of a statement by David G. Smith, one of my great teachers:

> The aim of interpretation, it could be said, is not just another interpretation but human freedom, which finds its light, identity and dignity in those few brief moments when one's lived burdens can be shown to have their source in too limited a view of things. (Smith, 1999, p. 29)

And then, from the Gelug tradition of Tibetan Buddhism, from Tsong-kha-pa's *The Great Treatise on the Stages of the Path to Enlightenment*, citing *Buddha-palita's Commentary on [Nagarjuna's] "Fundamental Treatise"*:

> What is the purpose of teaching dependent-arising? The master Nagarjuna ... saw that living beings are beset by various sufferings and assumed the task of teaching the reality of things ... *so that they might be free.* [my emphasis] What is the reality of things? It is the absence of essence. Unskilled persons ... conceive of an essence in things [something fixed and final and permanent] and then generate attachment and hostility with regard to them. (Tsong-kha-pa, 2002, p. 210)

And finally, from Dōgen Zenji, a lovely, obscure hint at how this bespoken freedom entails studying the self which entails forgetting the self and thereby become one with the myriad of things, those Ravens, this morning, yellow-eyed at the feeder, black-glint and squawking with no trace:

> To carry the self forward and illuminate myriad things is delusion. That myriad things come forth and illuminate the self is awakening. To study the Buddha Way is to study the self. To study the self is to forget the self. To forget the self is to be actualized by myriad things. When actualized by myriad things, your body and mind as well as the bodies and minds of others drop away. No trace of enlightenment remains, and this no-trace continues endlessly. (Dōgen, 2000, pp. 35–36)

References

Arendt, H. (1969). *Between past and future: Eight exercises in political thought*. New York, NY: Penguin Books.

Derrida, J., & Ferraris, M. (2001). *A taste for the secret*. Cambridge: Polity Press.

Descartes, R. (1955). *Descartes selections*. New York, NY: Charles Scribner's Sons.

Dōgen. (2000). *Enlightenment unfolds: The essential teachings of Zen Master Dōgen* (K. Tanahashi, Ed.). Boston, MA: Shambhala Publications.

Gadamer, H.-G. (1977). *Philosophical hermeneutics*. Berkeley, CA: University of California Press.

Gadamer, H.-G. (1983). *Reason in the age of science* (F. G. Lawrence, Trans.). Boston, MA: MIT Press.

Gadamer, H.-G. (1989). *Truth and method*. New York, NY: Continuum Books.

Gadamer, H.-G. (1992). *Hans-Georg Gadamer on education, poetry, and history: Applied hermeneutics* (D. Misgeld & G. Nicholson, Eds., L. Schmidt & M. Reuss, Trans.). Albany, NY: State University of New York Press.

Gadamer, H.-G. (2001). Aesthetics. In R. E. Palmer (Ed.), *Gadamer in conversation: Reflections and commentary* (pp. 61–77). New Haven, CT: Yale University.

Gadamer, H.-G. (2007). Text and interpretation. In R. E. Palmer (Ed.), *The Gadamer reader: A bouquet of later writings* (pp. 156–191). Evanston, IL: Northwestern University Press.

Hillman, J. (1983). *Healing fiction*. Barrytown, PA: Station Hill Press.

Jardine, D. (2006). What happens to us over and above our wanting and doing. In D. Jardine, P. Clifford, & S. Friesen (Eds.), *Curriculum in abundance* (pp. xxiii–xxviii). Mahwah, NJ: Lawrence Erlbaum Associates.

Jardine, D. (2012). *Pedagogy left in peace: On the cultivation of free spaces in teaching and learning*. New York, NY: Bloomsbury Publishing.

Jardine, D. (2016). *In praise of radiant beings: A retrospective path through education, Buddhism and ecology*. Charlotte, NC: Information Age Publishing.

Jardine, D. (in press). The ... readiness ... to be 'all ears.' In M. Quinn (Ed.), *From the echo of god's laughter: Essays on the generative and generous gifts of William E. Doll Jr*. New York, NY: Routledge.

Kermode, F. (1979). *The genesis of secrecy: On the interpretation of narrative*. Cambridge, MA: Harvard University Press.

MacPherson, C. B. (2010). *The political theory of possessive individualism*. Oxford: Oxford University Press.

Nishitani, K. (1982). *Religion and nothingness*. Berkeley, CA: University of California Press.

Smith, D. G. (1999). *Pedagon: Interdisciplinary essays on pedagogy and culture*. New York, NY: Peter Lang.

Smith, D. G. (2006). *Trying to teach in a season of great untruth: Globalization, empire and the crises of pedagogy* (pp. xxi–xxvii). Rotterdam, The Netherlands: Sense Publishers.

Snyder, G. (1980). *The real work.* New York, NY: New Directions.

Tsong-kha-pa. (2002). *The great treatise on the stages of the path to enlightenment* (Vol. 2). Ithaca, NY: Snow Lion Publications.

Wiebe, R., & Johnson, Y. (1999). *Stolen life: The journey of a cree woman.* Toronto: Vintage Canada.

CHAPTER 3

My Students' Stories Became a Gift: A Tale of Poetic Professional Learning

Kathleen Pithouse-Morgan

Setting the Scene: Teaching and Teacher Education against a Backdrop of Apartheid

I teach and supervise graduate students in a school of education at a university in South Africa. My students are practising schoolteachers and university educators with diverse educational backgrounds. During the apartheid era (1948–1994), most of them would have been classified as *African, Indian,* or *coloured,* while I was classified as *white.* The apartheid administration used these racial classifications to stratify South African society. A hierarchy of racialised privilege and dispossession ensured that people labelled as white benefited from high levels of government spending and access to superior facilities and resources in all domains (including education), while people labelled as African, coloured, and Indian were disenfranchised and oppressed (Clark & Worger, 2016). Of particular relevance to this chapter is how the apartheid government deliberately aimed to impoverish education for the majority of South Africans (Nkomo, 1990). Those of my students who are about my age (in their 40s) or older would have been educated in racially segregated schools during apartheid, and many of the younger students would have attended schools still marred by the residues of discriminatory apartheid policies.

As Southern African writer and poet Dorian Haarhoff (1998) emphasised, "the strategies of the apartheid state … locked doors between people and denied them access to each other's experience" (p. 10). Haarhoff advised that, when "we re-member (the opposite to dismember) our stories, we [can] reconstruct and reconnect our lives" (p. 5). Similarly, North American writer Andrew Solomon argued for "a moral purpose" for the writing and reading of personal stories of experience, pointing out that "it is nearly impossible to hate anyone whose story you know" and that "if you can give language to experiences previously starved for it, you can make the world a better place" (2015, p. 14). With this in mind, one of the consequences of my awareness of the miseducative apartheid legacy of social fragmentation is that I encourage my students to read and write personal history stories as an integral part of their graduate studies. My focus is on "personal history as those formative, contexualised experiences that have influenced teachers' thinking about teaching and their own practice" (Samaras, Hicks, & Berger, 2004, p. 909).

I bring personal history stories into my pedagogy through individual and group activities that provide support for writing and sharing such stories. Prior to becoming a teacher educator, I was an English language school-teacher with a particular interest in creative writing. Hence, I encourage my students to explore creative strategies for composing and responding to personal history stories. My pedagogic practices draw on the literary and visual arts, which can heighten engagement and deep thinking, dialogue and sharing, enjoyment, taking action, and emotional growth (Pithouse-Morgan et al., 2013). I also encourage reading and discussion of personal history narrative dissertations written by former students, and I invite these former students and other local authors who have published personal history narratives to come to talk with current students. I have found that such strategies bring to life reading as interaction with the author of a text as well as with the personal history narrative itself. Personal history stories written by local academics and student researchers offer relevant content presented in contexts and languages that are familiar and of interest to my students. Overall, my aim is to offer students opportunities and means to deepen and extend explorations of their personal and professional selves by reencountering and making meaning from personal stories of the past (both their own and others') and re-envisioning hopeful stories for the future. In so doing, I encourage students only to share stories that they are comfortable with disclosing and also to respect the privacy and dignity of others who are implicated in these stories (Nash, 2004).

Taking a Narrative Self-Study Stance in Researching Professional Learning

My academic work is located in professional learning, with a focus on teachers initiating and directing their own learning to enhance their continuing growth, in dialogue with others. I am drawn to understandings of professional learning that reconsider professionals as "self-directed" (Webster-Wright, 2009, p. 712) and "*self*-developing" (Easton, 2008, p. 756) learners. In essence, such understandings – which have been expressed as "authentic professional learning" (Webster-Wright, 2009, p. 702) and "powerful professional learning" (Easton, 2008, p. 756) – put emphasis on how professionals can develop vital insights into their own personal and professional selves and practice, with the intention of bringing about change for the better.

In taking a narrative self-study stance in this chapter, I am focusing on the experiential level of professional learning. Ideas about learning and teaching as experiential and contextual processes permeate the work of educational researchers who adopt narrative and self-study approaches (see, among others, Bullough & Pinnegar, 2001; Clandinin & Connelly, 1994). This is underpinned by a conception of inquiry by teachers and teacher educators as a significant and distinctive way of exploring and communicating the complexities of practice in educational settings (Samaras, 2011). I am working from a narrative understanding of the teacher or teacher educator as a protagonist situated amongst the plotlines, settings, and characters of an evolving life story and as able to take action to influence that story. I aim to engage critically and creatively with stories of my teacher educator-researcher self to enhance my professional practice and offer insights and possibilities for others (Pithouse, 2011; Pithouse-Morgan, 2017).

Exploring My Professional Learning in Relation to My Students' Stories

As I have described elsewhere (Pithouse-Morgan, 2016), an initially unforeseen effect of engaging closely for more than a decade with the writing of my students' personal history stories has been that my own professional learning has been troubled, deepened, and extended in critical ways. Recently, I have begun to employ "poetic professional learning" (Pithouse-Morgan, 2017, p. 63) as a literary arts-informed mode for exploring my professional learning in relation to my students' personal history stories. The work of scholars in a variety of social science fields (for example, Breckenridge, 2016; Furman, 2014; Pasquin, 2010) has illustrated how poetic professional learning can heighten self-insight, responsiveness, social awareness, and inspiration on the part of professionals such as nurses, social workers, and teachers, as well as offer others new understandings of the lived experiences of these professionals. The focus of such work is not primarily on creating poems that satisfy criteria for literary or artistic merit. Rather, the intention is to use poetic language and forms for the educative purposes of researching and enriching professional learning. I have used poetry as a way to grapple with my students' written stories of physically and emotionally painful experiences at the hands of their former teachers (Pithouse-Morgan, 2016), and as a means of facing a narrative tension in my teaching of academic writing (Pithouse-Morgan, 2017). Because of these poetic inquiries I have begun to re-member my teacher educator self in response to the lived experiences of my students.

The impetus for the inquiry described in this chapter was an increasing awareness that my journey of re-membering will be a lifelong process of discovery. As I have discussed elsewhere (Pillay & Pithouse-Morgan, 2016), I have an affinity to mystery novels, and I have come to see my narrative self-study explorations as an unravelling of a series of mysteries, with each one leading on to another. But, although I am drawing on tenets and devices of the literary arts, this work is not fiction and, at times, it feels distressing rather than pleasurable. Becoming more and more conscious of others' often painful personal history stories and my own obliviousness thereof or implication therein is not fun. However, I have realised that it is necessary, not only for continuing improvement of my professional practice, but also for a personal process of coming to terms with myself against a backdrop of the darkness of apartheid.

In this chapter, I offer an account of another episode in my continuing journey. At the outset, I did not have a clearly expressed research question; rather, I just had a feeling that there was more to find out about my professional practice and myself. In what follows, I illustrate how I used the literary arts-informed research practices of poetry and dialogue to connect with, and learn from, my students' stories of lived experience. I consider how mindfulness of what I have learned might enhance my future teaching and learning. I also draw attention to poetic professional learning as a generative practice for connecting with others' personal history stories.

My Poetic Professional Learning Process

I began the inquiry by deciding on my field texts (data sources). I went back to personal history stories written by my students to look for a narrative thread that I found emotionally, as well as academically, compelling (Conle, 2000). After time spent reading and rereading, I noted how, in 12 completed masters' dissertations on a range of topics, my students had chosen to describe childhood experiences of learning to read as a fundamental influence in their personal and educational development.

I copied and pasted relevant extracts from these 12 dissertations into a new document, which extended to 23 pages. I chose words and phrases in the dissertation extracts and played with rearranging these found words and phrases with the intention of composing a free verse found poem (Butler-Kisber, 2005). The process of composing and recomposing the found poem over several months helped me to move backward and forward through the dissertation extracts to find pieces that resonated emotionally and intellectually and, thus, seemed to hold promise for my learning (Clandinin & Connelly, 1994).

I started to see that a connecting thread running through the extracts was the positive influence of family members, most often mothers or grandmothers, who took on nurturing roles in my students' early experiences of learning to read. This was not in itself particularly surprising given the prevalence of research highlighting how the supportive influence of family members, particularly mothers, can be seen in literacy biographies (for instance, Boggs & Golden, 2009). Likewise, in my own childhood, my mother played a similarly supportive role in my reading development. However, what caught my attention was that, unlike my own mother and most of the mothers I had read about in published research, many of my students' mothers or grandmothers were illiterate or semiliterate.

Reading my students' stories of the vital contributions of their mothers and grandmothers reminded me of the beautiful metaphor poem by Guyanese poet, Grace Nichols, "A Praise Song for My Mother" (1984). Inspired by this,

A Praise Song for My Mother

My mother was
Illiterate
An uneducated person
Who could not read
Who never had a chance
Who sacrificed
To have an educated child

My mother was
Attentive
A walking dictionary
Who had a gift
Who never fell asleep
Who wished
To instil a love for reading

FIGURE 3.1   "A praise song for my mother" (inspired by Grace Nichols)

I eventually composed a 2-stanza poem (Figure 3.1) to make visible two noteworthy and ostensibly contradictory aspects of what I was beginning to see in the personal history stories: The mother as both an illiterate, "uneducated" person, and as "a walking dictionary."

As Furman and Dill (2015, citing Faulkner) explained, "characterized by compression, yet allowing for evocative and emotionally laden content, the research poem is a valuable means of condensing research data into its most elemental form" (p. 44). Creating a short 14-line research poem from a 23-page document helped me to begin to distill and develop my learning from my students' personal history stories.

I then started to merge the original two stanzas to create what I hoped would be a more nuanced and complex portrait. I went back to the dissertation extracts to find additional words and phrases to use in transforming my first poem into a second poem. This poem, "My Mother Had a Gift" (Figure 3.2), was written in the French Malaysian pantoum format, in which "repetitive lines

My Mother Had a Gift

My mother had a gift.
A walking dictionary,
She listened attentively.
She would praise me.

A walking dictionary,
She could not read.
She would praise me
To instil a love for reading.

She could not read.
She sacrificed.
To instil a love for reading,
To have an educated child

She sacrificed,
She listened attentively
To have an educated child.
My mother had a gift.

FIGURE 3.2   "My mother had a gift"

My *Teacher* Had a Gift

Kathleen:	*What does the poem say to you?*
S'phiwe:	I think it is saying that our parents are our first teachers, whether they are educated or not. My parents were not educated, but they sacrificed a lot in order for us to be what we are today. The poem brings up emotions because it speaks directly to my experience.
Ntokozo:	Yes, my grandparents were never at school, but they still checked my parents' homework.
S'phiwe:	And our parents *are* walking dictionaries. We go back to them, even as old as we are. Even though we know they are uneducated, we go and ask for their advice. They have knowledge and wisdom to share with us.
Khulekani:	It says that you learn everywhere, even at home. And you can learn from everyone. Family plays just as important a role as the school culture and community.
Nontuthuko:	I also think that concerned parents instil that love for reading, for education. They sacrifice a lot for their children.
Ntokozo:	My mother is very supportive. I wouldn't have studied further unless she had said to me, "You are capable. Do it." For our parents, our accomplishments are basically *their* accomplishments.
Kathleen:	*Is this worth saying? Why?*
Khulekani:	Reading this poem makes me do introspection. It tells me that, as teachers, we should emulate that love and those sacrifices that our mothers made for us. We should be like a mother and show children love, praise them, and give them all the support that they need.
Nontuthuko:	How I wish the poem said, "My *teacher* had a gift."
S'phiwe:	Yes! It's highlighting those important characteristics that we as teachers should have.
Khulekani:	And that we should never give up on children or ignore them.
Ntokozo:	Even recognising small things can encourage children to keep going.
Nontuthuko:	It gives a powerful message for us as teachers: Be there for your children, listen to them, praise them, and encourage them. Then they will go far, they will remember you as a mother who was there for them, and they won't forget you as a teacher.

FIGURE 3.3 "My *teacher* had a gift"

[allow] for the repetition of salient or emotionally evocative themes" (Furman, Lietz, & Langer, 2006, p. 28).

After composing the second poem, I decided to share it with four of my doctoral students: Khulekani Luthuli, S'phiwe Madondo, Ntokozo Mkhize, and Nontuthuko Phewa. They are all practising primary school teachers who are writing personal history stories as integral components of their self-study research. I wanted to see if and how the poem might resonate with them. Without giving any background to the poem or revealing that I had created it, I asked them to share their thoughts on what the poem conveyed to them. After they had offered their responses to the poem, I explained how and why I had composed it and we discussed that. With their permission, I audio recorded and transcribed their responses to the poem to create an additional field text to inform my inquiry.

Next, I created a dialogue piece (Figure 3.3) composed of lightly edited excerpts from the transcript. The editing was to enhance narrative coherence and flow and to highlight what I had gained from my students' responses. As a literary arts-based device, dialogue can help readers to come to understand more about the characters in a story and to see how growth happens through communication between characters (Coulter & Smith, 2009). In this case, I fashioned a dialogue piece to make visible how my students' conversation contributed to my professional learning.

Implications for My Professional Practice: A Shift Towards Multiplexity

The gradual process of creating the poems and the dialogue piece, along with the contributions from my doctoral students, helped me to become even more conscious of how my personal history of growing up as a white child during apartheid contributed to a grave ignorance of the lived experiences of the majority of people in South Africa. I also gained a heightened awareness of important ways in which my personal history is similar to, as well as different from, other South African histories. While highlighting some key differences, "My Mother Had a Gift" and "My *Teacher* Had a Gift" also illuminate a vital point of connection between many of my students and me: we all had mothers or other family members who were positive influences in our early learning years and who sacrificed and strove to further their children's education.

Looking back, I could see how, prior to engaging with my students' personal history narrative writing, I had assumed that being literate was a prerequisite for a family member's contribution to the literacy development of a young child. Yet, "My Mother Had a Gift" and "My *Teacher* Had a Gift" tell an alternative story. In this alternative story, family members who are not literate are portrayed as walking dictionaries with inestimable advice, wisdom, and encouragement to share. Because of my own immersion in an exclusive, literate social world, I had certainly been oblivious to the conception of oralate-ness as an educative capacity for families to draw on in supporting young children's literacy development, and which Conolly et al. (2009) described as:

> That biopsychological human capacity which enables the record and expression of human knowledge *without* scribal alphabetic writing, namely, *that which records in memory and expresses out of memory*. This complements literacy as that human capacity which records knowledge and expression *with* scribal alphabetic writing. Human "oralate" capacity predates literate capacity by an unknown and uncountable period of time. (p. 99)

The poems and dialogue piece, in conjunction with interaction with my students, brought the educative potential of oralate-ness to my attention and prompted me to reconsider my own use of the oral in my practice as a teacher educator. I started to see how my understanding of the role of the oral in my graduate teaching was largely as preparation for written, graded coursework, rather than as something of educative value in itself. In thinking about this, I went back to Conolly et al.'s work on oralate-ness (2009) and from there I started to explore Finnegan's research on orality and literacy (for example, 2003a, 2003b). I was fascinated to read about her conception of *multiplexity*, through which she emphasised the educative value of

> an increasing awareness of the multiplexities of human creativity. Not just the multiplicities of diverse viewpoints, genres, cultures, social situatedness, power relations, or historical specificities (all now rightly recognized themes in social and humanistic study), but more the move away from the narrowing ethnocentric models implied in the binarism of oral/ literate into the amazing range of multifaceted spectrums that people actively and creatively draw on in their communication and expression. (Finnegan, 2003a, p. 85)

I was intrigued by Finnegan's understanding of "multiplexities of human creativity" (2003a, p. 85) and "the multiplexity of human communication"

(2003b, p. 16) as crucial to better informed and more inclusive pedagogy. And I was inspired by her bold challenge to "the myth of the linguistic highroad to learning":

> Bringing into the open the myth of the linguistic highroad to learning can startle us into greater recognition of the other actors in our shared and varied human drama than the two pure verbally-clad heroes [Orality and Literacy]. As participants in education, in whatever role, we should capitalise joyfully – and knowingly – on that multiplexity both within and beyond the walls of our formal educational institutions. (Finnegan, 2003b, pp. 16–17)

Finnegan's work has prompted me to think deeply about how I might begin to make my own teaching and supervision more multiplex – having many folds or many parts (Multiplex, n.d.) – by integrating a wider "array of auditory, kinesic, visual, spatial, material, tactile, somatic, and olfactory resources" (2003a, p. 85). While supporting students in producing pieces of academic writing remains a key part of my professional practice, I have started exploring how this might be infused more consciously with multiplexity – as a valuable end in itself rather than only as a pre-writing activity. For instance, in preparing for a graduate course that I teach annually, "Understanding Teacher Education and Professional Development," I am now planning for students to submit portfolios of work that will include drawings, poetry, letters, mind maps, smart phone text messages, and performances of scripts for television commercials, rather than the usual two academic essays. Also, the course *readings* will include online talks, blog posts, and online magazine and newspaper articles as key texts for study, rather than just as additional material. It remains to be seen what the students and I will learn from this exploratory shift towards multiplexity, but I am hoping that we will all gain a heightened awareness of "'writing' in the context of, and working in tandem with, the many other media through which we actually educate and learn" (Finnegan, 2003b, p. 16).

It is important to stress, as Finnegan (2003b) does, that a shift towards multiplexity does not mean downplaying the importance of literacy in education and in society in general. Certainly, in the South African context, literacy still cannot be taken for granted. To illustrate, according to a recent report by the Progress in International Literacy Study, 78 percent of South African fourth grade children cannot read for meaning in any language (Mullis, Martin, Foy, & Hooper, 2017). Nonetheless, while the struggle for literacy as a fundamental human right continues, it seems to me that awareness of oralate-ness and multiplexity as resources for learning and teaching could strengthen efforts to make literacy education more widely relevant, interesting, and accessible.

Implications for My Continuing Professional Learning: My Students Became My Teachers

This inquiry has helped me to reconsider my students' personal history stories and my professional learning as a teacher educator in relation to Dewey's (1938/1963) vision of education as a social process of living to which all human beings can make a meaningful, distinctive contribution. Poetic engagement with my students' personal history stories has allowed me to see more distinctly how close encounters with others' stories of experience can facilitate personal and educational growth (Bruner, 1996). As expressed by Makaiau and Freese (2013), "[my] students' stories became transformational teaching texts" (p. 146) and, in this way, my students became my teachers. As work-in-progress, my teacher educator self continues to grow in relationship with my students and in response to my developing understanding of personal histories that are so unlike, and yet also akin to, my own.

A Poetic Closing

The two poems that I composed to facilitate my narrative self-study provided material for a third, interpretive poem, which offers a self-portrait, showing my subjective response to the study (Furman & Dill, 2015). I again used the pantoum format in creating "She Wished To Be Educated" (Figure 3.4). The poem expresses my learning about how students and other people can become walking dictionaries with gifts of personal history stories that can educate. It also conveys my heightened awareness of the pedagogic value of listening attentively to others' personal history stories. Furthermore, it highlights the necessity of not "falling asleep" and always trying to be open to being educated – no matter how many formal educational qualifications one might have. I offer my professional learning story and my poetic research practice as an invitation to other teacher educators and teachers who wish to never fall asleep.

She Wished to Be Educated

Listening
Attentively
For a gift,
A walking dictionary.

Attentively
Reading
A walking dictionary,
To be educated.

Reading,
She wished
To be educated,
To never fall asleep.

She wished
For a gift,
To never fall asleep
Listening.

FIGURE 3.4   "She wished to be educated"

Acknowledgements

I am beholden to all my students who have been my patient teachers. In particular, I thank Khulekani Luthuli, S'phiwe Madondo, Ntokozo Mkhize, and Nontuthuko Phewa for kind permission to include their words and names in this chapter.

I am appreciative of the constructive feedback from Ellyn Lyle and the helpful peer review by Sepideh Mahani. I thank Moira Richards for her professional assistance with preparing the chapter for submission.

I obtained ethical clearance from my institution to conduct research into my professional learning and my university-based teaching.

I gratefully acknowledge funding from the National Research Foundation (NRF) of South Africa (Research Grant Number 90380 and Incentive Funding for

Rated Researchers). Any opinion, findings, conclusions, or recommendations expressed in this material are those of the author and, therefore, the funders do not accept any liability in regard thereto.

References

Boggs, M., & Golden, F. (2009). Insights: Literacy memories of preservice teachers self-reported categories of impact. *The Reading Matrix, 9*(2), 211–223.

Breckenridge, J. P. (2016). The reflexive role of tanka poetry in domestic abuse research. *Journal of Research in Nursing, 21*(5–6), 1–14.

Bruner, J. S. (1996). *The culture of education.* Cambridge, MA: Harvard University Press.

Bullough, R. V., & Pinnegar, S. (2001). Guidelines for quality in autobiographical forms of self-study research. *Educational Researcher, 30*(3), 13–22.

Butler-Kisber, L. (2005). Inquiry through poetry: The genesis of self-study. In C. Mitchell, S. Weber, & K. O'Reilly-Scanlon (Eds.), *Just who do we think we are? Methodologies for autobiography and self-study in teaching* (pp. 95–110). London: RoutledgeFalmer.

Clandinin, D. J., & Connelly, F. M. (1994). Personal experience methods. In N. K. Denzin & Y. S. Lincoln (Eds.), *Handbook of qualitative research* (pp. 413–427). Thousand Oaks, CA: Sage Publications.

Clarke, N. L., & Worger, W. H. (2016). *South Africa: The rise and fall of apartheid* (3rd ed.). Abingdon: Routledge.

Conle, C. (2000). Thesis as narrative or "what is the inquiry in narrative inquiry?" *Curriculum Inquiry, 30*(2), 189–214.

Conolly, J., Desmond, S., Dullay, S., Gumede, J., Mnguni, E., Ngaloshe, C., ... Yeni, C. (2009). The self as a laboratory of awareness: Exploring the oralate-literate interface of memory. In K. Pithouse, C. Mitchell, & R. Moletsane (Eds.), *Making connections: Self-study & social action* (pp. 97–112). New York, NY: Peter Lang.

Coulter, C. A., & Smith, M. L. (2009). The construction zone: Literary elements in narrative research. *Educational Researcher, 38*(8), 577–590.

Dewey, J. (1963). *Experience and education.* New York, NY: Collier. (Original work published in 1938)

Easton, L. B. (2008). From professional development to professional learning. *Phi Delta Kappa, 89*(10), 755–761.

Finnegan, R. (2003a). "Oral tradition": Weasel words or transdisciplinary door to multiplexity? *Oral Tradition, 18*(1), 84–86.

Finnegan, R. (2003b). Orality and literacy: Epic heroes of human destiny? *International Journal of Learning, 10*, 1551–1560.

Furman, R. (2014). Beyond the literary uses of poetry: A class for university freshmen. *Journal of Poetry Therapy, 27*(4), 205–211.

Furman, R., & Dill, L. (2015). Extreme data reduction: The case for the research tanka. *Journal of Poetry Therapy, 28*(1), 43–52.

Furman, R., Lietz, C. A., & Langer, C. L. (2006). The research poem in international social work: Innovations in qualitative methodology. *International Journal of Qualitative Methods, 5*(3), 24–34.

Haarhoff, D. (1998). *The writer's voice: A workbook for writers in Africa.* Halfway House: Zebra Press.

Makaiau, A. S., & Freese, A. R. (2013). A transformational journey: Exploring our multicultural identities through self-study. *Studying Teacher Education, 9*(2), 141–151.

Mullis, I. V. S., Martin, M. O., Foy, P., & Hooper, M. (2017). *PIRLS 2016 international results in Reading.* Retrieved from http://pirls2016.org/download-center/

Multiplex. (n.d.). *The online etymology dictionary.* Retrieved from https://www.etymonline.com/word/multiplex

Nash, R. J. (2004). *Liberating scholarly writing: The power of personal narrative.* New York, NY: Teachers College Press.

Nichols, G. (1984). A praise song for my mother. In G. Nichols (Ed.), *The fat Black woman's poems.* London: Virago.

Nkomo, M. O. (Ed.). (1990). *Pedagogy of domination: Toward a democratic education in South Africa.* Trenton, NJ: Africa World Press.

Pasquin, L. (2010). Poetry as breath: Teaching student teachers to breathe-out poetry. *LEARNing Landscapes, 4*(1), 255–263.

Pillay, D., & Pithouse-Morgan, K. (2016). A self-study of connecting through aesthetic memory-work. In J. Kitchen, D. Tidwell, & L. Fitzgerald (Eds.), *Self-study and diversity II: Inclusive teacher education for a diverse world* (Vol. 2, pp. 121–136). Rotterdam, The Netherlands: Sense Publishers.

Pithouse-Morgan, K. (2011). "The future of our young children lies in our hands": Re-envisaging -teacher authority through narrative self-study. In C. Mitchell, T. Strong-Wilson, K. Pithouse-Morgan, & S. Allnutt (Eds.), *Memory and pedagogy* (pp. 177–190). New York, NY: Routledge.

Pithouse-Morgan, K. (2016). Finding my self in a new place: Exploring professional learning through found poetry. *Teacher Learning and Professional Development, 1*(1), 1–18. Retrieved from http://journals.sfu.ca/tlpd/index.php/tlpd/article/view/1

Pithouse-Morgan, K. (2017). Beginning to unravel a narrative tension in my professional learning about teaching writing. In M. Hayler & J. Moriarty (Eds.), *Self-narrative and pedagogy: Stories of experience within teaching and learning* (pp. 59–82). Rotterdam, The Netherlands: Sense Publishers.

Pithouse-Morgan, K., De Lange, N., Mitchell, C., Moletsane, R., Olivier, T., Stuart, J., Van Laren, L., & Wood, L. (2013). Creative and participatory strategies for teacher development in the age of AIDS. In J. Kirk, M. Dembélé, & S. Baxter (Eds.), *More and better teachers for quality education for all: Identity and motivation, systems and support* (pp. 75–90). Montreal: Collaborative Works. Retrieved from http://moreandbetterteachers.wordpress.com/

Samaras, A. P. (2011). *Self-study teacher research: Improving your practice through collaborative inquiry.* Thousand Oaks, CA: Sage Publications.

Samaras, A. P., Hicks, M. A., & Berger, J. G. (2004). Self-study through personal history. In J. J. Loughran, M. L. Hamilton, V. K. LaBoskey, & T. Russell (Eds.), *International handbook of self-study of teaching and teacher education practices* (Vol. 2, pp. 905–942). Dordrecht: Kluwer Academic Publishers.

Solomon, A. (2015, March 11). The middle of things: Advice for young writers. *The New Yorker.* Retrieved from http://www.newyorker.com/books/page-turner/the-middle-of-things-advice-for-young-writers

Webster-Wright, A. (2009). Reframing professional development through understanding authentic professional learning. *Review of Educational Research, 79*(2), 702–739.

CHAPTER 4

Being Indigenous in the Indigenous Education Classroom: A Critical Self-Study of Teaching in an Impossible and Imperative Assignment

Jennifer Markides

Beginning Where I Am and Considering the Whole

Both in my work and in my life, I walk in two worlds. I am cognizant of the irreconcilable tensions between Western and Indigenous worldviews (Little Bear, 2000) and how they play out in the academy. I navigate both settler and Indigenous lineages, and bring my complex identity into the classroom, wondering how will I be received. My role as teacher blurs the lines between my personal and professional identities. I am Métis. I am an educator. The institution asks me to bring my Métis-ness forward in the classroom, to be seen as an authority on Indigenous education. As an Indigenous Education instructor, I am conflicted: optimistic, reticent, humbled, honoured, and terrified, all at once. I strongly ascribe to the belief that "we teach who we are" (Palmer, 2017, p. 1). As such, I bring myself to my teaching – my history, my experiences, my values, my strengths, and my shortcomings. The content in the Indigenous Education course is daunting. It spans historical, political, philosophical, sociological, educational, and ethical issues. The students come into the course out of necessity, rather than by choice, as it is a mandatory part of their teacher education program. Some come in with open hearts, while others come in with closed minds. How can I be the teacher the students need me to be? Can I be enough? The university deems me to be a worthy candidate, but would my community? The Indigenous Education classroom is a contested space and a site of potential harm. Is being asked to teach this course an act of further oppression or an emancipatory opportunity?

Through self-study, I share my reflections, struggles, and discoveries in teaching a compulsory Indigenous Education course to pre-service teachers in the university setting. By way of deep introspection, I revisit the experiences that troubled me personally and pushed me professionally. I consider the many challenges associated with this important work in hopes of learning from and improving my practice. I also share my questions, observations, and stories as part of a larger reconciliatory conversation.

Self-Study as a Way of Being in Teaching

There are so many choices in teaching: what we teach; how we present the material; what resources we use; how we assess; and how we carry ourselves in relationship to the students. These are just a few of the many conscious and unconscious decisions we make in the act of teaching. In reflective practice, I have long considered the *why* behind the choices I make while planning and working with students. What really matters? How can I make the learning – of what really matters – engaging? How does my planning/vision measure up against the reality of what plays out in the classroom? As a reflective practitioner and researcher, I critique my self, my teaching, and my circumstances in a *self-reflective meaning-making process* (Kovach, 2009).

Inherently, the praxis of self-study is an integral part of teacher education. Teaching practice grows from an ongoing cycle of experience, reflection, and further action. In this way, I become the site of my study. Contrary to the connotation of *self* as being individual-focused, self-study is of a relational nature, involving "the elements of dialogue: inquiry, reflection, critique, evidence, or response ... [and,] through the negotiation of the tensions created by the elements of dialogue, meaning is forged" (Pinnegar & Hamilton, 2009, p. 90). Thus, I consider my observations and experiences in conversation with the teaching context, the course content, and my teaching practice.

Positioning My Self

As an Indigenous doctoral student, I negotiate the push and pull of expectations, preconceptions, and assumptions of what my scholarship *should* be – rigorous, academic, and Indigenous forward – and who I *should* be – rigorous, academic, and Indigenous forward. The expectations are not too different from those of non-Indigenous graduate students, with the noticeable exception being the near requisite articulation of my cultural identity.

An Indigenous positionality has become more common, safe, and even desirable since the Association of Canadian Deans of Education developed the *Accord on Indigenous Education* in 2010 and the Truth and Reconciliation Commission released the *94 Calls to Action* and *Summary Report* in 2015. The recent receptivity to Indigenous ways of knowing and being has opened opportunities for increased recruitment and enrolment of Indigenous students, greater numbers of hires of Indigenous faculty members, substantial growth in institutional, provincial, and federal financial support, and funding for Indigenous education scholarships and research project grants. While the changing social climate of the institutions may be seen as positive on the whole, Indigenous academics still face many challenges in the academy.

Peers and colleagues are sometimes disquieted by the increase of attention paid to Indigenous scholarship, leading to dismissive or discriminatory attitudes. *Being Indigenous has come into fashion, but for how long?* In some cases, the judgement and scrutiny comes from within our own community of Indigenous scholars – *membership checking* continues to be an unfortunate carry over from years of divisive rhetoric propagated within the settler narrative. In other writing, I have described the strength of standing together in mutually sustainable relationality (Markides, 2018, p. 194) – to be accountable to our communities and each other by holding ourselves to high standards and leading by example. We need to hold each other up as a community, rather than holding each other against arbitrary measuring sticks of Indigenous authenticity. We have more important work to do than to be fighting with and hindering each other.

Being Positioned as an Indigenous Educator in the Contested Space of Indigenous Education

I appreciate being able to teach in the undergraduate programs in education. It keeps me connected to my teacher self. Initially, I was nervous to accept a sessional position teaching Indigenous Education, but I felt compelled to say *yes*. It was only later that I learned that some Indigenous professors have refused to teach this course in other institutions. The backlash of resistance suggests that *Indigenous Education courses are contested spaces and sites of potential harm.*

With this knowledge, I began to question: Is this teaching assignment a further violation of my Métis identity? Who holds the power over Indigenous education and Indigenous educators? Am I a cog in the colonial wheel, further perpetuating oppression through narrow-representation (Absolon & Willett, 2005) and commodification of Indigenous knowledge (Smith, 2000)? Is my teaching an act of resistance or complacence? Or both? Could it be more? Might the struggle and hardship become a site of reconciliation and healing? Who will decide? Am I in any better position to teach this course than a non-Indigenous instructor, or will I fall short in the areas of deeply rooted knowledge and relevant relationships (Marom, 2017)? Can I be enough?

Being positioned as an Indigenous educator, by virtue of being Indigenous and an educator, is problematic. I find myself asking, "[Am I] not the Indian [you] had in mind?" (King, 2003, p. 31), and it troubles me. I imagine what the students *picture* an Indigenous educator to be, and I fall short on every account: I do not appear overtly or romantically Indigenous, as in the images of "Indians" on postcards, in movies, or in textbooks; I have not been gifted with an abundance of ceremonial teachings to share with the class; I do not speak an Indigenous language; I have not been given an Indigenous name through a traditional naming ceremony; and I do not have ties to a reserve community. To play on the students' expectations of me, I make a conscious effort to wear beaded earrings, feather prints, moccasins, and other recognizably Indigenous paraphernalia. I do this to quell any potential unrest – to garner approval and credibility – before disrupting the concept of an *authentic* Indigenous educator. While I am quite fond of these articles of clothing and jewellery, wearing them feels both disingenuous and necessary. It enables me to confront the preconceived notions of *what I should look like, what I should know, how I should teach,* and *who I should be for the course.*

I am not an expert of Indigenous peoples or cultures. There are so many Indigenous groups across North America and around the world that it would be impossible to be *an expert* on even a few of the communities, let alone know all of their languages, cultural practices, oral histories/stories, belief systems, leadership structures, roles of community members, teachings, and technologies. I can only speak from my own knowledge base and my own experience as a Métis woman, mother, and educator. I am learning from and with many communities as the opportunities arise, but I will never be more than a guest.

Is this Not the Indigenous Education Course You Had in Mind?

In addition to not being the Indigenous Education instructor the students may have had in mind, the content of the course is not likely what they expected either. In many ways, the teaching assignment is an impossible – yet imperative – task. Am I being set up to fail? There is simply too much to teach and too little time. The students might well anticipate that the course will be geared towards them as teachers and will introduce them to *how* to teach Indigenous topics and content in their own classrooms. Instead, Indigenous Education is very much designed for them as students and addresses *what* they might not know about the historical legacies of colonization. We look at the life experiences – the barriers and misfortunes perpetuated by systemic racism and colonial rule – of Indigenous peoples, that have contributed to the intergenerational traumas that are present today, and *why* this is important for them to know as teachers. They are being tasked with knowing more and knowing better – teaching more and teaching better – in order to begin the journey of reconciliation that must happen within our education system. *No pressure, though.*

Beyond the mismatched expectations of what the course is about, there is also the reality that everyone is coming into the learning with different knowledge and understanding. Unlike a levelled reading program, it is not as easy to differentiate the experience of learning about the pass system, residential schools, the 60s Scoop, and missing and murdered Indigenous women and girls. There is no *skipping ahead* when we are walking the path together. We must support the slowest, least knowledgeable travellers in the group, such that they will not be left behind. That is not to say that the students coming in with a lot of prior knowledge will not learn anything new from the course. It is as many Elders say, you take what you need to or are ready to learn from the teachings; the learning is not the same for all learners. These are very wise words.

While this is not a study that involves the students' experiences and perspectives, I am confident that both the teaching and learning in the course qualify as instantiations of *difficult knowledge* (Britzman, 1998, 2003); the learning involves a crisis of understanding, such that new learning is possible, but not guaranteed. How do I introduce historical events and racist realities that the students' life experiences and prior education have not prepared them to learn? How do I willingly expose them to the violence, hatred, and unimaginable hardship that Indigenous peoples have faced? The course content – learning outcomes, required readings, and supplementary resources – may challenge the students' personal beliefs, upbringings, religious positions, or understandings of Indigenous peoples and cultures. Is it right for me to expose the students to graphic incidents of abuse, rape, oppression, cruelty, torture, violence, and inaction? Is it ethical?

Conversely, some students may bring racist perspectives, foster misconceptions, ascribe to stereotypes, perpetuate stigma, display ignorance, or harbour hatred. How do I create safety for the students and for myself? In this teaching, I am shaken. I grapple with the wide range of challenges that are unlike any I have experienced before in my teaching career. It wears on me. I am eroded and exposed – left changed in unforeseeable ways.

Reading Myself in and against the Required Readings

In the first week, we read the Schissel and Wotherspoon (2003) chapter titled "Educational Dreams and Disappointments." It provides some context for the need, urgency, and importance of having an Indigenous Education course.

The authors describe the inadequacy of our education system and its inability to meet the needs of Indigenous students. While the students may sense the urgency for change, it is my responsibility to make the subject matter meaningful for them. I use questioning strategies to draw on the students' prior knowledge and experiences to determine *why this work is important.* I also share examples of inequities in funding for on and off reserve schools, and under-representation of Indigenous role models, educators, and community members within the public school setting. Making the work meaningful for the students is a familiar task in my teaching practice.

Next, the DiAngelo and Sensoy (2014) article frames the course as a social justice class that will address anti-racism, post-colonialism, critical pedagogy, multi-culturalism, social construction of knowledge, and the reproduction of inequality. I feel comfortable with these expectations. In another teaching context, I introduced animal rights issues into a classroom where most of the students and their families would have had traditional ivory carvings in their homes. I invited a guest speaker to talk about the importance of elephants as a keystone species and how they have become endangered from illegal ivory poaching. I also discussed concerns over the significant presence and dangers of pollution with students whose families owned factories that were undoubtedly contributing to the problem. As illustrated by these examples, I do not shy away from potentially controversial or uncomfortable situations in my teaching, positioning me in the role of *teacher as activist.* It is interesting for me to consider that I am more apt to consider myself as an activist educator than an Indigenous educator.

In reading Schissel and Wotherspoon (2003) and St. Denis (2007), I find myself in a difficult position. I am reading my self and my life experiences into the articles. St. Denis shares passages about her families who have reasoned not to teach their children their language or traditions in an effort to give them a better life. This was my grandpa's hope for his family, too. He wanted us to pass as non-Indigenous, so that we would not have to face the racism he had endured his whole life. As a result, we have very few traditions and cultural teachings passed down in our families. My grandpa would have seen this as a victory; but for most of us, it has been a resounding loss.

I also struggle with the reality of residential schools. Schissel and Wotherspoon (2003) and Poitras Pratt and Daniels (2014) describe experiences of life in residential schools with troubling honesty. With each line, I can picture my second cousins heading off to their *school lives* far away from home. I have made it personal for me and difficult to move on in the readings. I wonder if my underlying rage and deep sorrow come across as passion or vigilantism as I try to teach through my Indigenous identity – pain, loss, and lingering injustice.

Further Elaboration on the Challenges of Claiming an Indigenous Identity

With the same goals as residential schools, post-colonial institutions have long worked to break familial and cultural ties in Indigenous communities and create distrust among community members. Claiming an Indigenous identity – of any specific Indigenous group – has been dangerous for hundreds of years. Historically, the act of identifying one's self as Indigenous could lead to segregation, discrimination, persecution, mistreatment, and dehumanization. Thousands of communities have been isolated through the reserve system. Indigenous peoples are over-represented in prison populations. Indigenous children are over-represented in the foster care system. The numbers of Missing and Murdered Indigenous Women and Girls – moreover, Indigenous Persons, regardless of age, gender, or sexual orientation – reached innumerable and unprecedented proportions before gaining national attention.

Reconciling My Activist, Indigenous, and Educator Selves

I am motivated by the aforementioned colonial legacies to fight for better circumstances for all Indigenous peoples. I am tasked with knowing more and knowing better – with teaching more and teaching better. Reconciliation in education needs to be modelled and pursued. Struggling with the difficult knowledge has made me hungry for change in our education system. How might we disrupt the pervasive and long privileged colonial structures?

In teaching, I bring myself into relationship with my students. This requires self-knowledge, honesty, humility and, at times, courage. My years of teaching have led me to trust myself in this work. I trust that I can do well by my students. I have knowledge and experience to offer them. In these same ways, I am learning to trust myself, as an advocate for the reconciliatory change that is beginning in, and carrying forward from, the Indigenous Education classroom.

Becoming an Indigenous Educator

To make the learning meaningful, I draw on familiar strategies that suit my teaching style. I use media to bring other voices into the class, such as the film "We Were Children" (Irving, Christensen, & Wolochatiuk, 2012), documentaries including "Highway of Tears" (Smiley, Pope, Fernandez-Salvador y Campodonico, & Teegee, 2015) and "Elder in the Making" (Hsiung & Smithx,

2015), and Roy Henry Vicker's narration of Peace Dancer (Vickers & Budd, 2016). *I may not be the expert, but I know where to find a few whom I trust and value.* I was fortunate to have a guest speaker in to teach about their community and traditions. I drew from current events to spark dialogue around contentious issues, including the debates over changing the names of streets, sports teams, and buildings. We discussed the merit of removing monuments of people responsible for creating and supporting residential schools. While some ceremonies are difficult to explain and rarely observed, we watched the late Gord Downie's naming ceremony (Jancelewicz, 2016), which featured singing in the four directions, to the Earth, and to the Sky. I shared a message chain from an online discussion forum, where I defended someone who was being bullied online because of a pro-Indigenous rights comment. [This was new for me, but I felt the responsibility of having teachings that bound me to speak up and begin to educate people on the issues they clearly knew little about.] Along the same lines, we discussed the hate speech that found a home on a certain senator's website after she had posted a controversial letter espousing the many success stories that came out of the residential school system. We discussed surveillance footage of an Indigenous man being racially profiled as a shoplifter within a store, and a political cartoon that received a lot of on-line attention as it made light of the names changing on schools. There were so many examples of media and current events that made the learning feel timely. We were able to make rich connections between the course readings, additional readings, stories, and quotes, which collectively wove into the experiential fabric of our time together.

Teaching in an Impossible and Imperative Assignment

With humility and conviction, I have shared my questions, my stories, and my learning. I invited you along as I wondered how I might teach *Indigenous Education* well. Still, I wonder if it is even possible in the span of a semester … or in the span of a lifetime. Could I ever *be* enough? Outside of my own trepidations and shortcomings, I know that I have a responsibility that extends beyond me; how do I honour All My Relations, while supporting the students in this difficult learning?

In my writing, I draw on personal narratives to begin to answer these questions. My Métis teacher identity is a source of strength and apprehension. I inescapably teach who I am. For me, the required readings are a source of harm and unexpected healing. They hit too close to home and are hard to reconcile. *How much of my story should I share with the students and what do I keep for me?* I try to prepare for undertaking the difficult knowledge, but I am ultimately unprepared for the near violent workings of the experience. It is challenging to be the educator in this regard, putting students through potential turmoil to set loose their prior conceptions and provoke new learning – *if* they are ready.

In the Indigenous Education course, *I am not an expert.* As an Indigenous educator, I take a vulnerable stance by modeling *how to teach* without being an expert. I face this insurmountable task with hope that my students will go on to teach Indigenous education, too. Teaching Indigenous education is an imperative assignment that will take the commitment of many educators working mindfully and carefully to make real change.

References

Absolon, K., & Willett, C. (2005). Putting ourselves forward: Location in aboriginal research. In L. Brown & S. Strega (Eds.), *Research as resistance: Critical, Indigenous, and anti-oppressive approaches* (pp. 97–126). Toronto: Canadian Scholar's Press.

Association of Canadian Deans of Education. (2010). *Accord on Indigenous education.* Retrieved from http://www.csse-scee.ca/acde/publications

Britzman, D. P. (1998). *Lost subjects, contested objects: Toward a psychoanalytic inquiry of learning.* Albany, NY: State University of New York Press.

Britzman, D. P. (2003). *Practice makes practice: A critical study of learning to teach, revised edition.* Albany, NY: State University of New York Press.

DiAngelo, R., & Sensoy, Ö. (2014). Leaning in: A student's guide to engaging constructively with social justice content. *Radical Pedagogy, 11*(1), Article 2. Retrieved September 1, 2017, from http://www.radicalpedagogy.org

Hsiung, C., & Smithx, C. (Producers), & Hsiung, C. (Director). (2015). *Elder in the making* [Documentary series]. Calgary: Hidden Story Productions.

Irving, K., & Christensen, D. (Producers), & Wolochatiuk, T. (Director). (2012). *We were children* [Documentary film]. *Quebec*: National Film Board of Canada.

Jancelewicz, C. (2016, December 6). Gord Downie breaks down at an emotional first nations ceremony. *Global News.* Retrieved October 18, 2017, from https://globalnews.ca

King, T. (2003). *The truth about stories: A native narrative.* Toronto: House of Anansi Press.

Kovach, M. (2009). *Indigenous methodologies: Characteristics, conversations, and contexts.* Toronto: University of Toronto Press.

Little Bear, L. (2000). Jagged worldviews colliding. In M. Battiste (Ed.), *Reclaiming Indigenous voice and vision* (pp. 77–85). Vancouver: UBC Press.

Markides, J. (2018). Reconciling an ethical framework for living well in the world of research. In J. Markides & L. Forsythe (Eds.), *Looking back and living forward: Indigenous research rising up.* Leiden: Brill.

Marom, L. (2017). Tensions and intersections of self and subject: A new-settler teaching an aboriginal education course. In E. Lyle (Ed.), *At the intersection of selves and subject: Exploring the curricular landscape of identity* (pp. 19–29). Rotterdam, The Netherlands: Sense Publishers.

Palmer, P. J. (2017). *The courage to teach: Exploring the inner landscape of a teacher's life* (20th anniversary ed.). San Fransisco, CA: Jossey-Bass.

Pinnegar, S. E., & Hamilton, M. L. (2009). *Self-study of practice as a genre of qualitative research: Theory, methodology, and practice*. Dordrecht: Springer.

Poitras Pratt, Y., & Daniels, D. L. (2014). *Métis remembrances of education: Bridging history with memory*. Proceedings of the IDEAS: Rising to the Challenge Conference 2014, University of Calgary, Institutional Repository DSpace 2014, Calgary, Alberta. Retrieved from http://hdl.handle.net/1880/50137

Smiley, M., & Pope, C. (Producers), Fernandez-Salvador y Campodonico, L. F., Teegee, M. (Executive producers), & Smiley, M. (Director). (2015). *Highway of tears* [Documentary film]. Canada: Finesse Films.

Smith, G. H. (2000). Protecting and respecting Indigenous knowledge. In M. Battiste (Ed.), *Reclaiming Indigenous voice and vision* (pp. 209–224). Vancouver: UBC Press.

St. Denis, V. (2007). Aboriginal education and anti-racist education: Building alliances across cultural and racial identity. *Canadian Journal of Education, 30*(4), 1068–1092.

Truth and Reconciliation Commission. (2015a). *Honouring the truth, reconciling for the future: Summary of the final report on the Truth and Reconciliation Commission of Canada*. Retrieved February 18, 2016, from http://www.myrobust.com/websites/trcinstitution/File/Reports/Executive_ Summary_English_Web.pdf

Truth and Reconciliation Commission. (2015b). *Calls to action*. Retrieved February 18, 2016, from http://www.trc.ca/websites/trcinstitution/File/2015/Findings/Calls_to_Action_English2.pdf

Vickers, R. H., & Budd, R. (2016). *Peace dancer*. Madeira Park: Harbour Publishing.

CHAPTER 5

Leveraging Arts Integration to Transform Mathematics Praxis

Timothy M. Sibbald

Many years ago I lamented to a colleague that I was not sure how to maintain student motivation and engagement in a high school mathematics class as a holiday break approached. I was relatively new to teaching, but sufficiently experienced to anticipate that student interest would wane. My colleague suggested *Escher Art* as an activity that her students found both engaging and creative. This prompted me to engage in self-study where the activity provided a specific example that helped me understand changes in my own mathematics praxis over a long period of time.

The Escher Art task begins with a square of card stock. A side of the square is cut from one corner to another (see Figure 5.1). The piece cut out is removed and, being careful not to flip it upside down, is affixed to an uncut side of the template using tape (see Figure 5.2). The process is repeated for another uncut side to complete the template (see Figure 5.3). The template is used to create a pattern by tracing the outside edge of the template and then fitting the template in a new position, like a jigsaw puzzle piece. The template, in the new position, is traced and the process continues until there are no more positions for the template (i.e. the page is full). The resulting tessellation can then be adorned with aesthetic aspects that transform the pattern into a piece of art. Often the template shape appears with multiple orientations and some orientations facilitate creative interpretation. Strictly speaking this is only

  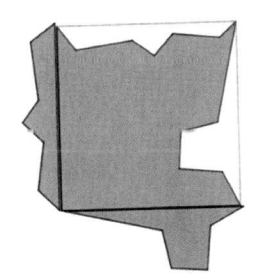

FIGURE 5.1 A side of the template is cut corner to corner

FIGURE 5.2 Affixing the cut piece onto another side

FIGURE 5.3 Example of a complete template

© KONINKLIJKE BRILL NV, LEIDEN, 2019 | DOI:10.1163/9789004388864_005

loosely what Escher did in his artwork (see www.mcescher.com), but can be a viable way for students to gain an understanding of the tessellation aspect of Escher's work.

In my earliest adoption of Escher Art, I focused on solving a pragmatic issue around motivation and engagement as a holiday approached. I was not aware of the mathematics of tessellations but interpreted the end result as analogous to patterns made by jigsaw puzzles. The artistic aspect was something I had seen at the National Gallery of Canada. At this stage of my career, I was content with a new activity that could be enacted to address a particular issue. It was more a matter of "going through prescribed motions" (Wight, 2015, p. 184) than praxis.

A year later I used the same activity again to address the same concern. However, I had misplaced the instructions and made the prescriptive assumption (Brandenburg, 2008) to forgo the instruction sheet because the instructions had not been that complicated. I instructed students to cut corner to corner, remove the piece, and tape it onto another side of the square. They repeated the process for another side and they had a template. Time ran short and students were asked to finish tessellating the pattern for homework so that they could focus on the artistic aspect the next day. When I reflect on this detail I find it demonstrative that I did not shy away from the artistic aspect that I considered a personal weakness. In fact, I was promoting engagement in the artistic aspect during class to further my own understanding of how to develop my praxis around the art component, unaware of an opportunity to learn considerable mathematics. I was viewing it as an opportunity to learn about artistic creativity from my students.

The transformation of my praxis began in earnest when some students arrived to class very upset that their patterns did not work. I had students who had built new templates because the pattern from their original templates would not work – a novelty as the activity had worked the previous year. Many students had created tessellations that were fine. As I inquired about why some did not work I was unsure whether it was due to student error or the lack of strict instructions. I made the prescriptive assumption, once again, that a minor change in the instructions could not lead to a major change in the result. However, I could not reconcile the assumption with the collection of reliable students with seemingly errant results. Perhaps there was more to the instructions than I knew.

A student showed me his tessellation where a U shape formed with two lines of traced templates showing a clear crack in the pattern – too narrow to fit the template, and yet, the pattern seemed to be valid and reproducible with their template. Another student had a pattern with a three by three block where the middle was missing because the template could not fit into the hole; however, the eight surrounding pieces legitimately fit together.

I was thrilled that opening up the possibilities beyond the basic instructions had led to such rich outcomes. The activity was showing that "I needed to move away from what was known (for me) into situations where I became a learner alongside [my students]" (Brandenburg, 2008, p. 172). Mathematically I could not explain the results because I did not know enough about tessellation. However, I was inclined to agree with Skovsmose that "mathematics as a school subject refers to a rather well-defined body of knowledge parcelled out in bits and pieces to be taught and learned according to preformed criteria. Mathematics could, however, also refer to domains of knowledge and understanding that are not institutionalized through research priorities or curricular structures" (2016, p. 1).

It was also exciting that the task could fit within the problem solving process outlined in the curriculum. This strengthened the potential curriculum connection, though I did not have sufficient details to properly place the activity. There was a possibility of using the activity as an exploration of unanticipated geometric behaviour that could be brought together with a creative artistic component. This could portray mathematics as having elements that are not thoroughly known or established with textbook rigidity. It was evident that there was considerably more mathematics available through the activity, which could resolve my concern about the activity's curriculum connection.

I was in an early stage of forming my identity as a teacher, and it was fortunate that I was able to connect the observed mathematical behaviour with "interruption to the habitual and a degree of living with the discomfort and uncertainty of not predetermining learning outcomes" (Brandenburg, 2008, p. 172). The unusual outcomes gave students an authentic sense of discovery. There was a candid admission to the students that they were being given the opportunity to explore something I did not fully understand mathematically. Some students found my stance exhilarating where others clearly believed a teacher should know all the answers – they did not appreciate a teacher who had "the confidence to challenge the status-quo" (Brandenburg, 2008, p. 172) in mathematics.

Later reflections highlighted that the sense of discovery is something I view as supremely important in mathematics. Discovery facilitates students constructing an understanding in their own way; however, when a teacher engages content they do not fully understand, it provides an opportunity for students to collaborate with the teacher in the co-construction of an understanding. It was an experience where "I found that as I engaged in inquiry, my discoveries changed both my teaching and me" (Marin, 2014, p. 24). There was authenticity to this approach because I was not simply creating an artificial scenario where I pretended not to know – I genuinely did not know and, to this day, remain uncertain about some of the mathematical nuances.

The task when taken in a general sense generates some wonderful patterns. I identify with using the general process because, pedagogically, I believe that math teachers should be bringing novelty to their classrooms. The activity is at the junction between conforming to standard math teaching practices and the way I identify with math teaching. It is a relationship between creativity and maintenance (Cunha, Pacheco, Castanheira, & Rego, 2015) within math teaching praxis. It was a personal belief that too much of mathematics was being taught in a manner that promoted following instructions, as opposed to having students exercise choice and addressing the consequences of the choice.

The Ontario mathematics curriculum was being reformed to have greater emphasis on student-centered teaching where students would be "actively engaged with subject matter" (Marin, 2014, p. 22). The reform supported undoing (Iszatt-White, Kempster, & Carroll, 2017) the teacher-student power structure in favour of facilitating student exploration. Pedagogically, it was a difficult negotiation with students who lacked self-efficacy to explore a process.

The reform changed the position of Escher Art because mathematical discoveries occurring in my classroom were necessarily student-centered. Using the activity reinforced the undoing of the power structure that Brandenburg (2008) refers to as the "sleeper issue of the impact of my authority of position" (p. 135). Collective classroom effort was slowly revealing more than the teacher knew of the content. It was, as Marin (2014) describes, an inquiry activity that was changing the way I taught and my own view of what I could achieve within teaching.

However, while the changes to the curriculum were serendipitous, it was only one example from a period with several significant transitions in terms of developing my own praxis. The power negotiation was not clear at the time because the particular activity was my first significant experience in changing the subject authority. The instructional center and authority changes also facilitated the artistic element that contrasted with the mathematical component – an ongoing tension where I learned from both opportunities. While I was not aware of the underlying mathematics, I knew how to determine the mathematical structure, which contrasts with the artistic element where I was inexperienced and unsure of my capacity to understand the activity. Students pursued artistic inspiration that did not occur to me, and I had the opportunity to learn about the process of developing artwork. For example, mathematically I assumed one would complete a tessellation (i.e. fill the page), however, some students tessellated regions (i.e. clouds) without necessarily tessellating between regions.

Over the course of a decade I revisited the task each time exercising reflexive thinking (Cunha, Pacheco, Castanheira, & Rego, 2015). The activity informed the transformation of my instruction, and I continued to learn from the activity. It was no longer a set of instructions to achieve a product; rather, it was a process where I came to understand the activity better and was able to advise students based on prior enactments of the activity. The nature of the mathematics, partially revealed by variations in the instructions, was illuminating because of increased tacit knowledge (Pinnegar & Hamilton, 2009, p. 17) and confidence when setting students up for the task. Students who wanted an end result with a definitive pattern were instructed to carefully avoid flipping the cut pieces when making their templates. Students who felt more adventurous were forewarned that flipping one or two cut pieces would give them a chance to explore the unknown. This approach was transformative because it offered "an intellectual playground" (Greer & Mukhopadhyay, 2012), both artistically and mathematically. The artistic opportunity led some students to challenge their own conception of mathematics as a subject leading to definitive end results. Other students were intrigued by the process of generating patterns and motivated by the mathematics rather than the artistic possibilities. However, the approach was, as Korthagen and Vasalos (2010) have described, a quick and superficial solution that facilitated classroom utility but did not clarify the underlying mathematics.

The transformation of praxis was not neat or linear. The lessons about pedagogy and changing the power structure of the classroom were early messages from the activity. The impact "pushed comfort zones" (Brandenburg, 2008, p. 150) and contributed to ongoing remodeling and reframing of my role as a teacher. This occurred in conjunction with curriculum changes that promoted student-centered learning over teacher-centered approaches. Addressing the changing curriculum was a focus of the department, and the pedagogical shift in my praxis was rapid. Altering power structures was slower in coming, largely because an authentic power shift in a mathematics classroom requires structures that facilitate discovery approaches and student ownership of knowledge. These are challenging when the high school curriculum contains considerable abstraction and, in Ontario, quite a lot of busy work.

Ultimately, I joined a faculty of education and included the activity during my first year because "pre-service teachers are to be encouraged and feel more empowered to negotiate aspects of their learning about teaching mathematics" (Brandenburg, 2008, p. 134). However, academia provided professional autonomy (Brandenburg, 2008) for research time to delve into the details of how the different templates led to different outcomes. After using the activity in my new environment, I had a request to run a professional development session for in-service teachers. I used the occasion to engage some students in the process of providing the workshop. In addition, when I run workshops, I aim to add something new for anyone who is familiar with the concept being taught. So I suggested a couple of students should explore what happens when a template is made from a hexagon rather than a square. The hexagon, like the square, tessellates to fill a page without requiring gaps.

The introduction of hexagons was something that I knew was feasible in principle, but wasn't something I had done. I was continuing to transform my praxis by making it clear to the students that I did not know what would result. All I knew was that hexagons, unlike pentagons, do tessellate to fill the plane. It was an example of "our obligation to create practice environments that enable our teacher candidates to flourish in ways that, in turn, contribute to deeper learning for their future students" (Pinnegar & Hamiltion, 2009, p. 57). I knew I was taking a risk that it might not go well but, pedagogically, I was experienced with addressing the risk and felt it would model that aspect of my praxis for the teacher candidates.

Beyond the classroom, I collaborated with a graduate student in a community event that was for children aged five to ten. Activities needed to be hands on, relatively quick, but engaging and interesting. Square patterns would have been too complicated, but I was not opposed to using Escher Art with a young age group provided I could ensure their success. So, I made a template out of an equilateral triangle and cut twenty pieces out of foam board. In the process, I realized that there was only one other unique template possible with equilateral triangles and I made 20 pieces based on it. The two collections of pieces provide very different outcomes: one makes hexagons, while the other makes linear chains. This extended the thinking on Escher Art by providing a simplest case and highlighting the relevance of the number of distinct templates.

A pre-service candidate, who had investigated hexagonal templates, was sufficiently intrigued to collaborate on investigating the activity. It became an opportunity to work with someone who could "mediate, provoke, and support new understandings" (Samaras, 2011, p. 6). A significant challenge was the development of a method for communicating results and conveying the findings in a manner that could be comprehended by teachers. A lettering system was adopted to identify where a cut was made and how the cut piece was affixed. The system led to clarification of the different characteristic behaviours and resonated with experience. We began drafting a paper that provided details of all the possible outcomes (Sibbald & Wheatstone, 2016).

Working through the details that informed the paper served as a pivotal point in the transformation of my praxis because we summarized the different behaviours succinctly for the first time. It also summarized the "creation of new knowledge and the subsequent challenges to my conceptualizations of learning and teaching" (Brandenburg, 2009, p. 196). Of the five unique templates identified, four produce uniformly tessellated patterns. There are differences in how they tessellate and their aesthetic qualities, but they are complete tessellations. Only one case gives rise to unusual behaviour – this explains why only some students experienced anomalies. The details of the unusual case are astonishing. Firstly, I mentioned some students produced tessellations with holes and others generated patterns with cracks (a gap that can never be filled). These arise from the same method of producing the template and correspond to choices made when tessellating the template (see Figure 5.4). Imagine a jigsaw puzzle where assembling the pieces in different ways can result in different overall characteristics for the puzzle. Artistically it is fascinating that the same template can lead to different tessellated behaviours that have different aesthetic qualities.

I had assumed the different behaviours were due to the different templates, but the investigation established that one template gave rise to distinctly different tessellations. For example, it can produce a very compact tessellation with holes at regular intervals, which was consistent with what a student had showed me early in my adoption of the activity. Another solution results in a U shape with two tessellated arms emerging in a manner where the template can never fit between the arms. Again it was consistent with results students had generated. In both cases, the large-scale behaviour was a repeating pattern. Mathematically I knew that there were tessellations that did not repeat, and I wondered if it might be an undiscovered possibility for this unusual case. The remarkable outcome of exploring the tessellating process was the realization that a repeating pattern could be generated that allowed a component that did not have to repeat – it is akin to having a chain of cells with each having unique DNA. While the overall pattern repeats, each instance can have a non-repeating "signature" component.

The examination had shown that only one case needed to be separated out for effective praxis. It also pointed to the option of having students consider multiple ways they could tessellate the template pattern for the one unique case. There were details to be determined for instruction, and it evolved as the teacher candidate and I arranged to present at a teacher conference. We wanted the presentation to be available to a wide range of teachers and decided we needed to tier the task. A relatively simple entry point to Escher Art used equilateral triangles that had been developed for the local

D C / A B	B C / A D	A B / D C			C D / B A
		C D / B A	D A / C B	B A / C D	C B / D A
B A / C D	C B / D A			A D / B C	D C / A B
A D / B C	D C / A B	B C / A D	A B / D C		
A B / D C		C D / B A	D A / C B	B A / C D	

B C / A D	A B / D C	A D / B C	D C / A B	B C / A D	A B / D C	A D / B C	D C / A B	B C / A D	
C D / B A	D A / C B								C D / B A
		B A / C D							
A B / D C	A D / B C								A B / D C
D A / C B									D A / C B
B A / C D	C B / D A								B A / C D
A D / B C	D C / A B	B C / A D	A B / D C	A D / B C	D C / A B	B C / A D	A B / D C	A D / B C	
	B C / A D			A B / D C		C D / D A	D A / C B		
	A B / D C			B A / C D		D A / B A	C B / C D		
		C D / B A	D A / C B		D A / C B	B A / C D	C B / D A		
A B / D C			B A / C D		B A / C D		D C / A B	B C / A D	A B / D C
D A / C B		A D / B C		A D / B C	D C / A B	B C / A D			D A / C B
		A B / D C		A B / D C		C D / D A			
	C D / B A	D A / C B		D A / C B	B A / C B	C B / D A			

FIGURE 5.4 Two different tessellation outcomes for one template. ABCD is the template and side AB connects to BC, while side CD connects to AD. (Reproduced from Sibbald & Wheatstone, 2017, with permission from the Ontario Association for Mathematics Education)

event to exhibit distinct behaviours. It was an important point in terms of praxis because preparing the presentation developed a scaffold making more elaborate patterns accessible.

With teacher candidates I had also tiered the task. However, in that instance, I needed to create more challenging scenarios for students with stronger mathematical backgrounds. I achieved that by encouraging students to consider what happens with hexagons. Interested in what we were discovering, the teacher candidate I continued to formally investigate the hexagon problem. Ultimately we resolved the hexagon version of Escher Art, but it was not overly transformational in the sense that there were few new surprises (Sibbald & Wheatstone, forthcoming). It did yield a mathematical problem of a spiral tessellation where it is unclear if the spiral will continue indefinitely.

Simultaneously, I began exploring a related problem that required tessellation in three dimensions. While I produced models, the lack of precision of modeling materials left *wiggle room* that created uncertainty about the mathematical concepts behind the patterns. Essentially, the process has reached an impasse where the abstraction entailed to understand the underlying research mathematics conception of tessellations is required.

It was serendipitous that a student in the university mathematics department gave a presentation about research she had done regarding a particular kind of tessellation. It had a jarring effect, as a key focus of the presentation was clarification using mathematical results from the field of topology. It held a personal message: that if I wanted to go further with my development, the next step was to adopt the formal machinery of topology as an organizing medium. The details of this unfamiliar branch of mathematics offered an opportunity to continue the transformation of my own praxis.

An interesting parallel can be drawn between the development of the article that explained Escher Art outcomes to teachers (Sibbald & Wheatstone, 2016) and the language and organization for communication of the ideas, which was a crucial aspect of the article. The parallel is that the mathematics of topology requires substantial conceptual clarity that provides a framework for developing a broader base for further thought. In the case of tessellations, the conceptual base is rich and complicated, which is why Escher found it rewarding as a grounding aspect of many pieces of art.

As Pinnegar and Hamilton (2009) note, the approach taken for teacher instructional research is not conducive to acceptance of the research findings within the traditional mathematics community because it has not been conveyed within the norms of their community. This renews the critical issue surrounding authoritative power within mathematics, except that this time it is not the teacher-student divide, it is the teacher-researcher divide. In effect, the work done does not inform mathematics research and, because of the level of abstraction, it is not readily informed by mathematics research. Further transformation of my praxis requires bridging the practitioner-instructional focus with the researcher-abstraction focus.

The placement of the task has evolved over 15 years. It is informative to align it with the hierarchal onion model of reflection (Korthagen & Vasalos, 2010) that uses teaching environment, teacher behaviour, capacity, beliefs, identity, and mission. Simply put my attitude has been that the task has interesting facets (environment) that help convey a sense of intrigue in multiple ways (behaviour) that will engage student thinking (capacity). I hold a fundamental belief that I do not have to maintain full control of what happens when students explore territory where I do not know all the answers (beliefs). Nurturing teacher-student respect and providing students with power over their learning is fundamental (identity) to developing student recognition that learning is a lifelong endeavor (mission).

From a critical perspective, I claim mathematics is a field that is developing new ideas and is not dissimilar to science. However, there is very little in the way of popular dissemination of mathematics and few people who can provide interpretations of research mathematics for teachers. Where there are difficulties bringing modern mathematics to the classroom, Escher Art leverages the artistic element to provide an interdisciplinary circumstance that facilitates the development of mathematical concepts around tessellation processes while not making the teacher entirely reliant on the thoroughness of their knowledge of the underlying mathematics.

The example of Escher Art, and the way the activity has transformed my praxis, is important because it highlights that teachers can explore new ideas leading to understandings that open up new areas for mathematical exploration. It has also been important as an indicator of the powerful use of interdisciplinary pedagogy where a different transformation of personal praxis is underway. The connection of mathematics praxis to its research community remains difficult and needs attention. The connection is challenging because "mathematics is critical but in both a significant and undetermined way" (Skovsmose, 2016, p. 8).

References

Brandenburg, R. (2008). *Powerful pedagogy: Self-study of a teacher educator's practice.* New York, NY: Springer.

Brandenburg, R. (2009). Assumption interrogation: An insight into a self-study researcher's pedagogical frame. In D. Tidwell, M. Heston, & L. Fitzgerald (Eds.), *Research methods for the self-study of practice* (pp. 195–211). Berlin: Springer.

Cunha, M., Pacheco, M., Castanheira, F., & Rego, A. (2015). Reflexive work and the duality of self-leadership. *Leadership, 13*(4), 472–495.

Greer, B., & Mukhopadhyay, S. (2012). The hegemony of mathematics. In O. Skovsmose & B. Greer (Eds.), *Opening the cage: Critique and politics of mathematics education* (pp. 229–248). Rotterdam, The Netherlands: Sense Publishers.

Iszatt-White, M., Kempster, S., & Carroll, B. (2017). An educator's perspective on reflexive pedagogy: Identity undoing and issues of power. *Management Learning, 48*(5), 582–596.

Korthagen, A. J., & Vasalos, A. (2010). Going to the core: Deepening reflection by connecting the person to the profession. In N. Lyons (Ed.), *Handbook of reflection and reflective inquiry: Mapping a way of knowing for professional reflective inquiry* (pp. 529–552). New York, NY: Springer.

Marin, K. (2014). Becoming a teacher educator: A self-study of the use of inquiry in a mathematics methods course. *Studying Teacher Education, 10*(1), 20–35.

Pinnegar, S., & Hamilton, M. (2009). *Self-study of practice as a genre of qualitative research: Theory, methodology, and practice.* London: Springer.

Samaras, A. (2011). Understanding self-study research: What and why? In A. Samaras (Ed.), *Self-study teacher research: Improving your practice through collaborative inquiry* (pp. 3–22). Thousand Oaks, CA: Sage Publications.

Sibbald, T., & Wheatstone, M. (2016). Advancing Escher art through generalization. *Ontario Association for Mathematics Education Gazette, 54*(4), 23–26.

Sibbald, T., & Wheatstone, M. (forthcoming). Escher art with hexagons. *Saskatchewan Mathematics Teachers' Society the Variable*.

Skovsmose, O. (2016). Mathematics: A critical rationality? In P. Ernest, B. Sriraman, & N. Ernest (Eds.), *Critical mathematics education: Theory, praxis, and reality* (pp. 1–22). Charlotte, NC: Information Age Publishing.

Wight, I. (2015, January–February). From practice to praxis – as transformative education: Leading at the integral/professional interface? *Integral Leadership Review*, 184–191.

CHAPTER 6

The Transformative Becomings of a Nature-Based Educator

Cher Hill and Laura Piersol

As in-service teacher-educators working in a graduate program based on a self-study methodology (Pinnegar & Hamilton, 2009; Samaras, 2011), we have witnessed the transformative nature of engaging in reflexive inquiry. While reflexive inquiry is oriented towards future transformation (see Pinar, 1975), traditionally it involves a retrospective analysis. We are interested in how an emergent sense of self might evolve from self-study methods that are non-linear and forward reaching, as well as retrospective. We wonder how we, as educators, move beyond our dominant narratives and learn to tell new stories about ourselves. In the words of Ben Okri (1997), "we live by stories, we also live in them ... If we change the stories we live by, quite possibly we change our lives" (p. 46). The goal of this inquiry was to use collaborative self-study to change the stories that Cher told about herself as an educator, thereby creating openings for transforming practice. We endeavoured to create new stories not only informed by what has happened, but also what is yet to occur.

In this work, identity is viewed as a material assemblage (de Freitas & Curinga, 2015), and a process of becoming. Central to this is Barad's (2007) conception of relational ontology in which phenomena, such as identity, are regarded as material expressions that are continuously constituted and reconstituted through the entanglement of various elements. Here the focus is on "identity-in-action" and "the series of co-constructions that unfold, fold over, and refold in the becomings of a teacher" (Strom & Martin, 2017, p. 8). Within this work we embrace a nomadic sense of self (Braidotti, 2011) as practitioner that involves exploring new terrain, while returning to familiar patterns of movement.

Context

This year Cher unexpectedly became involved with Laura's Master of Education in Nature-based, Place-conscious Practices cohort, which is outside Cher's usual teaching assignments. Laura's cohort meets in various locations within natural environments and works collaboratively with nature as co-teacher. Laura, unlike Cher, has worked as an ecological educator for over 20 years, helping to start two ecological public schools that are rooted in place, and she is most comfortable teaching outdoors. Laura has spent a long time considering the many ways in which she is connected to the more-than-human world and how it has shaped her identity and sense of self. While Cher appreciates her colleague's scholarship and pedagogies, and has philosophical connections to her work through feminism and new materialist perspectives, when she began this project she felt she had few personal connections to that natural world. Her initial characterization of her childhood was one that was primarily spent indoors, in which she chose pools over lakes and whizzed through nature on a pair of skis. In the beginning, Cher felt a lack of personal connection to this work. This unusual teaching assignment provided a meaningful opportunity for Cher to explore new pedagogical possibilities and identities.

Method

This work is grounded in self-study methodologies, involving the disciplined study of one's own actions, identities, experiences, beliefs, and values situated within the context of professional practice (Pinnegar & Hamilton, 2009; Samaras, 2011). This self-study involved a living inquiry into Cher's becomings as an instructor within nature-based and place-conscious education, as well as her practice as a teacher to her children (ages 5, 8, and 10). Self-study methodologies exist at the very intersection of theory and practice, reconfiguring the usual boundaries between the two and disrupting hierarchies between professional and academic knowledge. "Critical friends" who question, support, extend, and suggest, are essential to knowledge development and validation (Pinnegar & Hamilton, 2009; Samaras, 2011). Within this project, Laura served as a mentor and critical friend to Cher, and their co-teaching arrangement provided an ideal context for learning collaboratively from and through practice.

We used reflective methods, which involve a re-viewing of actions and interactions and examining values and assumptions (Bolton, 2010; Brookfield, 1995), as well as reflexive methods, which involve revisiting events and experiences that contribute to the ongoing and relational development of self (Lyle, 2013). As Lyle (2017) explains, "reflection is after and individual whereas reflexivity is ongoing and relational" (p. vii). Both are part of an iterative process of becoming that can contribute to the ongoing development of self and can catalyze personal and professional transformation. Our reflective and reflexive methods included Cher's autobiographical writing, an inquiry journal documenting teaching and learning experiences and discussions, as well as photos and reflections of Cher's visits to her micro-site located within an urban forest.

We also engaged in diffractive methods, which involve reading insights "through one another" (Barad, 2007, p. 30) to create openings, inspire questions, and illuminate how differences are made. These methods exist on the edge of the future and resist the foreclosure of knowledge. They attempt to transcend the level of critique and instead aim for "respectful engagement" through transdisciplinary exploration (Barad, 2007, p. 93). We diffracted ideas from Laura's article, *Listening Place*, through Cher's paper, *More-than-reflective practice: Becoming a diffractive practitioner*, allowing different concepts and issues to interfere with, inform, and build on one another. When reading our papers through each other we identified more resonances than we initially imagined, as well as gentle interference patterns. The experience felt akin to looking through a kaleidoscope in which each twist forefronted particular aspects of patterns that were always part of the configuration but were previously backgrounded. We hoped that these diffractive methods would uncover new possibilities for Cher among the many potentialities within the context of her challenging teaching assignment.

Transformative Becomings

Reflective and Reflexive Practices: Building Relationships with the Natural World

In order to develop her connection within the natural world, three months before Cher began her teaching assignment, she took up the practice of visiting a micro-site on a regular basis. Micro-sites, often part of Laura's pedagogy, are bio-diverse places that learners visit in order to form relationships with the natural world (see Piersol, 2014). Cher's micro-site is located in Mundy Park – an urban forest near to her home within the unceded territory of the Kwikwetlem First Nations people. It is primarily a new growth forest comprised of 178 hectares of land. The park includes multiple trails, a small lake, as well as a recreational area. Within her micro-site, Cher is learning how to develop respectful relationships with/in the natural world and to support others in doing so, producing shifts in her practice and her sense of self. At the beginning of her inquiry, Cher decided that she would visit her micro-site while running through the park. While it is difficult to develop a relationship with place while in motion, it is not surprising that this was her initial entry point, as there are few places in the forest that invite stillness. In this regard, the trails serve as molar lines, dominant forces that regulate ways of thinking and acting (Deleuze & Guatarii, 1987), keeping bodies in motion, and limiting opportunities for forming deep connections with place. Cher chose a 50-year-old Douglas fir tree as the epicenter of her micro-site because initially she intended to stretch against this tree at the end of her run. The material world however has an agential vitality; that is objects possess an efficacy "in excess of the human meanings, signs, or purposes they express or serve" (Bennett, 2010, p. 20). Once Cher slowed down enough to look closely at the Douglas fir, noticing his delicate bark that hosts other non-invasive entities (see Figure 6.1), she realized that it was not ethical to push her body up against the tree, potentially altering the bark and others who lived there (Inquiry Journal, 30 September 2017). The bark was communicating with her in ways that had previously been invisible. Cher continues to visit with the tree (which she cheekily calls Stretch) but in more collegial ways. With Laura's encouragement to learn *with* place, Cher began to see Stretch as a subject helping her to inquire into her becomings as a nature-based instructor and to think and act in new ways.

Laura encourages instructors to plan lessons in place and contends that "making an effort to play, rest and linger in the places where one teaches, not as part of work but as a part of coming to know the wild voices around us, can assist in learning what these places have to offer" (Piersol, 2014, p. 46). Indeed, Cher has found that, through building a relationship with the forest, she is able to support others in developing similar relationships. Her micro-site has been

FIGURE 6.1

The vitality of Stretch's bark

FIGURE 6.2   Stretch, Fishtail, and Hugging Trees

a powerful place for supporting her children in forming their own respectful connections with the natural world.

> Feb 24th, 2018, Mundy Park, Kwikwetlem Nation
> I took Alex with me to the park today. I told him that I had a special friend who lived in the park and asked if he would like to meet him. Alex nodded and appeared to be curious. We walked to the beginning of the trail and I said, "This is my friend, Stretch." Alex immediately hugged Stretch and then decided to make his own tree friends including Fishtail and Hugging Trees (see Figure 6.2). This was very different from the time I took the children into the ravine. Some of the kids whacked sticks on the tree trunks, attempting to break the sticks ... Today there was no whacking, and Alex even questioned how the snow felt when he stepped on it.

Through Laura's questioning, Cher has come to see that projecting human qualities on to trees and bestowing them with names can be viewed as a colonial practice. Understanding *tree-as-friend,* however, has dramatically shifted Cher and her children's relationships within the natural world and their identities in relation to the land. They now come to the forest to learn with it, play with it, care for it, and heal themselves, rather than travel through it. They are learning to see and feel the natural world not simply as backdrop or something that serves humans, but rather as an agent with something to offer in and of itself.

Reflective and Reflexive Practices: Belonging and Becoming

When Cher visited the MEd cohort for the first time and heard the students' (all practicing teachers) autobiographical presentations, she was surprised by the diverse entry points that fuelled their connections with the natural world, including sports, relationships with others who inspired a love of the land, art, animals, and fear of the anthropocene, as well as the capacity of the natural world to heal and calm (Inquiry Journal, 24 November 2017). Some of the stories shared "hung on the edges" (Downey & Clandinin, 2010) of Cher's stories in unexpected ways, both heightening and disrupting her sense of not belonging within this space. Mimicking George Ella Lyon's poem *Where I'm From* (a pedagogical method used in our program), Cher created an account of her dis/connection with the natural-world, which she shared with the cohort.

"I am From" Poem
I am from vineyards and pine needles
 From still lakes and full moons
 sunburned cheeks and cherry earrings
 cracked earth
 and cracked feet
I am from immigrant settlers
 From "this land is my land"
 my Canadian dream
 funded by a small fortune
 hidden inside a doll's head
I am from the Valley
 From containment and homogeneity
 sexism and racism
 the erasure and mythologizing
 of those who walked these paths first
I am from the Japanese garden
 From the secret pathway, sacred rock, and coy pond
 maintained by arthritic hands
 dreaming only of this place
 and never of her
I am from the farm
 From acres of rolling hills of green foliage, heavy with dew
 daisy chain crowns in my hair
 distracting from the cobwebs of cruelty
 hanging in corners
I am from days spent in fishing boats
 From my parents obsession
 my head in book
 praying no fish would be caught and killed
 in front of my eyes

I am from fear of the Wild
  From the safety of civilization
  affirmed by the gun
  residing in our trailer days after a family mirroring mine
  was murdered at their campsite
I am from the mountains
  From the solace found in snow and ice
  escaping allergies and asthma
  and experiencing a fleeting spirituality in the peaks
  Is it coincidence that I carry this name?

This rendering became part of the material expression of Cher's identity, providing "traces of what might yet (have) happen(ed)" (Barad, 2014, p. 168), and who she might be/come. Within this entanglement Cher's identity was reconfigured, creating a foundation for what has been and is yet to come, laying the groundwork for her pedagogical practice. This re-visiting of memories contributed to Cher's evolving sense of self and, in particular, her feelings of belonging within the cohort.

Diffractive Practices: Full Body Sensory Engagement

Within Laura's scholarship, full body sensory engagement achieved through "discipline, practice and the humility to surrender some control" (Piersol, 2014, p. 46) is described as a possible way to deepen human-land relationships. There is a resonance here within Cher's writing about what it means to be a diffractive practitioner, as informed by new materialist perspectives. She writes, "the diffractive practitioner moves away from cognitive reflections of self and other to engage their bodymind sensibilities (Lenz Taguchi, 2012), intra-acting with forces and flows within educative assemblages, becoming-with the world" (Hill, 2017, pp. 7–8). Attunement among humans and more-than-humans is an area of overlap within our scholarship that incites possibilities for practice. Within new materialist perspectives, all physical bodies are thought to have a vitality and creative force (Bennett, 2010). Likewise, Laura views nature as a co-teacher, full of subjectivity and agency.

As an indoor educator, however, Cher's practice has typically focused on materials found within classrooms, such as pencils, whiteboards, and balls. One exception involved her observations of the beach co-teaching her daughter to swim, an experience that inspired her to hold her graduate class at the beach (see Smythe, Hill, MacDonald, Dagenais, Sinclair, & Toohey, 2017). Previously Cher viewed natural landscapes as powerful in a pedagogical sense because they are predominantly smooth spaces that enable open and fluid movement

(Deleuze & Guattari, 1987). She compares this to classrooms, which she understands as typically striated spaces because they channel movement along predetermined linear pathways. Inherent within Cher's outdoor pedagogy, however, was a hierarchical divide in which the natural environment is distinct from, and in service to, humans. As Barad asserts, all practices involve particular ways of knowing and being that have ethical consequences as "epistemology, ontology, and ethics are inseparable" (p. 69). Our diffractive reading revealed how differences between our pedagogies are produced and why they matter. Laura's pedagogy goes beyond Cher's focus on the ontology and epistemology of learning within natural environments to emphasize the ethical dimension of disrupting hierarchical relationships between humans and the natural world. This interference pattern marked the new terrain that Cher grew to occupy and informed the development of her pedagogical practice.

In her becoming as a nature-based educator, Cher is learning to develop more ethical relationships with the land through full bodily engagement, as well as how to support others in doing the same. Unlike classrooms that can erupt in e/motions that commend attention and are often visible or auditory, becoming attuned to flows of energy within and among organic bodies, for Cher, involved noticing more subtle energies. Participants in Laura's study used creative practices such as photography and poetry as tools that supported their bodily engagement in place. Cher found that arts-based practices described in Flowers, Lipsett, and Barrett (2014), particularly left-hand drawing and eyes closed drawing, were helpful in attending to the vitalities of bodies as well as their teachings. For example, in Figure 6.3, through left-handed drawing, Cher sensed a friendly, invitational, and caring presence of a cedar tree. She noticed how its branches appeared to be shielding a broken bow. The second sketch, some of which she

FIGURE 6.3   Friendly the Tree and Mountain as Witness

completed with her eyes closed, focused her attention on the commanding presence of a collective of trees on a mountain that were silent and still, in comparison to the river at its base and the clouds at its peak that were constantly in motion. This experience left Cher with a sense of *mountain as witness*, attending to all the events that have occurred in this place since creation.

As with diffractive reading, when listening for subtle energies, the goal is not to ascertain *Truth* but rather to uncover one of the many potential existing realities within the human and more-than-human entanglement that create openings and allow for something new to occur. Although these examples involved anthropomorphizing, for Cher, they were an entry point in attending to the vitalities of the more-than-human, knowing nature-as-teacher, and developing a respect for the natural world, as well as a sense of humility. When attending to the subtle energies, the impact of human interference within the natural world becomes apparent, as does an awareness of how small changes can have major repercussions (both positive and negative).

Cher has been taking up this practice of sketching entities within the natural world with her students and her children. In doing so, her pedagogy has shifted to support more affective, aesthetic, and spiritual components of nature-based learning as well as intellectual and cognitive aspects. She is learning to provide students with private quiet time on the land with fluid entry points to engage with the place, including Indigenous knowledge and history, poems,

FIGURE 6.4   Learners along the bank of the river sketching, drumming, or contemplating

and arts-based practices, and coming to understand ritual and ceremony as pedagogies that connect humans with the natural world through awareness, gratitude, and appreciation (see Figure 6.4).

Diffractive Practices: Fluid Boundaries

Another reverberation that became apparent through diffracting our scholarship is the blurring of boundaries between bodies and an immersion of self within the natural world. Laura writes, "self is always embedded in a web of relations rather than presuming to dangle outside of it" (p. 45). Participants in her research described immersive experiences with the natural world in which they are in place and place is in them. One participant referred to this sort of blurring of material boundaries when they ate and drank from the land and wondered, "how does the 'I' change when the place is literally 'part of me'?" (p. 49). This overlaps with the relational ontology that is foundational within Cher's scholarship. Cher writes, "... bodies are viewed as open systems with fluid boundaries. Realities are not a priori but emerge as human and non-human bodies assemble to produce particular phenomena" (Hill, 2017, p. 7).

Laura's scholarship provides phenomenological accounts of this sort of expansion of self, theorized within the context of the natural world. New material perspectives illuminate the perpetual becoming of the world in which all boundaries between and among humans and more-than-humans are constantly transformed producing different phenomena. Barad (2007) refers to these ethico-onto-epistemological practices of world making, in which socio-material entanglements are continuously reconfigured to produce and order bodies, as agential cuts. Cher has experienced this sort of shifting of boundaries and sense of self within human-human relationships as she came to a place of journeying with her son rather than standing outside of him, trying to control him, and imposing her intentions on him (Hill, 2016). This reverberation created an opening for Cher, informing the development of her pedagogical practice. Her work, then, was to decentre herself and participate in becoming-with the natural world while supporting others in doing so. She first experienced this sort of diffusion between the usual boundaries between self and the natural world one day when skiing.

Feb 12, 2018, Big White Mountain, Syilx Nation
I am experiencing the mountain differently today. I feel a different way of being in relationship, a different ontological stance. Going up the chair lift it is incredibly windy. People around me were turning away from the wind and wishing it wasn't so windy. This is how I would normally feel but today is different. Today I face the wind head on and feel it stinging my cheeks. I feel its power and I feel alive and humbled in its presence.

Instead of viewing it as an annoyance ruining an otherwise perfect blue bird day, I am experiencing it on its terms rather than imposing my desire for it to be serving my own needs – to be tamer, warmer or coming from a different direction. I am with wind ...

Cher was struck by the vitality of the wind and its agential force, impacting people and the landscape in both potentially creative and destructive ways. This story of becoming *with-wind* flowed into other human-land assemblages, producing similar shifts in her practices and her identity. Cher found that she could become *with-tree*, for example, breathing in and out as the symbiotic flow of oxygen and carbon dioxide permeated their bodies and sharing the same orientation and stance within the forest (Inquiry Journal, 11 March 2018). Once she experienced this ontological shift, she was able to support others to enact similar practices.

March 17th, 2018, Mundy Park, Kwikwetlem Nation
Today in the park I practiced becoming-with the natural world and tried to teach the kids how to do so. I asked them to pick a tree, close their eyes and imagine what it feels like to be the tree. The boys wouldn't or couldn't engage in this way. They playfully shouted, "I'm a tree, I'm a tree!" My daughter however described how she made shade, and that things grew on her, which tickled. She spontaneously picked up a clipboard and drew a picture of a Douglas fir tree covered in moss and algae (which she called Peach) that was not in her current visual field (see Figure 6.5).

Cher compared these experiences of *becoming-with* the natural world to other profound experiences within natural spaces in which she maintained a distinct sense of self, for example the time she went out on the land with the cohort in the dark

FIGURE 6.5

Becoming with Peach the tree

during a rainstorm. Through the light of her headlamp, she watched rain collecting and departing from cedar's saturated bows and saw tiny particles floating in the air. She experienced the forest as she never had before and was in complete awe of her surroundings – it was an exhilarating experience (Inquiry Journal, 2 February 2018). Cher initially valued complete sensory immersion within that natural world over the feelings of awe and wonder she experienced in the presence of place while feeling separate and distinct from the land (Inquiry Journal, 16 February, 2018). Mindful of Deleuze and Guattari's (1987) critique of tree thinking, which encourages linearity and the creation of binaries and hierarchies in which one perspective is adopted over the other, she tried to embrace rhizomatic thinking, in which concepts are connected and intertwined and thinking expands and emerges in multiple and unpredictable directions. She wrote a poem called *Ontological Bridge*, disrupting this dichotomy between the two orientations with/in nature and viewing difference as a positive phenomenon and a generative creative force.

Ontological Bridge

Learning as breathing in[1]
And breathing with
My breath
Our breathing
Becoming with the world
And then separate again
Journeying with wind
Through branches of trees
Across the face of the mountain
Witnessing rainstorms after dark
When nature is closed for the day
Framed through the illumination of a headlamp
As there is light in dark
There is dark in light[2]

The poem highlights the agential cuts in which the boundaries of self are expanded and contracted, producing distinct ethico-onto-epistemological, as well as agential, implications. In this regard, we are constantly unmeshed within and in a process of becoming with the natural world.

Changing Stories – Changing Lives

Through this self-study Cher is learning to tell new stories about herself and her work as a practitioner. In changing the stories she lives by, she has quite possibly changed her life (Okri, 1997). This is the power of self-study methodologies – to catalyze transformative praxis both epistemologically and ontologically, changing not only the way practitioners think but also their ways of being within the world. For Laura witnessing Cher's journey, she was struck by her openness to engage in this type of inquiry as exploring the unknown can be a vulnerable space into which to enter. It inspired Laura to think of the ways she might do this within her own practice, and she was humbled by Cher's courage to constantly evolve self and while modeling genuine inquiry.

Through this project we have come to understand the usefulness of diffractive methods to augment and extend our usual methods of reflection and reflexivity. Identifying resonances and inviting interferences within our scholarship uncovered new possibilities for practice, allowing us to cycle through quasi-familiar places on our journeys to unknown destinations. Reflecting and dialoguing about our diffractive (as well as reflexive) texts contributed towards the production of our *identities-in-action* (Strom & Martin, 2017). In this regard, diffractive reading has much potential as a method of self-study for educators who are new to a particular teaching practice and may lack a personal grounding within a particular curriculum or specific discipline. This is a resting place for us, and we offer just one of many stories that could be told about our self-study. These stories will continue to grow and take form as we continue our wayfaring (Ingold, 2011) along the paths in which life is lived.

Acknowledgements

We would like to acknowledge our human and more-than-human teachers, in particular Alex, Mia, and Kai, and the teachers enrolled in our Master's program.

Notes

1   From Cajete (2005).
2   From Barad (2014).

References

Barad, K. (2007). *Meeting the universe halfway: Quantum physics and the entanglement of matter and meaning*. Durham, NC: Duke University Press.
Barad, K. (2014). Diffracting diffraction: Cutting together-apart. *Parallax, 20*(3), 168–187.

Bennett, J. (2010). *Vibrant matter: A political ecology of things*. Durham, NC: Duke University Press.

Bolton, G. (2010). *Reflective practice: Writing & professional development*. Thousand Oaks, CA: Sage Publications.

Braidotti, R. (2011). *Nomadic subjects: Embodiment and sexual difference in contemporary feminism* (2nd ed.). New York, NY: Columbia University Press.

Brookfield, S. D. (1995). *Becoming a critically reflective teacher*. San Francisco, CA: Jossey-Bass.

Cajete, G. (2005). American Indian epistemologies. *New Directions for Student Services, 109*, 69–78.

de Freitas, E., & Curinga, M. I. (2015). New materialist approaches to the study of language and identity: Assembling the posthuman subject. *Curriculum Inquiry, 45*(3), 249–265.

Deleuze, G., & Guattari, F. (1987). *A thousand plateaus: Capitalism and schizophrenia* (B. Massumi, Trans.). Minneapolis, MN: University of Minnesota Press.

Dolphijn, R., & van der Tuin, I. (2012). *New materialism interviews & cartographies*. Ann Arbor: Open Humanities Press.

Downey, C., & Clandinin, D. (2010). Narrative inquiry as reflective practice: Tensions and possibilities. In N. Lyons (Ed.), *Handbook of reflection and reflective inquiry* (pp. 383–397). New York, NY: Springer.

Flowers, M., Lipsett, L., & Barrett, M. J. (2014). Animism, creativity, and a tree: Shifting into nature connection through attention to subtle energies and contemplative art practice. *Canadian Journal of Environmental Education (CJEE), 19*, 111–126

Hill, C. M. (2016, May 28–June 1). *Mad I'm mad: Parental action research*. Paper presented at the Annual Meeting of the Canadian Society for the Study of Education, May 28–June 1, 2016, Calgary, Alberta.

Hill, C. M. (2017). More-than-reflective practice: Becoming a diffractive practitioner. *Teacher Learning and Professional Development, 2*(1), 1–17.

Ingold, T. (2011). *Being alive: Essays on movement, knowledge and description*. London: Routledge.

Lenz Taguchi, H. (2012). A diffractive and Deleuzian approach to analysing interview data. *Feminist Theory, 13*(3), 265–281.

Lyle, E. (2013). Overcoming disconnectedness: Reflexive narrative inquiry as it informs the development of an adult learning centre. In E. Lyle (Ed.), *Bridging theory & practice: Pedagogical enactment for socially just education* (pp. 3–28). Halifax Big Tancook Island, NS: Backalong Books.

Lyle, E. (2017). *Of books, barns, and boardrooms: Exploring praxis through reflexive inquiry*. Rotterdam, The Netherlands: Sense Publishers.

Okri, B. (1997). *A way of being free*. London: Phoenix House.

Piersol, L. (2014). Listening place. *Australian Journal of Outdoor Education, 17*(2), 43–53.

Pinar, W. F. (1975). *Autobiography, politic and sexuality: Essays in curriculum theory, 1972–1992*. New York, NY: Peter Lang.

Pinnegar, S., & Hamilton, M. L. (2009). *Self-study of practice as a genre of qualitative research*. New York, NY: Springer.

Samaras, A. P. (2011). *Self-study teacher research: Improving your practice through collaborative inquiry*. Thousand Oaks, CA: Sage Publications.

Smythe, S., Hill, C., MacDonald, M., Dagenais, D., Sinclair, N., & Toohey, K. (2017). *Disrupting boundaries in education and research*. Cambridge: Cambridge University Press.

Strom, K. J., & Martin, A. D. (2017). *Becoming-teacher: A rhizomatic look at first year teaching*. Rotterdam, The Netherlands: Sense Publishers.

CHAPTER 7

Negotiating Fear and Whiteness

Elizabeth Kenyon

"You have to betray your ancestors,"[1] she said, and I didn't understand what that meant. Now I know it means turning in my race card, the white one, the one I was born with. Just like I was born with United States citizenship, I was also born with a white citizenship, one that my ancestors fought to construct – so that we could be above, the elite, the ones with the money, and the power and the ones who tell and shape the story. The moment I explicitly confront racism, name it, name white supremacy and demand (not ask) that my students grapple with it, I shed the membership to the white club – sort of – at the very least I break the rules; I am put on probation. Of course, you cannot really leave the white club when you are born into it, and you cannot enter the white club if you are not born into it. You might pass through, get past the front desk, sit at the table for a bit, but membership is forbidden. The rules of the white club are primarily to pretend that it doesn't exist, to make the walls that guard it invisible, to make the whiteness innocent. The whiteness my ancestors created. So yes, naming the club is the primary infraction and, with committing this infraction, I may temporarily shed some of the privilege my white skin affords me – my students may feel betrayed. When they walked in they saw a nice white lady, someone like them who wants to create safe spaces, avoid discomfort or tears, who is there to be a cheerleader and a guide, but not to challenge something that is foundational to their existence – to our existence. This foundational belief is that our whiteness does not matter, that it does not exist, that we are innocent of whiteness. And the thought of turning in this race card, of even momentarily losing some of the advantages my creamy white skin has wrapped me in my entire life, terrifies me.[2]

This self-study delves into my own ambivalence and fear, both of which are deeply grounded in my identity as a white middle-class woman, when it comes to teaching about and against racism. It relies on several semesters of field notes, conversations with critical colleagues, student work and feedback, and my own journaling and artwork. This study was initiated as a self-study to answer two specific questions: how do I (not) teach against racism in my methods course; and what factors promote or inhibit my teaching against racism? I took this study up after several moments of realizing that I would shy

© KONINKLIJKE BRILL NV, LEIDEN, 2019 | DOI:10.1163/9789004388864_007

away from opportunities to engage students in discussions about race and racism despite it being something that is important to me. Working in a primarily white institution with groups of students who are overwhelmingly white means that, although race and racism is always present in the classroom, I can choose the extent to which we confront racism in ways that my colleagues of colour, for whom racism is an ever-present threat, cannot.

Early in the research I was confused about the fear my students were expressing about teaching against bias in their future classrooms. They expressed concerns about backlash from parents primarily. As I struggled to understand their fears, I realized that my own fears were almost overwhelming and equally confusing to me, so much so that I struggled to even identify them. As I have worked to better understand my own fear through reflection, reading, and writing, I am discovering the ways in which my whiteness, and a desire to protect the advantages of that whiteness, are at the heart of my own fear, and perhaps that of my students (Applebaum, 2008; DiAngelo, 2011; Leonardo & Porter, 2010). Therefore, this chapter explores the role of self-study in better understanding the role of whiteness in my teacher identity.

One of the functions of whiteness is that it constructs certain expectations, beliefs, and assumptions about all people, including white people. As a youngish white woman[3], my students expect me to be nice, pleasing, and comfortable. They may identify with me because of our multiple shared identities. To a certain extent, I am all of those things. I have excelled in fulfilling the construct, meeting expectations and, for the most part, it has worked well for me. However, these expectations conversely create fears. What will happen if I step outside of the expectations? How will my students react when I stop playing the part?

My students are majority white and female and have fulfilled similar expectations in their lives. As early childhood educators, they express interest in spending their days with children and doing good in the world. As soon as the topic of anti-bias education comes up, their fears around offending parents almost explode, as do my fears of offending the pre-service teachers. And yet, this is what whiteness relies on – that for white people, the discomfort, the fears, the landmine laced field will all feel too dangerous, or simply not worth the lives of those who are not white. Whiteness relies on our love of comfort.

In this chapter, I describe the process of confronting how my own fear plays a large role in my teaching against race. I also discuss the work I have done and am doing to negotiate the fear and whiteness in my teaching. A part of this has been revisiting my own narrative and identity as a white, middle class, US American woman who has been working on issues of race and racism for most of her adult life. Interspersed throughout the chapter are internal monologues of my own struggles as I negotiate the whiteness of myself in my role as an educator. These monologues are drawn from my reflections and notes and are inspired by reading, conversations with critical colleagues, work with data, and lived experiences.

Getting Started

Issues of race and racism are important to me, or so I have always thought. As a teacher educator, I realized that I would shy away from discussions on race, or dive into a discussion on race only to get lost or change direction soon after. This troubled me. Why did I keep retreating? I decided to conduct a self-study of my own teaching about race in the early childhood social studies methods course that I taught.

> What have I been wondering about with my teaching throughout this process? It all started with wondering how to move past my fears and really push an anti-racism agenda (do I want to use that word?) in my early childhood classes – this was a class where I felt a little crippled by the expectations of the nice white lady .... I can't remember the event that sparked the question, just that it was something important. So much of it has to do with all that has been present in the media of late [Philando Castille, Eric Garner, Sandra Bland, and so many others.] .... Throughout my adult life in particular, I have had varying levels of awareness of the ways in which a plethora of fears impede my ability to act with integrity about the things that are most important to me. The post it note on my laptop reminds me "Be fearless in the pursuit of what sets your soul on fire." Well, a lot of things set my soul on fire, getting rid of racism is one of those things, and I am almost never fearless. I have read a lot of studies about our students' resistance to talking about or admitting issues of race explicitly but much less on our successes teaching against racism – this is my attempt to better align my teaching with my beliefs and principles.

As I embarked on this journey I realized that it would be much more than just jotting down a few notes about my teaching every now and then. It became, at times, an all-consuming work of self-discovery, of learning about whiteness and how it functions in my life, in the classrooms in which I teach, and about fear and how it can shape my thoughts and actions. Using a copy of Samaras' (2011) *Self-Study Teacher Research: Improving your Practice through Collaborative Inquiry*, I started writing notes on my teaching, creating documents like "my living educational theory," diving into conversations with critical colleagues, reading articles, and listening to podcasts.

As I read through Samaras' (2011) book, I came to see the work of self-study as expansive and full of options. For example, every semester I draw something, as I ask my students to do, during a particularly fraught moment around race in the course, so I found the drawings as a source of data. I had conversations with new colleagues, old colleagues, and with myself. And I wrote, and wrote, and wrote. I thought about whiteness, my life, and my teaching while out running, while driving around, while trying to sleep in the middle of the night. I combed my Facebook feed for blog posts and articles on whiteness and education, revisited certain articles, and found new research to challenge and support my thinking. I have been teaching the same methods course throughout this research project, so each iteration has provided new opportunities to try things out, to better understand the students I work with, and to watch and study my own fear.

In addition to my own notes, I collected data from students. Students in the course fill out weekly *take-away sheets* with the major things they learned from the day and any questions or concerns they have. During the first class, where we go in depth on discussing racism, they write questions or concerns they have on blank pieces of paper without their names. They then crumple up the paper and have a *snowball fight.* Everyone collects a paper and responds to the question or comment with the support of their table group. They then crumple the paper up and do another snowball fight before a final response or comment is made. We follow this with a whole class discussion. What is shared in the snowballs is often quite revealing so I saved them. I developed a habit of writing my own notes immediately after class, reading through students' take away sheets, and then making more notes. This allowed me to get my own impression of the class and then check it against what the students were taking away. I took the many forms of data (my notes, students responses to class, course PowerPoints,[4] and the snowball responses) and put them in chronological order.

This cacophony of data seeped through my mind as I read it over and over, adding layers of my own notes and memos with each read. As I worked with the data, I changed as well. I slowly became more familiar with the regional context in which I teach. My own understanding of whiteness continued to evolve and, at times, devolve as my engagement with the project ebbed and flowed. Every time I have written for this project, new insights have developed including while writing the following narrative about the role of whiteness in my life.

Whiteness in My Life

*I have always wanted to save the world. The thing I have never known com-
pletely is where or how. This, too, is a symptom of whiteness – the hubris to
think that I would have something to offer. This hubris was apparent many
places and times including when, after graduating from college, I did a
yearlong volunteer program in Buenos Aires, Argentina, where I worked at
a home for street boys. It seemed like the perfect place to save the world and,
yet, I barely spoke Spanish, and knew nothing of what it was like to live on
the streets or come from the families that these boys came from. I thought
my good intentions and college education were sufficient. A piece of that
belief, I now see, was that my whiteness was also enough. While I began to
understand the faulty nature of my assumptions that year, it did not stop
me in my drive to save the world.*

A year after returning from Argentina, I did another yearlong volunteer program at a youth crisis shelter in Washington DC. Again, I assumed I had something to offer when, in fact, I had very little. I once told a group of students that
these things were perhaps my most racist acts. It all reflected the racism that
saturates our society in the United States, the narrative that white, middle class
people, can transform others into themselves, bringing them out of poverty
into a life much like their own. This assumes that the white middle-class life
is the best and that everyone wants to be saved. It completely dismisses the
cultural values and strengths of marginalized communities and assigns super
hero status to white people.

There was one experience during this year that highlighted for me the
deeply embedded aspects of racism within our society. Working with the after-
school program at the shelter, I realized that my middle class white English
was extremely valuable. The director of the program was a black man who had
completed some college but, when students needed help with a paper or a
writing task for school, he would always refer them to me. I already talked the
way they were expected to write. This was one moment I saw the racism that is
inherent in the education system, of all the systems in the United States, that
white English is right while all other English is wrong (Collins & Blot, 2003).

Following this experience, I went to get a degree in intercultural service
leadership and management, still determined to save the world, perhaps by
being a project manager in South America. During this program, I slowly and
painfully started to realize that the problem was us: middle class, white, U.S.
Americans. The seed that had been planted by my previous experiences in
Argentina and Washington DC was germinating. I went from that program to

an education degree in secondary social studies and, from there, to a job in Washington DC at a high school for emotionally and behaviorally disturbed students. In part, this was just the job I was able to get, but perhaps that desire to save someone had not yet died completely. Instead, I found myself trying to mitigate the damage that the school was doing while also just trying to survive. Another two years teaching at a middle school affiliated with the high school, and I couldn't stomach it anymore, so I fled to a PhD program, full of rage, frustration, and anger over what racism and the racist education system had done to the students I worked with, and yet still not fully understanding.

Whiteness in My Teaching: Facing Expectations and Fears

The challenge of whiteness is that it is so present, persistent, and pervasive. It never stops inundating everyone with its messages and this becomes more powerful when one is in a majority white context where the functionings of whiteness and racism are powerful but expected, making them all but invisible. Because of this, eradicating whiteness and white supremacy becomes a violent act (Leonardo & Porter, 2010). You must extract from the mind something that is deeply embedded.

> A humanizing form of violence is a pedagogy and politics of disruption that shifts the regime of knowledge about what is ultimately possible as well as desirable as a racial arrangement. It is not violent in the usual and commonsensical sense of promoting war, injury, or coercion. Insofar as the theory of violence we put forth is positioned against racial domination, it is violently anti-violence. To the extent that racial violence is structured discourse, we argue that dislodging it will require a violent undertaking in order to set pedagogy on a humanizing trajectory. (Leonardo & Porter, 2010, p. 140)

Committing violence of any kind is not something I have ever been very comfortable with. I would much rather stay within the safe boundaries of the *nice white lady* expectations. However, I agree with Leonardo and Porter: racism has deep roots that must be violently extracted. For me, that means moving through my own discomfort with violence and confrontation, even humanizing violence, so that I can challenge my students and make them uncomfortable.

Taped to the wall above my desk is a reprint of a 1934 photograph of a lynching protest on the National Mall. Several people, some white, but mostly black, stand with nooses around their necks, wearing the names of people who have been lynched. That is uncomfortable. That is courage. It both inspires and shames me. People who fought in the many forms of the Civil Rights Movement regularly put their lives, their health, their general well-being, and often that of their families, on the line. My major risk is bad student evaluations which, while they play a role in my tenure process, would probably not cause me to lose my job. I must step out more bravely, and risk making my students uncomfortable.

I have fears that go beyond my own personal wellbeing and need for comfort. I fear that students will disengage, become defensive, or stop hearing what I am saying. While I try to guard against it, there is also the fear that my students will become stymied by guilt or overwhelmed with the immensity of it all and throw up their hands in defeat. Perhaps my largest fear is that they will not like me, and that their dislike will make me less legitimate. These fears result in the above-mentioned diving into issues of racism and then often retreating. As I have become more intentional, it often feels like walking a tight rope, attempting to push the students but not too far. Below is a description of what I currently do in regard to teaching about and against racism.

There are structured components and less structured components. Much of it is spontaneous and flustered, something I believe is the result of my own discomfort and fear (DiAngelo, 2011). Often, I have hoped that my own commitments and disposition would fill the gaps in the formal curriculum of the course, leading me to respond to the spontaneous in a way that would push the antiracism work. Through this self-study, I discovered that fear and flustering too often get in the way, that while certain aspects of my teaching against racism will always be flexible and responsive to students, other aspects must be more intentional.

Most references to race the first few weeks of class are tangential and informal. Then, leading up to the fourth week of class, the "anti-bias" week, I have students listen to the This American Life podcast (Hannah-Jones, 2015), "The Problem We All Live With," in order to establish that racism still exists. In addition, I include articles on the importance of doing anti-bias work with young children and various approaches to doing it. The following week we explore articles about using children's literature about difference in early childhood classrooms (Cipparone, 2014; Elija, 2014; Lara & Leija, 2014; Lembo, 2014). None of these books focus specifically on race. Instead they focus on gender roles, immigration, and cultural identity. The following two weeks we focus on teaching history, explore the Rosa Parks myths (Kohl, 1994), and take a critical look at Christopher Columbus (Cowhey, 2006) all the while exploring the way historians do their work. During the citizenship week, we sometimes focus on the activism of the Civil Rights Movement. For economics, we look at wealth inequality with a note to the disparities between White, Hispanic and Black families. For geography, there is a turn to the global, watching and thinking about how and where t-shirts are made (Blumberg, 2013) in preparation for global citizenship week when we try to look critically at the idea of helper and helped within the context of the United States and its many roles internationally. Finally, we talk about difficult topics and circle back again to the anti-racism work.

Moments of Fear

This field note after the first and, in some ways, most intense anti-racism class of the semester, reflects my concerns that I am not doing enough. I reference the above-mentioned snowballs as well as the students' reflections on their daily take-away forms. In reflecting on Leonardo and Porter's (2010) article on the need for humanizing violence, I am concerned that I do not push students enough. It also highlights some specific fears that I have:

> *A lot of people said they loved class or it was a great class. I kind of want them feeling uncomfortable instead of great, so I need to do more to challenge them perhaps?*
> *There was also a comment about having to respect everyone's opinions that is disturbing. I confess that I feel unprepared for such discussions. I want to say that is why we have public schools, because we hope that we keep getting better, and school is a way to prepare kids to be better citizens than their parents are. But I, of course, mean better in a particular way. I struggle to think though that wanting students to be less racist is at all biased or a matter of opinion. RACISM IS WRONG, people; it isn't a matter of opinion.*

In here is a fear of being accused of being biased, something that has only happened a few times openly. Once a student questioned why, when doing current events, I only talked about black individuals being shot by police and not about police being shot by black individuals. However, what comes out in the snowball responses over and over is that, as teachers, students will need to respect and be open to the opinions of racist parents. One student even went so far as to suggest that if parents are against anti-bias teaching, perhaps you could give their student an alternative assignment to do in the hallway. That is where the above frustration came from. And yet, I am not exactly sure how to approach this challenge. I struggle to understand the concerns parents would have in regard to teaching against bias even as I work to understand my own fears about it.

In one of the final classes I play a clip from another *This American Life* podcast (Bell, 2015), in which W. Kamau Bell tries to figure out when and how to talk to his four-year-old daughter about race and racism. There are some great metaphors and descriptions but there is one person in the podcast, Clift, who makes me nervous. Bell talks to Clift because he meets Clift's daughter, an outspoken activist against racism. He finds out that Clift started explaining the racist history of this country to his daughter when she was just four, including the horrors of slavery, the violence of Jim Crow, and the resistance of African Americans throughout. When asked if he worried that his daughter would not like white people, Clift responds that he isn't worried about the white man. As Bell himself admits, Clift is hard, and yet we all need more Clift in our lives. This clip always makes me deeply uncomfortable and I worry how the students will respond.

> ... we then listened to the Birds and Bees podcast and the students drew. I went and stopped it before Clift talked about not caring how white people felt, and I said something about "maybe this is enough." But the students wanted to finish it, so I did. But first I said that there were things that made me uncomfortable in the next part. Why did I do that? I struggle so much with that podcast. One concern I shared with the students is that I didn't want them to fixate on Clift's response – I didn't want them to think that this is how all black people feel.

Every semester I struggle with this particular moment, this particular listening activity. It is one of the moments where I see myself retreating against my better judgement. I ask students to draw, write, and colour on big pieces of white paper while we listen to this segment, and I always sit down and do the same. One semester of the study my ambivalence about the podcast and about the students listening to it, was prominent in my drawing. In it there is an expression of guilt for not talking about a whole host of issues. There is also a drawing of a *sea of isms* with two people talking inside of the sea, tension between and around them, a listing of my fears. There is a lot of red and orange highlighting the warmth and intensity of my thoughts and feelings. The word "Anger" is written in red letters down the middle. I remember I was wondering about the purpose of anger, how to use it, how to acknowledge its necessary existence. I was also worried that the students would be put off by Clift's anger. I worry that students will dismiss him and everything else in the podcast as stereotypical rantings of angry black people.

There is so much in the podcast clip that speaks to the continued prevalence of racism, of the harm that it does. This puts emphasis for me on the need to continually address it in my teaching. Then there is Clift, and my concerns about the students' response to Clift reflect so many of my own fears. Just as I fear that they will dismiss the whole podcast because of Clift, I fear they will dismiss not only the work we have done in our class, but also the work that has been done throughout the program to address issues of racism. This brings back some of the ways in which whiteness is designed to perpetuate itself. By making a white perspective the only rational, neutral, and unbiased perspective, it dismisses anything that would challenge white supremacy and racism. This makes whiteness a particularly insidious entity and my deep knowledge of this only adds to the fear.

Perhaps the most powerful finding of this process is that my fears, just like my whiteness, are constructed. Whiteness, white femaleness, creates a certain set of expectations, beliefs, and assumptions that are constructed around that whiteness for both myself and my pre-service students. These expectations create fears regarding how others will respond to explicit teaching against racism (Loughran & Russell, 2002; Samaras, 2011). Every semester I push myself to be more courageous, more clear. I have worked to add structure, systematically tying issues of race and racism to the various social studies disciplines we explore. Sometimes I leave class with what feels like elevated blood pressure as I work to push through these fears of mine and say what I believe I must say. I remind myself that for my colleagues of colour, this extra stress is a regular and unavoidable occurrence. In addition, I continue to read literature, continue to challenge myself through conversations with colleagues, and continue to engage myself in conversations about my teaching. While the formal time of the self-study has ended, the process has not.

Notes

1 These words were spoken by Janaki Natarajan in a teacher education course in which I was a student.

2 This is taken from my own journaling that was an aspect of the self-study.

3 Important here is the intersectionality of my race, class, gender, age and sexuality. Our constructed expectations of each other are created around multiple identities.

4 While my PowerPoints serve as more of a guide for discussions and activities as opposed to a source of content, they are still important reminders of the intended curriculum each week.

References

Applebaum, B. (2008). White privilege/White complicity: Connecting "benefiting from" to "contributing to." *Philosophy of Education Archive*, 292–301.

Bell, W. K. (2015, May 15). If you see racism, say racism, act two of birds & bees. *This American Life*. Retrieved from https://www.thisamericanlife.org/557/birds-bees/act-two

Blumberg, A. (producer). (2013, December 2). Planet money makes a t-shirt: The world behind a simple shirt in five chapters. *Planet Money*. Retrieved from https://apps.npr.org/tshirt/#/title

Cipparone, P. (2014). Reading poncho rabbit and the coyote: An allegory of immigration sparks rich discussion. *Social Studies and the Young Learner, 27*(2), 9–13.

Collins, J., & Blot, R. K. (2003). *Literacy and literacies: Text, power, and identity*. New York, NY: Cambridge University Press.

Cowhey, M. (2006). *Black ants and Buddhists: Thinking critically and teaching differently in the primary grades*. Portland, ME: Stenhouse Publishers.

DiAngelo, R. (2011). White fragility. *The International Journal of Critical Pedagogy, 3*(3), 54–70.

Elija, R. (2014). Discovering and constructing our identities: Reading the favorite daughter. *Social Studies and the Young Learner, 27*(2), 5–8.

Hannah-Jones, N. (2015, July 31). The problem we all live with. *This American Life*. Retrieved from https://www.thisamericanlife.org/562/the-problem-we-all-live-with-part-one

Kohl, H. (1994). The politics of children's literature: What's wrong with the Rosa Parks myth. In B. Bigelow (Ed.), *Rethinking our classrooms: Teaching for equity and justice*. Milwaukee, WI: Rethinking Schools.

Lara, G. P., & Leija, M. G. (2014). Discussing gender roles and equality by reading Max: The stubborn little wolf. *Social Studies and the Young Learner, 27*(2), 22–25.

Lembo, C. (2014). Who does the housework? Gender roles and consciousness raising with piggybook. *Social Studies and the Young Learner, 27*(2), 26–28.

Leonardo, Z., & Porter, R. K. (2010). Pedagogy of fear: Toward a Fanonian theory of "safety" in race dialogue. *Race Ethnicity and Education, 13*(2), 139–157. Retrieved from http://doi.org/10.1080/13613324.2010.482898

Loughran, J., & Russell, T. (2002). *Improving teacher education practice through self-study*. London: Routledge.

Samaras, A. P. (2011). *Self-study teacher research: Improving your practice through collaborative inquiry*. Thousand Oaks, CA: Sage Publications.

CHAPTER 8

A Self-Study of Culturally Relevant Pedagogy in a Higher Education Institution in the United Arab Emirates

Sepideh Mahani

My professional and personal journeys have intertwined placing me in a unique position to write this chapter. For nearly a decade I taught at the largest women's college in Abu Dhabi, United Arab Emirates. The majority of my students were first-generation female students, meaning they were the first one in their families to pursue higher education. I engaged in this self-study in an attempt to understand my students' experiences and academic needs as well as my own praxis (Samaras & Freese, 2006; Whitehead, 2004). Through this self-study, I examined my pedagogical practices in order to become a more culturally competent instructor. I learned there was a great need for culturally relevant pedagogy that recognizes the importance of including student's cultural knowledge and prior experiences in all aspects of learning, thus enriching students' learning experiences and engagement (Landson-Billings, 1994).

Personal Context

Before sharing the stories of my students, it is important for me to share my own. My parents immigrated to Canada when I was an adolescent and, on the first day that I attended middle school, I realized that I would need to learn not only a new language but also a new culture. Even at a young age I recognized that the stories I read in books and the subjects we discussed in class were different than my culture at home. Thankfully, my learning occurred in an inclusive environment where cultural diversity was valued and the curriculum was designed to include students' different cultures and prior experiences. Hence, as I learned a new language alongside a new culture, I had caring teachers who encouraged me to integrate my cultural background into various projects and activities, and this was significant in shaping my identity as an Iranian-Canadian. Twenty years later, and after graduating from university, I moved with my husband to the United Arab Emirates and began a teaching position at a women's college. I vividly recall waking up in the early hours of my first

© KONINKLIJKE BRILL NV, LEIDEN, 2019 | DOI:10.1163/9789004388864_008

morning in Abu Dhabi and looking out the hotel window to a view that felt so different yet inexplicably familiar.

The Emirati Context

Understanding the experiences of Emirati students and appreciating Emirati women's status, requires an understanding of the history of the UAE, specifically prior to the discovery of oil and the independence of 1971. Prior to this time, the United Arab Emirates, which consists of seven Emirates today, was known as the Trucial States, where each Emirate was governed by a different ruler (Kazim, 2000; Tuson, 2003). After the discovery of significant oil reserves in the 1980s and 90s, the UAE witnessed rapid development and became a modernized and multicultural society (Bristol-Rhys, 2009). Only few decades after the discovery of oil Abu Dhabi, the capital of UAE, is now one of the wealthiest cities in the world; the days of water and food shortage are a distant memory in the minds of the older generation of Emiratis. Oil revenues have transformed the city and the division of wealth has left many Emiratis enjoying a lavish lifestyle (Davidson, 2009). The new generation of Emiratis, who are currently enrolled in federal colleges or universities, were born in late 1980s and many were born into wealthy families and comfortable lives (Bristol-Rhys, 2010). Today, Emiratis represent only 19% of the UAE's 9.27 million population and the 81% remaining are expatriate workers who have moved to the UAE for work opportunities (Langton, 2017). Emirati citizenship is not given to foreigners who live in the UAE regardless of being born in the UAE or living in the country for decades (Bristol-Rhys, 2010). In a wealthy country such as the UAE, which has a relatively a small population, citizenship represents access to free education, tax-free income, free healthcare, social welfare, government housing, pensions, subsidized water and electricity, and access to a variety of financial resources such as wedding funds, agricultural lands, and the right to sponsor workers (Bristol-Rhys, 2010). Although more than 80% of the country's population is expatriates, the foreigners and the Emiratis rarely interact and socialize, with the exception of some professions, such as teachers (Blair & Sharif, 2011; Bristol-Rhys, 2010).

Educational Opportunities for Emirati Women

One of the major contributions of the oil discovery has been the expansion of educational access to Emirati citizens, particularly Emirati women (Kirk, 2010). Prior to the discovery of oil, Emirati women acquired education through

Koranic schools and learned to read and write Arabic and the Koran (Bilkhair, 2007). Since the discovery of oil, instrumental social and political reform implemented by the UAE government has empowered women to partake in and influence society (Bilkhair, 2007). In 1975 the Ministry of Higher Education was established, which led to the opening of the United Arab Emirate University (UAEU). The UAEU offered education to both male and female students in a gender segregated environment and ensured families that, by sending their daughters to a segregated institution, they were not compromising their traditional values and beliefs (Bilkhair, 2007). Thus, by the 1980s, many Emirati families started to accept that women could obtain higher education and integrate slowly into the workforce without comprising their traditional roles and values (Mayers, Sonleitner, & Wooldbridge, 2007).

The College Environment

As a new faculty member at the college, I was required to complete a one-week orientation to become familiar with the college system. The workshop was designed to introduce new faculty to the structure of the academic year and college policies. While I was expecting there would be an extensive introduction to the Emirati culture, I was surprised that there were limited discussions on the topic. As new hires, my colleagues and I were briefly informed of certain cultural restrictions. For example, male instructors were informed to always knock before entering the classroom, allowing enough time for students to cover their heads, and to avoid all physical contact with female students. We were also informed to follow the syllabi strictly and never discuss certain topics in class such as premarital sex, religion, or government critique. Following this one-week orientation, new instructors began teaching without having received any further introduction to the Emirati culture.

The mission of the college was to prepare the female Emirati students to meet international education standards. A great emphasis was placed on ensuring the quality of education offered was comparable to Western standards, through an English-based curriculum. The curricula used for instruction were published in Western countries and the content was of relevance mainly to Western societies.

Despite my initial anxieties, I felt at ease in my new position and around the female students; I was also surprised to see how comfortable they appeared to be around me, particularly because communication was sometimes challenging given I did not speak Arabic and English was a second language for the students. The official language of the UAE is Arabic, and most Emirati students attend secondary schools where courses are taught in Arabic. This made it all the more astonishing that public higher education institutions prefer English as the language of instruction (Ashencaen Crabtree, 2010). I was further baffled by the inconsistency with pedagogical approach between preparatory feeder schools and the college: the dominant teaching style in these high schools was teacher-centric, and students were required to memorize facts and perform well on examinations. This was in contrast with the teaching style at the college, which followed a student-centric model where students were required to become independent learners and develop critical consciousness while exhibiting originality and self-confidence (Shaw, Badri, & Hukul, 1995; Sonleitner & Khelifa, 2005). In addition to the new student-centric learning environment, students had to follow a Western curriculum in English and use textbooks that were not written with the Emirati culture in mind. This practice meant learning and teaching took place "in a cultural and educational environment where students and staff often perceived each other across ethnic, cultural, and socio-religious divides, creating a challenge to all parties" (Ashencaen Crabtree, 2010, p. 88).

At the college, I taught a variety of undergraduate English and Liberal Arts courses. Because of my own cultural background, I was more familiar with the Emirati culture than most of my Western colleagues and, as a result, I could identify subjects that were foreign to my students and recognized when certain textbook-driven discussions made them uncomfortable. I was also aware of my restriction to make any changes to the course content, but I often noticed the need for more culturally relevant material. I noticed students seemed disconnected from the subjects discussed in class. They seemed uninterested and disengaged. I suspected this was more than a language barrier since students who took Liberal Arts courses were in their third or fourth year of studies and had become quite lingually proficient. In discussions with colleagues, I began to wonder again if the students' disengagement was largely because their learning did not relate to their life experiences and culture. I noticed that when I shared my cultural background and personal experiences with the students, they were suddenly more absorbed and engaged, and effortlessly shared their own insight and experiences with me, which often led to very interesting discussions.

As their instructor I found myself questioning my own pedagogical practices and wondered how I could possibly make the course content more relevant to students in order to enhance their learning experiences. However, I was limited by the approved course textbook and required adherence to the syllabus. In discussions with my department Chair I often expressed the need to incorporate the Emirati culture in the curriculum, and to provide students with opportunities to connect to the content, consequently improving their engagement and academic success (Gay, 2000; Ladson-Billings, 1995).

I decided to engage in a self-study in order to examine my assumptions about learning, enhance my pedagogical practices, as well as provide a more relevant learning experience to my students.

Self-Study Methodology

Bullough and Pinnegar (2001) state "the aim of self-study research is to provoke, challenge, and illuminate rather than confirm and settle" (p. 20). Upon starting my teaching at the college, I soon realized that I had two choices: I could accept the curriculum and pedagogical practices that seemed irrelevant to the environment we were a part of; or I could challenge and improve them so that I could deliver a valuable learning experience for my students. I assumed that, if I demonstrated sensitivity to student needs, interests, learning preferences, and abilities, we would have a more effective classroom. Because of the Emirati cultural background, it was crucial that changes include culturally relevant pedagogy. I realized that to become a culturally competent educator, I had to change my attitude and beliefs about teaching.

According to Samaras and Freese (2006) self-study is crucial to developing teacher efficacy. My goal for engaging in this self-study was personal and professional development, in addition to enhancement of the learning experiences of the Emirati students. Bullough and Pinnegar (2001) explain "to study a practice is simultaneously to study self; a study of self-in-relation to other" (p. 14). I wanted to critically examine my own assumptions about teaching and concurrently improve my teaching practices in the hope of delivering culturally relevant pedagogy. By being observant to my own views and practices, I wanted to recognize my strengths and weaknesses in this new environment and so that I might establish ways to help students reach their academic goals.

After engaging critically with the literature and gaining a better understanding of self-study as a methodology, I had to personally situate myself in the inquiry and draw on my own experiences as an educator. I also needed to collaborate with colleagues with different backgrounds who could apply different lenses to the self-study. Samaras and Freese (2006) state that a successful self-study is based on collaboration of a professional community. Loughran and Northfield (1998) highlight the significance of collaboration in self-study and point to the importance of discussing and checking the data and analysis with colleagues. They argue that, through collaborative self-studies, educators can better highlight existing issues within their educational contexts and construct new ideas to enhance their professional learning. Another benefit of collaborative self-studies is their ability to give educators a mutual assurance to challenge existing practices while inspiring them to take risks with new ideas and pedagogical practices (Loughran, Mitchell, & Mitchelle, 2002).

Bullough and Pinnegar (2001) provided guidelines for quality in self-study when using journaling as a method of data collection. They argue that, in order to bring validity to the study, journaling should give the reader a good sense of the researcher's thoughts and feelings. While taking these guidelines into consideration, I kept a journal and noted the frequencies where I felt the students appeared disengaged with the content. I also noted every time I taught a class where students were more engaged and focused, and those were often the days where we discussed a more culturally relevant topic. I made notes about how I reacted when students asked question about my personal background and the reactions I received when I shared my personal stories with them. Based on my notes and reflections, I suspected the students' disengagement was more deeply rooted in their inability to connect with the curriculum. For example, I noticed that when we discussed the history of the UAE, students often showed great pride in their nation's history, particularly the Bedouin tribe who, prior to the discovery of oil, lived difficult lives in the harsh desert climate. I also learned that Emiratis, in general, are very proud of their Bedouin heritage, which they consider a foundation of the Emirati society and a fundamental part of their national identity (Heard-Bey, 2001, 2007).

In discussions with some colleagues, I learned they shared the same experiences and frustrations with the lack of culturally relevant course content. We also problematized that the majority of the instructors were not familiar with the students' culture, history, language, or community. Gay (2002) argues that instructors' lack of knowledge about students cultural backgrounds may suggest to the students that their culture and experiences are not important.

We recognized that students often felt misunderstood by the expat dominated society, including some of their own instructors. We also knew UAE women did not benefit from equal rights as men do in the legal areas of divorce, marriage, child custody rights, and inheritance (Kazemi, 2000). However, the status of Emirati women has evolved significantly over the past decade. Despite their late arrival in the education system, and despite the cultural and traditional constraints on women in the UAE, female Emirati students are outnumbering and outperforming male Emirati students (Khine & Hayes, 2010). We felt that, while it was important for educators to inspire and empower these women, it was equally important that these topics were approached with sensitivity because cultural boundaries and predetermined gender roles were deeply rooted in their culture and religious beliefs. Villegas and Lucas (2002) suggest that teachers can support students' construction of knowledge by involving them in personally meaningful learning. Hence, it is essential for educators to create a learning environment in which students are inspired to make sense of new ideas and form their own understanding by using their personal experiences.

The self-study confirmed that, in order to encourage and engage students in learning, teachers must understand their experiences and cultural background. When educators are familiar with the student's family dynamics, culture, language, and communities, they are better prepared to incorporate these experiences into their classroom activities and discussions (Moll & Gonzalez, 1997). Equally, educators who are familiar with their students' interests and hobbies outside of the classroom are better able to incorporate their interests to support their teachings, thus improving students' engagement and motivation to learn (Ladson-Billings, 1994). Villegas and Lucas (2002) state "If teaching involves assisting students to build bridges between their preexisting knowledge and experiences and the new material they are expected to learn, then teachers must know not only the subject matter they teach but also their students" (p. 26).

Significance of Cultural Relevant Pedagogy

Having a sense of the recent history of the UAE helps contextualize the significant advancements made by female Emirati students. Because of the residual adherence to tradition, though, this progress would be further supported by culturally relevant pedagogy (Ashencaen Crabtree, 2010). Culturally Relevant Pedagogy (CRP) is a theoretical framework that was conceived by Gloria Landson-Billings in 1994. She argued that, in order to promote a more nurturing learning experience, educators must ensure they offer opportunities for students to connect their cultural backgrounds to the content. Landson-Billings (1995) insists that culturally relevant pedagogy "not only addresses student achievement but also helps students to accept and affirm their cultural identity while developing critical perspectives that challenge inequalities that schools (and other institutions) perpetuate" (p. 469). Gay (2002), an advocate of CRP, extends Ladson-Billings' framework to discuss Culturally Responsive Teaching and presents educators with strategies on how to improve the performances of culturally diverse students:

> Using the cultural characteristics, experiences, and perspectives of ethnically diverse students as conduits of teaching them more effectively, it is based on the assumption that when academic knowledge and skills are situated within lived experiences and frames of reference of students,

> they are more personally meaningful, have higher interest appeal and are learned more easily. (Gay, 2002, p. 106)

Unlike some of the early scholars and advocates of CRP, Gay (2013) insists that culturally relevant pedagogy should not merely focus on historical knowledge and cultural experiences; rather, it should emphasize "cultural and contemporary content, with historical experiences as foundational influences" (p. 49).

Gay (2000, 2002) discusses three components of culturally responsive teaching: cultural competence; critical consciousness; and engaging academic success. According to Gay (2002, 2013) culturally competent teachers incorporate cultural characteristics, experiences, and perspectives of culturally diverse students in their curriculum. Furthermore, culturally competent teachers value diversity and provide opportunities for students to integrate their experiences in their work. Klump and McNeir (2005) discuss the importance of utilizing the student identities and cultural background to develop an open and expressive learning environment so that students feel comfortable discussing their own experiences. They add, "being culturally relevant is more than being respectful, empathetic, or sensitive. Accompanying actions, such as having high expectations for students and ensuring that these expectations are realized, are what make a difference" (Klump & McNeir, 2005, p. 11).

One of the main principles of CRP is that teachers must uphold high expectations for their students' achievement (Ladson-Billings, 1994). Many advocates of culturally responsive pedagogy believe that students bring with them knowledge and experience that is often rooted in their culture (Ladson-Billings, 1994; Moll & Gonzalez, 2001). Thus, teachers must value student knowledge and experiences by providing them opportunities to apply this knowledge to their learning. This empowers students by affirming that their teacher values their cultural background and life experiences, yet has high expectation for their achievement (Ladson-Billings, 1994; Gay, 2000).

Howard (2003, p. 197) argues that culturally diverse students often bring "cultural capital to the classroom," which may be very different from the conventional norms and teacher's own culture. This left me worried that Emirati students were at a disadvantage because curricula and pedagogical practices did not reflect their cultural capital, practices, and ideologies. Howard (2003) states that culturally diverse students may be at a great disadvantage if they are learning in an environment where their cultural background and experiences are disregarded. He argues that "one of the central tenets of culturally relevant teaching is a rejection of deficit-based thinking about culturally diverse students" (Howard, 2003, p. 197). Further, in order for educators to become culturally relevant, they must critically reflect on their positionality (Howard, 2003; Ladson-Billings, 1994).

Teachers must also recognize the importance of culturally relevant pedagogy and the clear relationship between culture and learning. Moreover, teachers must be knowledgeable about cultural relevant pedagogy and find ways to incorporate learners' cultural background into their pedagogical practices.

Toward a More Culturally Relevant and Responsive Pedagogy

Through conscious and deliberate self-study, coupled with impressions of student (dis)engagement in response to particular pedagogical practices, I became convinced that we needed to integrate the Emirati culture into the curriculum and to provide students with better opportunities to connect to the content. The inquiry process also helped me to understand that culturally responsive educators must recognize and value their students' cultural background and adapt teaching practices to reflect the student culture. When the opportunity finally arrived, I was pleased to work closely with a team of curriculum developers in reconceptualizing several of our Liberal Arts courses. After having witnessed students frequently struggle to connect to course content, I wanted to ensure the redesigned content was relevant to their lives. I also wanted to ensure they were given opportunities throughout the course to connect the learning to their cultural background. As a member of the curriculum committee, I ensured there was room for teachers to adjust their teaching practices to accommodate students' needs in order to support a more meaningful learning experience. To meet these aims, we were guided by Gay's five essential components for culturally relevant content which include: developing a knowledge-base about cultural diversity, including ethnic and cultural diversity content in the curriculum; demonstrating caring and building learning communities; communicating effectively with ethnically diverse students; and responding to ethnic diversity in the delivery of instruction" (2002, p. 106). While working on creating new content, our goal was to encourage students to utilize their life and cultural experiences, interests, and hobbies. We were aware of the topics and discussions that excited and motivated our students, so we created activities, assignments, and content in that spirit.

Conclusion

The self-study influenced my noticing the importance of CRP. I also learned that feeling more fulfilled in my teaching through connecting with my students enhances my pedagogical practices as well as students learning experience. Analyzing my own notes and exploring cultural relevant theory helped me understand Emirati students' needs better. Learning that my colleagues had encountered similar issues as me, made me feel less isolated in my teaching and part of a group who were willing to improve our practices. Furthermore, I learned that in order to engage and motivate Emirati students, I must first gain a clear understanding of the Emirati culture and the needs of students in order to create an inclusive and respectful learning environment where students' cultural background and prior experiences are valued. I believe that it's through my self-study research that I became a more conscious educator, colleague, and expatriate in the United Arab Emirates.

References

Ashencaen Crabtree, S. (2010). Engaging students from the United Arab Emirates in culturally responsive education. *Innovations in Education and Teaching International, 47*(1), 85–94.

Bilkhair, A. (2007). Political reforms for access and equity: Women's education in the United Arab Emirates, from 1938 to the present. *On Campus with Women, 36*(3), 6.

Blair, I., & Sharif, A. (2012). Population structure and the burden of disease in the United Arab Emirates. *Journal of Epidemiology and the global health, 2*(1), 1–13.

Bollough, R. V., & Pinnegar, S. (2001). Guidelines for quality in autobiographical forms of self-study research. *Educational Researcher, 30*(3), 1–21.

Bristol-Rhys, J. (2009). Emirati historical narratives. *History and Anthropology, 20*(2), 107–121.

Bristol-Rhys, J. (2010). *Emirati women: Generations of change.* London: Hurst & Co. Publishing.

Davidson, C. (2009). *Abu Dhabi: Oil and beyond.* New York, NY: Columbia University Press.

Gay, G. (2000). *Culturally responsive teaching: Theory, research, and practice.* New York, NY: Teachers College Press.

Gay, G. (2002). Preparing for culturally responsive teaching. *Journal of Teacher Education, 53*(2), 106–116.

Gay, G. (2013). Teaching to and through cultural diversity. *Curriculum Inquiry, 43*(1), 48–70.

Heard-Bey, F. (2001). The tribal society of the UAE and its traditional economy. In I. Al Abed & P. Hellyer (Eds.), *United Arab Emirates: A new perspective* (pp. 98–116). London: Trident Press.

Heard-Bey, F. (2007). The United Arab Emirates: A study in survival. *International Journal of Middle East Studies, 39*, 679–682.

Howard, T. C. (2003). *Culturally relevant pedagogy: Ingredients for critical teacher reflection.* Columbus, OH: The Ohio State University.

Kazemi, F. (2000). Gender, Islam and politics. *Social research, 67*, 453–475.

Kazim, A. (2000). *The United Arab Emirates: A.D.600 to the present*. Dubai: Gulf Book Centre.

Khine, M., & Hayes, B. (2010). Investigating women's ways of knowing: An exploratory study in the UAE. *Issues in Educational Research, 20*(2), 105–118.

Klump, J., & McNeir, G. (2005). *Culturally responsive practices for student success: A regional sampler*. Portland, OR: Northwest Regional Educational Laboratory.

Ladson-Billings, G. (1994). *The dreamkeepers: Successful teachers for African American children*. San Francisco, CA: Jossey-Bass.

Ladson-Billings, G. (1995). Multicultural teacher education: Research, policy, and practices. In J. A. Banks & C. M. Banks (Eds.), *Handbook of research on multicultural education* (pp. 747–759). New York, NY: Macmillan.

Loughran, J., Mitchell, I., & Mitchell, J. (Eds.). (2002). *Learning from teacher research*. Crows Nest: Allen & Unwin.

Loughran, J., & Northfield, J. (1998). A framework for the development of self-study practice. In M. Hamilton, S. Pinnegar, T. Russell, J. Loughran, & V. LaBoskey (Eds.), *Reconceptualising teaching practice: Self-study in teacher education*. London: RoutledgeFalmer.

Mayers, G., Sonleitner, N., & Wooldridge, D. G. (2007). Next step: From internship to workplace participation in the United Arab Emirates. *Delta Kappa Gamma Bulletin, 74*(1), 12–16.

Moll, L. C., & Gonzalez, N. (2001). Lessons from research with language-minority children. In E. Cushman, E. R. Kintgen, B. M. Kroll, & M. Rose (Eds.), *Literacy: A critical sourcebook* (pp. 156–171). New York, NY: Bedford/St. Martin's.

Samaras, A. P., & Freese, A. R. (2006). *Self-study of teaching practices: Primer*. New York, NY: Peter Lang.

Shaw, K. E., Badri, A. A. M. A., & Hukul, A. (1995). Management concerns in United Arab Emirates state schools. *International Journal of Educational Management, 9*(4), 8–14.

Sonleitner, N., & Khelifa, M. (2005). Western-educated faculty challenges in a Gulf classroom. *Learning and Teaching in Higher Education: Gulf Perspectives, 2*, 1–20.

Sonleitner, N., & Khelifa, M. (2005). Western-educated faculty challenges in a Gulf classroom. *Learning and Teaching in Higher Education: Gulf Perspectives, 2*, 1–21.

Tuson, P. (2003). *Playing the game: Western women in Arabia*. London: I.B. Tauris.

Villegas, A. M., & Lucas, T. (2002). *Educating culturally responsive teachers: A coherent approach*. Albany, NY: SUNY Press.

Whitehead, J. (2004). What counts as evidence in self-studies of teacher education practices? In J. J. Loughran, M. L. Hamilton, V. K. LaBoskey, & T. Russell (Eds.), *International handbook of self-study of teaching and teacher education practices* (pp. 871–903). Dordrecht: Kluwer Academic Publishers.

CHAPTER 9

Seeing Ourselves on the Walls: Teacher Identity and Visual Displays in Schools

Sherry Martens

A conversation is not merely a human interaction,
it is also a display of something,
and the success and failure of the conversation,
is a success or failure in the manifestation
of the thing in question. (Sokolowski, 1997, p. 231)

Concealed within each story
Is more than a life
Waiting to be told
It is living itself
Lived out
Striving for expression

It is a transformative event
Engaging
Who we are
With who we might become.

M. FREEMAN (2001, p. 649)

∴

Be/coming

I have revisited the photographs of my classroom spaces to ascertain if who I was in the process of becoming as a teacher was displayed on my bulletin boards and classroom walls. As a new teacher, I was *all eyes,* taking my cues by watching more experienced mentors craft their visual displays. I did not ask questions; striving to be an ideal apprentice, I mimicked the walls of those who I assumed knew what they were doing and, yet, I never questioned what it might mean to *know* something. I recall wanting my displays to look like theirs, perhaps because of an innate desire to please those around me or perhaps to be recognized as someone who knew what she was doing. I hung the commercially purchased borders, posters, art prints, and student work as I had seen on the walls of other classrooms. I wanted to be seen as the teacher who valued student work by creating multiple displays that showcased not only the end product but the process that students had engaged in as they completed their work. I enjoyed poetry and quotes and filled my classroom walls with inspirational posters that I hoped, in turn, would inspire students to love words in the same way. Many years later, I have come to see that the walls were a representation – a portrait – of me, of how I saw myself, and of what I wanted others to notice about my learning and expertise as a teacher. This realization has led me to wonder about the role that identity plays in what appears on classroom walls.

So, Now You Are a Teacher ...

I was five years old when I knew for certain that I wanted to be just like Mrs. Schwartz, my first grade teacher. In my young mind, I did not separate her from her role as teacher; they were one and the same. Several other former teachers also influenced my future career path. Unlike other professions, those of us choosing a career as a teacher have been observing teachers and visual displays for about 16,000 hours (assuming six hours per day over the course of 12 years of schooling and an estimated 2,000 hours for an undergraduate degree). We have been exposed to a variety of teachers, philosophies, and school experiences that have helped shape not only who we are as individuals, but also who we may be as teachers.

A review of the educational literature on teacher preparation highlights the significance of identity within teacher professional development. Beauchamp and Thomas (2009) specifically noted the difficulties in "defining the concept; the place of self and related issues of agency, emotion, narrative and discourse; the role of reflection; and the influence of contextual factors" (p. 181). Although researchers have explored the transition from student to teacher, there is no single story of learning to teach. As Britzman (2003) observed,

> The story of learning to teach begins much earlier than the time that one first decides to become a teacher. The mass experience of public education has made teaching one of the most familiar professions in this culture. Implicitly, schooling fashions the meanings, realities, and experiences of students: thus those learning to teach draw from their subjective experiences constructed from actually being there. Students have learned the formal and hidden curriculums. (p. 26)

What does Britzman's (2003) observation also say of visual displays in schools? In the early 1990s, teacher preparation programs focused on the skills of teaching rather than the teacher as a holder of "personal, practical knowledge" (Connelly & Clandinin, 1999, p. 1). Connelly and Clandinin (1999) coined this phrase to reflect their epistemological curiosity connecting an individual's experiences of becoming a teacher to the practices of teaching, pinpointing a crucial gap in teacher education. They located personal, practical knowledge as a narrative of teaching – a story that is informed by the teacher's personal history. Connelly and Clandinin (1999) situated this narrative in the context of "in" and "out" of classroom places:

> Classrooms are, for the most part, safe places, generally free from scrutiny, where teachers are free to live stories of practice. These lived stories are essentially secret ones. Furthermore, when these secret lived stories are told, they are, for the most part, told to other teachers in other secret places. When teachers move out of their classrooms onto the out-of-classroom place on the landscape, they often live and tell cover stories, stories in which they portray themselves as experts, certain characters whose teacher stories fit within the acceptable range of the story of school being lived in the school. Cover stories enable teachers whose teachers' stories are marginalized by whatever the current story of school is to continue to practice and sustain their teacher stories. (p. 3)

Teachers continually move between complex and sometimes contradictory places, often portraying themselves to match the story being told because they want to be seen as "good teachers" (Danielewicz, 2001, p. 3). Much about the experience of students becoming teachers, according to Britzman (2003), has been negative, casting teaching as a set of rules of what to do and not do, as well as what not to become.

Although I chatted with several teachers about visual displays over the course of many months, Aimee's (a pseudonym) story about visual displays tugged at me. She had just begun her fourth year as an elementary teacher. She was passionate about literacy and English language acquisition because of her own positive early school experiences. She had been determined from a young age to become a teacher because of the many teachers who had inspired her love of reading and the arts.

I met with Aimee twice. Our first conversation was based on some of my initial questions about visual displays, her own practice, and what she had noticed about the topic. After this first talk, more questions arose, and more of the topic revealed itself. A person's relationship to language and to understanding is ontological. Through practice and engagement with others within specific contexts, understanding and meaning take shape (Freeman, 2006). Because understanding is constantly evolving and is dependent on context (Gadamer as cited in Fleming, Gaidys, & Robb, 2003), I spoke with Aimee, over a period of several months, transcribing the conversations and sharing my understanding of previous conversations prior to our next session.

Drawing on the work of several scholars, I used poetic transcription as an artful way to bring forth key ideas and perceptions from lengthy transcripts. I then used these interpretations as catalysts for future conversations. I have been using poetry for many years to reflect upon and make sense of the world around me. Poetic inquiry rooted in an arts-based inquiry tradition allow me access into the entanglement of the words that are spoken and not spoken, particularly teacher identity. As a researcher interested in aesthetics and the arts, this approach offered me different ways to frame the topic in a language I am readily able to hear and understand. I thought about Aimee's story of teaching, how she learned to navigate the role of teacher, and how she came to understand visual displays.

Early Stages: Growing into the Profession

I arrived at Aimee's school as the last bell of the day was ringing. Walking in, I was immersed in the familiar smells of damp shoes, paper, and crayons so viscerally associated with elementary schools. I noticed several displays in the hallway adjacent to the office; those that singled out the accomplishments of the individual juxtaposed against the artwork of the many. I looked forward to talking with Aimee about how displays in the school were constructed.

My reverie was interrupted by Aimee's cheerful voice. She welcomed me enthusiastically to her school. As we walked to her room, I noticed the artwork that adorned the corridors. One wall held papier mâché animals that were colourfully painted and hung at different angles; across the hall, renderings of winter nature scenes were displayed in straight lines. On closer inspection, I saw that numerous media and styles were employed, and the work was made meaningful by artist statements written by both children and teachers. Ushered into Aimee's room, I was once again met with the winter aroma of children: damp wool from afternoon recess and indoor shoes. The classroom was awash in late afternoon February light.

I asked Aimee to tell me about what she had displayed in her classroom. She thoughtfully contemplated the space that she occupied daily with 20

10-year-old learners, and she began cataloguing the objects and images that I had already noticed. Aimee began to paint a portrait of herself and her classroom:

> I like displaying things that children need to know. So, I have things like my no-excuse word wall. I also like to display work that they are proud of, ... work that is a reminder of what we have created together that I would call a masterpiece. (Aimee)

I was instantly captured by the word "masterpiece." What does this word mean? *Masterpiece* suggests that the work is a creation of a master artist. Has Aimee been schooled to regard displayed work as *the best* work? Is this how school walls should appear? I wondered about Aimee's personal story of teaching and if it appeared on the classroom walls. Was her identity as a teacher displayed? What or who had influenced her decisions?

Aimee: At first, I didn't notice all the things on my wall were literacy based. I just thought that it was something that I would normally put up, that I got used to [putting up] over the past three years. I didn't know what to put up on walls as a first-year teacher. I looked at other classrooms, and I thought there were expectations of every teacher to have a word wall ... I noticed that every classroom needs to have this, this, this ... It just started becoming a part of me, that I needed to have certain things on the wall, in a certain way.

Sherry: Who do you think decides that those certain things are displayed in a certain way?

Aimee: I was told [by my mentor in my previous school] that I was expected to have them [literacy-focused items] there on the wall. As for the other walls in my classroom, my mentor told me that he really liked seeing a subject on each wall or at least a portion of the wall and that it should stay there for a month.

Sherry: Whose beliefs and values are displayed when you see what is on your classroom walls?

Aimee: I think it is the values and beliefs of the people who taught me ... I have followed the advice that I was given, and it has just become a part of my own teaching practice.

Sherry: Do you think that teachers learn to construct classroom displays in the same way that you have?

Aimee: I think about why I have put certain things up, and I think it is either because I was used to seeing those things, like the alphabet line in my own classroom as a child, or because of my mentor. I think sometimes that the walls are a complete reflection of him, and it makes me feel safe. I know that may sound weird, but it is a part of me and yes, [she begins to cry] it does make me feel safe.

Sherry: Do you recall any guidance from your teacher education program in this area?

Aimee: It was not something we talked about, but I do remember asking about what we could put up on the wall.

Sherry: Do you mean asking for permission?

Aimee: Yes, I do, from the people in charge ... [such as] partner teachers, my professors, my field people. I didn't feel that I could decide that on my own.

Sherry: Do you think that you may still be seeking permission as a teacher?

Aimee: I think that I need to meet the expectations of the school, which is that art should be displayed frequently and be changed several times ... the expectations that you are constantly changing it, constantly demonstrating that you are "doing" art in your room, because that is the school philosophy.

Sherry: Are those expectations expressed in writing?

Aimee: No, at least I have never seen them. It is just something that we talk about as a school.

Sherry: Do you talk about classroom displays as a school staff?

Aimee: Not really. I think that it was something that was established early on, before I came here ... I am assuming that was happening.

Sherry: How much of the display is about the teacher showing the work and how much of the display is about showing student work?

Aimee: I would say that it is more about the teacher than the student. For example, if I change the hallway bulletin board when Person A does, then I think I am perceived as doing more art, as they seem to do. I think that my colleagues and my administration will think that I am meeting the school expectations. I don't always think that I am because there is so much more to art than just producing work and putting it up. If you are telling the students that you just need to keep producing something, it changes what the philosophy of this school is supposed to be. That is about a process, and how do you display that?

Sherry: Do you think it matters if that work is in the hallway or inside the classroom?

Aimee: I think that when the work is displayed inside the classroom, it's about me and a reflection of what I value as a teacher. When it is in the hallway, I think it is about accountability to parents and to administration.

Sherry: Do you think that [distinction] has changed since you first entered the profession?

Aimee: I think the younger and more inexperienced the teacher is, the more willing they might be to show more of themselves on the walls but, the longer you stay in a school, the more the philosophy of the school seeps into you and what you might think or feel may not matter so much anymore ... I felt dictated to, as to what [went] up on the walls.

Sherry: Do you think that teachers may just go along with what others want them to do?

Aimee: I think you go along and follow what others tell you, as much as you may want to do something else, because you don't want to do anything that will impact your role in the school or how people view you because you are new. And in my case, maybe a little unsure and scared.

Sherry: So, do these walls resemble those of your earlier experiences?

Aimee: Maybe a little bit, but I am always trying to develop. Wherever I go, I take my experiences and perhaps the expectations of others with me. Maybe I still see some meaning to what I learned that first year, so I can see evidence of it up on the walls today. But I don't put up other things because I might have been directed to do so in my last school, but I don't feel compelled to do that here. I guess I am changing and growing.

Taking up the Portrait: A First Glimpse

The conversation with Aimee illustrated how visual displays in schools may be connected to a teacher's identity. I came to see that I could not discuss the pedagogical practice of creating visual displays without consideration of how Aimee – and so many of us – arrived at those decisions and how we are bound by them. Several things resonated for me in our discussion. I was struck by Aimee's declaration of the expectations she perceived surrounding visual displays. She spoke of how, in the first school she had worked, visual displays were directed by the school administration and fellow colleagues. She felt detached from what was expected of her, perhaps because her identity as a teacher was not invited into the decisions. Aimee produced the visual displays as she had been guided, not because she was convinced that they were the ones she should construct. It is difficult for a first-year teacher to resist the narratives of a school in favour of including also the moral, emotional, and aesthetic dimensions of their history (Connelly & Clandinin, 1999).

In her previous school context, Aimee did as she was told; she constructed visual displays about literacy in a way that was familiar and acceptable to those around her. There was no opportunity to question or consider what the displays might mean, nor were there any specific explanations from school administrators. Her identity as a teacher was shaped by the values, mandates, and mission of the school. Britzman (2003) connects this habitus to voice: "the surprise is that one's voice, whether we call it the voice of experience or the voice of the beginner, seems to come from the outside in, even if it is intimately felt from the inside out" (Britzman, 2003, p. 21). This led me to wonder if beginning teachers are in danger of *becoming the language they speak* (Aoki as cited in Pinar, 2004). Where does simply following the educational directives of others lead us as educators?

As we spoke, I listened for Aimee's voice by looking for her presence. It occurred to me, then, that Aimee was revealing parts of herself through the topic of visual displays. I began to see each of them as an artistic portrait. Gadamer (2007) defined a portrait as

> a likeness [*Abbildung*], the image [*Bild*] of an individual that would enable us to recognize it, if we know it … a portrait is not just a random shot, such as today's camera take. Nor does it come about simply as a result of sitting for someone, as one says so quaintly … only thus, namely through becoming one's image in such a way, can a person have an image, and it is precisely this image which, in the portrait, has become valid for everyone. (p. 294)

I thought about the purpose of the portrait in its original intent, as a way of capturing not only what someone looked like, but also how that person portrayed his or her identity – socially, economically, and politically. West (2004) wrote that the portrait belies more than a simple definition of a likeness of an individual. Rather, it can be a representation of the subject's "inner life, probing the uniqueness of an individual that sets the sitter apart from his or her context" (West, 2004, p. 21). I mused over the artistic metaphor that appeared to me in the classrooms that I had visited and reflected on Aimee's experiences. She met the topic with differing experiences and understandings not only because of who she was, but also because her experience had revealed something else to her about the topic, especially in the influence of her mentor. I likened the honing of her abilities to those of the artist who creates a portrait and prepares for the work first as an apprentice. Although I often feel uncomfortable with the implications of power, gender, and hierarchies embedded in the titles of master and apprentice, I left them there, lingering, as another aspect that needed to be considered.

Returning: Re/Framing the Portrait

Following the work of Freeman (2001), I wondered what process Aimee might have gone through as she considered the walls. Returning to my own roots, I relied on poetry to help be seek understanding and prompt our second conversation:

> The walls, once empty, now speak
> with the voice of one
> who responded with care and nurture
> when a young teacher needed just that.
> Now, surrounded by different walls,
> his voice still echoes
> reverberates from the word wall
> and she catches her reflection
> of him in the mirror
> recognition of rightness
> honouring of what has come before
> and she feels safe.

When I showed it to Aimee, she was silent at first and then she smiled. Had the poem taken her back to the hours of conversation that she and her mentor had shared?

Aimee: I look around the room and I wonder how much of it is still him and how much of it is me. I have wondered over the last while how much of it will change as I don't speak as often with him. Will my classroom change? Will how I teach change as a result of that? There is some fear there. Will his voice still be in my head as it is now?

Sherry: Perhaps you look to others now as well, here in this school, when you spoke of changing hallway displays. Competing with them? Consider the origins of the word *compete*, which means to "strive together," as well as the roots of *display*, which means to "unfold" or "reveal."

Aimee: I think that a lot of time, we put work up for each other. They notice something new and they may compliment me on it, and it encourages me to just keep doing something a certain way. Maybe that is how we are "striving together."

Sherry: What about the work that we don't display? Are we concealing something by not revealing it to others?

Aimee: I think that we are okay with work that has "met expectations" but not with the work that may not look that good. I think that people would wonder why it was there. I think that I would maybe even feel uncomfortable with it because I was displaying something that might not be deemed beautiful enough.

Sherry: I have been thinking about how you considered the outside walls looking a certain way.

Aimee: I liken it to a stage. Being on a stage and being someone else because you have to meet the ideals of the audience watching you. I think that is kind of the way that I view education; you always have to show something, something, *something*. You have to be accountable, and you have to show it to somebody. Inside, I feel free to make it about something else, but I'd better do a good job of what others see.

I considered Aimee's words months after I left her. I have pursued the topic of visual displays down many paths and it has unfolded in particular ways, bumping up against pedagogy, curriculum theory, history of curriculum, art history, and visual culture. I wonder now how it impacts teacher identity. I hope, much like through the conversation Aimee and I have shared, that we might individually and collectively become more aware to the meanings evoked by these images. Like Rose (2001) says, seeing an image must necessarily intersect with the social context of its viewing and the lenses spectators bring to their viewing.

In this regard, visual displays in elementary schools are not only reflective of teacher identity, they are also critical tools in constructing, disseminating, negotiating, and representing knowledge.

References

Beauchamp, C., & Thomas, L. (2009). Understanding teacher identity: An overview of issues in the literature and implications for teacher education. *Cambridge Journal of Education, 39*(2), 175–189.

Britzman, D. (2003). *Practice makes practice*. Albany, NY: New York Press.

Connelly, F. M., & Clandinin, D. J. (1999). *Shaping a professional identity: Stories of educational practice*. New York, NY: Teachers College Press.

Danielewicz, J. (2001). *Teaching selves: Identity, pedagogy, and teacher education*. Albany, NY: State University of New York Press.

Fleming, V., Gaidys, U., & Robb, Y. (2003). Hermeneutic research in nursing: Developing a Gadamerian-based research method. *Nursing Inquiry, 10*(2), 113–120.

Freeman, M. (2001). "Between eye and eye stretches an interminable landscape": The challenge of philosophical hermeneutics. *Qualitative Inquiry, 7*(5), 646–658.

Freeman, M. (2006). Nurturing dialogic hermeneutics and the deliberate capacities of communities in focus groups. *Qualitative Inquiry, 12*(1), 81–95.

Gadamer, H.-G. (2007). *The Gadamer reader: A bouquet of later writings*. Chicago, IL: Northwestern University Press.

Pinar, W. (2004). *What is curriculum theory?* Mahwah, NJ: Lawrence Erlbaum Associates.

Rose, G. (2001). *Visual methodologies*. London: Sage Publications.

Sokolowski, R. (1997). Gadamer's theory of hermeneutics. In L. E. Hahn (Ed.), *The philosophy of Hans-Georg Gadamer* (p. 213). Chicago, IL: Open Court.

West, S. (2004). *Portraiture*. Oxford: Oxford University Press.

CHAPTER 10

Negotiating Identity in a Relational Pedagogy: A Cross-Cultural Perspective

Chinwe H. Ikpeze

Successful teaching depends mostly on building relationships (Davis, 2006; Huang, 2010; Margonis, 2004; Newberry, 2010; Ritter, 2017). In order to build relationships and teach successfully, teachers must be cognizant of the classroom cultures that affect student behaviour, their learning styles, unique circumstances, ways of being and communicating, as well as the political context in which the work of teachers is situated. Davis (2006) observed that students who perceive supportive relationships with their teachers generally reported feeling more motivated in their classes and received higher grades. In contrast, conflictual relationships are often accompanied by student misbehaviour, expressions of disrespect, and use of the poor relationship quality as an excuse to quit. Relationship building can be very challenging because it includes becoming cognizant of our observations of the other's personality, our interpretation of their motives, as well as our reactions to all of it (Newberry, 2010). The situation may be exacerbated in a cross-cultural teaching context because students may view teachers as a *cultural other* and act out in resistance to them. As a result, relationship building between the two takes more time and energy (Ikpeze, 2013). Relationship building in a cross-cultural context could be a site where interpersonal and institutional relations intersect (Gomez, Allen, & Clinton, 2004) with possibility for tension and conflict. Faculty in such contexts may go through both external struggles with their students and internal struggles with themselves due to several factors that include personality, otherness, noviceness, and cultural dissonance (Huang, 2010). In addition, feelings of vulnerability and credibility are common due to differences in the social and cultural identities of the teacher and students. These observations speak to my experiences as a foreign-born faculty of colour in the first years of teaching. Successful teaching in a cross-cultural context not only involves building pedagogical relationships, but also involves attending to identity issues.

Identity Construction and Relationship Building

Teachers' personal and professional identities have been widely studied (Beauchamp & Thomas, 2009; Clark, 2009; Edwards & Burns, 2016). Identity

© KONINKLIJKE BRILL NV, LEIDEN, 2019 | DOI:10.1163/9789004388864_010

is an ongoing process and comprised of what a teacher is (and is not), what a teacher does (and does not do), and who a teacher is (and is not) in relation to self and others (Clark, 2009). Identity is dynamic, complex, negotiated, and co-constructed (Clark, 2009; Edwards & Burns, 2016). Teacher identity is a site for exploring teachers' teaching lives as it involves the complex, shifting interplay between several power structures, both internal and external, to the individual teacher. Teacher educators are constantly developing their cultural and professional identities based on past experiences; these identities help shape their dispositions and commitments to certain norms within their practice. In a bid to negotiate classroom relationships across cultural, racial, and linguistic differences, identities can be disrupted, constructed, or deconstructed. As a foreign-born faculty of colour, I had to negotiate multiple identities as I worked to build pedagogical relationships with my students.

In this chapter, I first discuss my background and the tensions that I faced as an African-born faculty of colour. Then I discuss how I transformed my practice through self-study and through deliberatively engaging in a relational pedagogy and identity renegotiation. In doing this, I sought to explore how I reframed my practice to engage in a relational pedagogy, and how this process was informed by identity.

Background and Study Context

I was born in Nigeria where I had my early and college education. I was a high school English teacher for a few years before my family migrated to the U.S. When I got to the U.S, I enrolled in doctoral studies. I was later employed in the School of Education in a Liberal Arts college. Although I came into college teaching with years of prior teaching experience in both college and high school levels in Nigeria, I was soon to learn that my prior teaching experiences were inconsequential in my new context. I was constantly in search of an identity that would both reflect my cultural background and enable me to be successful in my new context. My Nigerian schooling experience conveyed to me that teacher-student relationships were hierarchical: teachers dominate the educational process; and teacher-student relationships were generally characterized by power distance. The teacher was the sole authority figure and students simply obeyed and followed directions. Teachers were highly respected and hardly challenged, contradicted, or criticized publicly by students. In short, the teacher's authority was never questioned. The curriculum was more or less teacher-centered, and there was little or no room for students to negotiate the curriculum with teachers. On the contrary, the

American educational system emphasized closer relationship between teachers and students. In addition, the institutionalized culture of student empowerment meant that students not only felt entitled to several privileges, they were also bold and sometimes assertive, which had potential for tension and conflicts.

Data for this chapter were obtained from a larger study – cumulative self-studies conducted within the context of a Graduate Literacy Program at a medium-sized college in North Eastern U.S.A. between 2007 and 2014. The participants were graduate teacher education candidates enrolled in a master of literacy program. Data were collected across seven years, across courses, studies, and in multiple formats. During this period, there were four Institutional Review Board (IRB) approved studies in which I examined my teaching and students' learning. The analysis of the cumulative self-studies was recursive. Rudimentary and ongoing analyses were conducted as the data were collected. This enabled me to refine my research questions. Grounded theory (Glaser & Strauss, 1967) was used to analyze all the data. Grounded theory is a way to generate theory from data through inductive and constant comparative analysis.

Toward a Relational Pedagogy

Findings from the cumulative self-studies indicated that tensions and conflictual relationships were a major motivation for engaging in self-study. Identifying the tensions in my practice became an impetus to rethink my pedagogy and relationships with students. I first discuss the tensions that I identified, and then how I reframed my practice through self-study and relationship building.

Navigating Tensions

Learning to solve many common pedagogical problems leads to practical dilemmas and tensions. Tensions are "problematic situations" (Berry, 2007, p. 27), especially those that cause doubt, perplexity, or surprise, that lead one to question otherwise taken-for-granted practices. Within my first few years of teaching, cultural and linguistic differences as well as pedagogical issues became the major challenge. One of the major tensions arose from identity perception gap, which is the difference between who teachers think they are and who the students think the teachers are (Toshalis, 2010). Tokenism and linguicism also constituted major challenges. *Tokenism* is a subtle presumption of incompetence, inferiority, inadequacy, and intolerance by native-born students toward foreign-born scholars of colour (Ukpokodu, 2013). *Linguicism* is discrimination due to accent. In addition, there were some misunderstandings and miscommunications as a result of differences in socialization, which resulted in different ways of looking at the world, and what one considered acceptable or unacceptable behaviour. I was also affected by the entitlement culture. The entitlement culture involves a belief by students that some reward is deserved that is not justified based on one's actual academic achievement. In an entitlement culture, students' expectations about the role of their teachers go above and beyond expectations of providing normal instructional guidance. It was also challenging for me to deal with other issues in building pedagogical relationships, such as balancing between care and control, or balancing high expectations with student interests. It also appeared that the prospective teachers and I had different cultural models and expectations of teacher-student relationships. These necessitated that I engaged in self-study.

Engaging in Self-study: Toward Transformation

The journey toward transforming my pedagogy and bridging the teaching gaps started with a self-study. Self-study is a necessary pedagogical exercise that can improve teaching and learning in teacher education learning contexts (Dikelman, 2003; LaBoskey, 1997; Loughran, 2014). Self-study enables teacher educators to conduct intentional and systematic inquiry into their own practice that yields knowledge about practice (Dinkelman, 2003). In doing that, teacher educators are able to carefully review and reflect on their actions, ideas, pedagogies, and decisions taken in order to improve their practice. Rather than simply uncovering an answer to a research question, self-study research tends to facilitate more nuanced kinds of learning that can be in relation to others, by seeing practice from the students' perspective. Self-study therefore enables teacher educators to question certain assumptions, consider multiple perspectives, avoid judgments, recognize complexity, and focus on the needs of their students (LaBoskey, 1997) Self-study opened a way for me to interrogate, construct, and reconstruct my identity to align with the realities of my new cultural context, thereby transforming my practice. I understand transformational learning as a process whereby individuals engage in critical reflection that results in a deep shift in perspective toward a more open, permeable, and better justified way of seeing themselves and the world around them (Dyson, 2010). It involves heightened awareness of how social, contextual, and cultural factors impact our beliefs and worldviews, a critical self-analysis of these factors, and an understanding of how they have shaped our beliefs and feelings. Transformational learning led to rethinking my pedagogy.

Rethinking Pedagogy

Self-study enabled me to uncover the relational gaps in my interaction with students. Like Ritter (2017), the relational challenges I experienced revolved around the relationships I was attempting to forge with my students and the associated issue of how to structure learning opportunities framed by those relationships. From a relational perspective, I struggled to forge educative relationships in the first few years of teaching. Self-study enabled me to purposefully examine these educative relationships so that alternative perspectives on my intentions and outcomes might be better realized. In doing that, identity negotiation was critical.

Negotiating Identities

My identity as an African-born woman of colour influenced my beliefs about the role of the teacher as the sole authority figure in the classroom and how a teacher should act and interact with students. The first step toward building relationships was to reflect on my own values, beliefs, and assumptions and how I might look differently at the world. I realized that succeeding in my new context would involve some form of identity renegotiation, rethinking of assumptions and beliefs, as well as understanding how my background might impact my thinking about teaching and learning. I agreed with Milner (2010) that it is no longer acceptable for teachers to assume that either their identities or their students' identities are generic as if their race, ethnicity, social class, language, gender, sexual orientation, or their markers of identity did not influence their ideas and practices. I realized that before a teacher can transform the lives of her students, she must first become transformed because beliefs, values, and attitudes, are critical and connected to a teacher's effective practice. Indeed, my race, gender, social class, language, and ethnicity all impacted my teaching identities in a certain way and influenced my choice of textbooks and activities. The first thing I did was to study and understand who my students were. While I worked to understand my students' identities, I reflected deeply about some of my pedagogical practices that had worked in other contexts and wondered if they constituted an obstacle to building relationships in my present context. I then positioned myself as a certain kind of teacher; one that prospective teachers would see as knowledgeable, approachable, friendly, and understanding of their hybrid identities as students, teachers, and parents. Far from being a strict teacher, I invested in the ethics of caring. This involved listening to students and understanding their identities. However, this identity shift did not mean that I completely changed my belief in quality teacher education. I resisted replacing challenging and developmentally appropriate course work with entertaining activities. Instead of conceptualizing practice as being technical, I worked to thoughtfully engage in practice in ways that elucidated deep thinking, reasoning, and informed decision-making that underpins effective pedagogical practice (Loughran, 2014). In all, I moved toward relationship building as I constructed and reconstructed my identities, negotiated authority, reconciled expectations, and reframed my pedagogy (Ikpeze, 2015).

Reframing Pedagogy

My self-study taught me that building relationships depend on being an effective teacher. Indeed, teachers' ability to provide affective support and a positive classroom climate impacts the quality of their relationship with students. In line with Lampert's (2010) assertion that teachers relate with students through the content, I worked hard to improve my teaching effectiveness in order to build relationships. I invested in activities that foster teaching effectiveness such as presenting the material well, making my courses interesting, stimulating interest in the subject, and motivating students to learn. In order to capture students' perspectives about their learning and help them better comprehend course materials, I utilized a variety of strategies. These included use of student reflections, making my personal life visible, individual conferencing, and modeling best practice. Others included maintaining rigour and negotiating authority. I utilized a variety of students' reflections such as individual lesson reflections as well as the midterm and end-of-semester reflections. These were very effective in monitoring students' learning. Another tool that I used to monitor students' learning and build relationships was the exit ticket. This is a technique that helps the teacher collect instant assessment of students' perception about their learning at the end of a lesson. Exit tickets helped me check students' understanding by having them summarize key points from the lesson, ask questions, and finally write what they liked or did not like about the lesson. In addition, I discussed my background, cultural upbringing and personal life, and used my minority background as a teaching tool. I worked to model best practice as well as behaviours and attitudes. As the students got to know me better, they were better able to connect with me. In addition, I negotiated authority and the curriculum with students.

Negotiating Authority

A major strategy that I used to build relationships with students was negotiating authority and the curriculum with students (Brubaker, 2010; Calderwood & Amico, 2008). Teachers by their position have some authority, which is defined as the power to give instructions and to expect others to follow those instructions (Calderwood & Amico, 2008). However, authority requires social cooperation; people recognize and affirm it by confirming or rejecting authority. Authority is also a reciprocal issue; teachers can influence students just like students can influence teachers. The biggest challenge I faced was balancing care and control and students' interests with the expectations of the curriculum. Balancing between care and control involves negotiating authority and encompasses procedural dimensions of classroom life such as issuing instructions, making decisions, and establishing and enforcing rules. At the same time, infusing care while maintaining control involves constructing relations of democratic authority (Brubaker, 2010) in which teacher and students jointly construct their relationships. This was not an easy task for me. For once, I quickly learned that I had to negotiate authority and relationships differently with different groups of students. What worked with one group of students did not always work with another group. Different student groups responded to care and control differently.

It appeared that, while students wanted some form of relationship with the teacher, they also wanted leadership and structure based on authority. My syllabus was very clear about when topics would be taught and the required readings and assignments. I expected students to submit their assignments on the due dates, according to the syllabus. But, some of them would come up with excuses and would not submit these papers. Initially, I had insisted that they submit their papers on the due dates or face penalty. This did not go down well with some students who felt that I was not flexible or did not demonstrate understanding of their unique situations. To build relationships, I was more flexible with due dates, and I let the students use their initiative to follow rules and structures of the classroom. However, I was surprised when another group of students in another semester complained that I was complacent. Some students commented, "We want check stops," "you need to push us more," and "the instructor should stand her ground." What they meant by check stops was that I should enforce the rules and designate some due dates as stops so that whatever was due on or before that date must be submitted or the student is penalized. I agreed with them and implemented the check stops and the students adhered to the rule and submitted all their papers on their designated check stops. The check stops were student initiated rules, which they all obeyed. I agree with Birgham (2004) that, as teachers, we should treat "authority as interplay between proximity and distance" (p. 35). This means we should learn when to exercise authority and when to allow students to co-construct authority, during which we keep our own authority at bay.

Reconciling Different Cultural Models of Care and Relationship

My conception of teacher-student relationships emanated from my Nigerian schooling experience and earlier socialization with my own professors, which conveyed to me that teacher-student relationships are hierarchical. Influenced by prior experience, I thought that my decision as a teacher was final, and students should not complain about course work or seek to negotiate the curriculum in any way with me. I was shocked when students argued with me, demanded less work, tried to negotiate the curriculum, course attendance, and even their grades. In addition, I had to deal with the hard-to-relate to and difficult students. In essence, I noticed that the students and I had different cultural models of care and relationships. To reconcile these differences, I took a number of steps that included carefully studying the students' and peer culture and understanding their perspectives about learning. I then came up with some strategies to build relationships with these students. These included forging new relationships, demonstrating professionalism, and meeting with students one-on-one to talk things over or for individualized instruction.

A major relational shift occurred when I began to document what the prospective teachers valued in teacher-student relationships versus what I valued. For example, while I took pride in being a serious-minded, no-nonsense teacher, the prospective teachers preferred to deal with a carefree, laid-back teacher in a relaxed course environment. They also wanted their teachers to take their perspectives about their learning very serious. This forced me to move toward authority relationships that were neither authoritarian nor permissive but somehow democratic. In doing this, I adopted Reeve's (2006) ideas about teacher characteristics that can lead to high quality relationships. These included attunement, relatedness, supportiveness, and gentle discipline. In a survey that I administered to ascertain how the students perceived classroom interactions and relationships, a few of the comments, like the one below, made me stop and ponder:

> I have taken this professor before during a normal semester and honestly I could not to relate to her at all, and I felt as if she had little connections with her students. However, during this summer session, I was impressed.

> I learned a lot of useful information and she was always there for clarifications. Even though her expectations could be clearer, I feel as if she did a good job the second time around and now, I would recommend her to other students, whereas before, I would not have. All in all, this was a good class and a good instructor. (Ikpeze, 2015, p. 108)

Based on this student's comments, learning useful information, having the teacher clarify things, and making expectations clear were the major reasons this student was able to have a better relationship with me. While it was important to understand students' perspectives about teacher-student relationships, my study of this topic indicated that most students perceived relationship building as one-directional – something that the teacher does. As a result, they fail to take control of their learning. Taking control of one's learning can take many forms, including being proactive, asking questions, seeking for clarification, meeting with the instructor one-on-one, among others. The caring work of teaching is premised upon having a reciprocal relationship between students and teachers. Reciprocity entails "teachers and students continually developing, negotiating, and maintaining a social connection" (Gomez, Allen, & Clinton, 2004, p. 483). An important lesson that I learned about teacher-student relationships was that there is no ready-made answer to relationship challenges. Relationship is constructed differently with regard to different students and different groups of students. I had to constantly negotiate relationship boundaries, balance between care and control, as well as balance students' interest with the demand of the curriculum.

Using Identity-Perception Gap as a Resource

As part of my relational shift, I began to view and use identity-perception gap as a resource, instead of an impediment, by examining what was at stake in teacher-student relationships within a cross-cultural context. It was clear that certain ways of interacting and communicating can promote relationship building. In realization of this, I moved through a cyclic process that involved changing from *doing teaching* to building relationships (Loughran, 2007). Instead of having my values dictate my teaching practice, my experience with students informed my values and dictated the changes that I made. I deliberately adopted the caring pedagogy through listening to students, using autonomy supportive strategies, showing gratitude, encouraging students' efforts, as well as being friendly. It appeared that the identity-perception gap persisted because many of my students did not know much about my background and had limited knowledge of people from other cultures. I also let students know that relationship building is not a one-way process. I expected them to warm up to teachers who do not look like them, ask questions, and initiate friendships. This relational shift yielded good results as many of the students wrote in their course reflections about their excitement of learning more about my background. They acknowledged that they enjoyed the thorough introduction of my past and present, and appreciated how I injected many of my stories with details from my past, "both in a cultural sense as well as professional" (personal communication, anonymous student).

Conclusion

The centrality of relationship, especially within the context of small to medium-sized colleges and universities, cannot be overemphasized. Relationships are complex, unpredictable, and unique in every context. Building relationships requires treating teaching as an object of study. Self-study promotes self-awareness, which results in being more conscious of teaching and learning, more vigilant about the nuances of classroom interaction, and more thoughtful in assessing what works or does not work as well as goals, practices, students, and contexts. My self-study process started with questioning my assumptions and beliefs and acknowledging cultural, racial, and linguistic differences as well as differences in lived experiences and social realities. In a cross-cultural context, faculty and prospective teachers may have different cultural models of caring that can create conflict. The complexity of relationship building lies in the fact that relationship with content is constructed differently among different students and groups of students. Therefore, there is no singular solution for relationship challenges that might arise. Building good relationships first require enacting responsive pedagogy and continuously adapting to the unique needs of students at any given time.

References

Beauchamp, C., & Thomas, L. (2009). Understanding teacher identity: An overview of issues in the literature and implications for teacher education. *Cambridge Journal of Education, 39*(2), 175–189.

Berry, A. (2008). *Tensions in teaching about teaching: Understanding practice as a teacher educator*. Dordrecht: Springer.

Birgham, C. (2004). Lets treat authority relationally. In C. Birgham & A. Sidorkin (Eds.), *No education without relation* (pp. 23–37). New York, NY: Peter Lang.

Brubaker, N. (2010). Negotiating authority by designing individual grading contracts. *Studying Teacher Education, 6*(3), 257–267.

Calderwood, P. E., & D'Amico, K. M. (2008). Balancing acts: Negotiating authenticity and authority in a shared reflection. *Studying Teacher Education, 4*(1), 47–59.

Clarke, M. (2009). The ethico-politics of teacher identity. *Educational Philosophy and Theory, 41*(2), 185–200.

Davis, H. A. (2006). Exploring the contexts of relationship quality between middle school students and teachers. *Elementary School Journal, 106*(3), 194–223.

Dinkleman, T. (2003). Self-study in teacher education: A means and ends tool for promoting reflective teaching. *Journal of Teacher Education, 54*(1), 6–18.

Dyson, M. (2010). What might a person-centered model of teacher education look like in the 21st century? The transformism model of teacher education. *Journal of Transformative Learning, 8*(1), 3–21.

Edwards, E., & Burns, A. (2016). Language teacher–researcher identity negotiation: An ecological perspective. *TESOL Quarterly, 50*(3), 735–745.

Glaser, B., & Strauss, A. (1967). *The discovery of grounded theory: Strategies for qualitative research*. Chicago, IL: Aldine.

Gomez, M. L., Allen, A., & Clinton, K. (2004). Cultural models of care in teaching: A case study of one pre-service secondary teacher. *Teaching and Teacher Education, 20*, 473–488.

Huang, Y. P. (2010). International teachers' cross cultural teaching stories. *Curriculum and Teaching Dialogue, 12*(1–2), 89–103.

Ikpeze, C. H. (2013). In retrospect: Navigating culturally responsive pedagogy in teacher education. In I. Harushimana, C. Ikpeze, & S. Mthethwa-Sommers (Eds.), *Reprocessing race, language and ability: African-born educators and students in transnational America* (pp. 45–57). New York, NY: Peter Lang.

Ikpeze, C. H. (2015). *Teaching across cultures: Building pedagogical relationships in diverse contexts*. Rotterdam, The Netherlands: Sense Publishers.

LaBoskey, V. K. (1997). Teaching to teach with purpose and passion: Pedagogy for reflective practice. In J. Loughran & T. Russell (Eds.), *Teaching about teaching: Purpose, passion and pedagogy in teacher education* (pp. 150–163). London: Falmer Press.

Lampert, M. (2010). Learning teaching in, from and for practice: What do we mean? *Journal of Teacher Education, 61*(1–2), 21–34.

Loughram, J. J. (2007). Researching teacher education practices: Responding to the challenges, demands, and expectations of self-study. *Journal of Teacher Education, 58*(1), 12–20.

Loughram, J. J. (2014). Professionally developing as a teacher educator. *Journal of Teacher Education, 65*(4), 271–283.

Margonis, F. (2004). From student resistance to educative engagement: A case study of building powerful student-teacher relationships. In C. Birgham & A. Sidorkin (Eds.), *No education without relation* (pp. 39–53). New York, NY: Peter Lang.

Milner, H. R. (2010). What does teacher education have to do with teaching? Implications for diversity studies. *Journal of Teacher Education, 61*(1–2), 118–131.

Newbery, M. (2010). Identified phases in the building and maintaining of positive teacher-student relationships. *Teaching and Teacher Education, 26*, 1695–1703.

Reeve, J. (2006). Teachers as facilitators: What autonomy-supportive teachers do and why their students benefit. *The Elementary School Journal, 106*(3), 225–236.

Ritter, J. (2017). Those who can do self-study, do self-study: But can they teach self-study? *Studying Teacher Education, 13*(1), 20–35.

Toshalis, E. (2010). The identity-perception gap: Teachers confronting the difference between who they (think they) are and how students perceive them. In H. R. Milner (Ed.), *Culture, curriculum and identity in education* (pp. 15–35). New York, NY: Palgrave Macmillan.

Ukpokodu, O. N. (2013). A synthesis of scholarship on African-born teacher educators in the U.S. colleges and schools of education. In I. Harushimana, C. Ikpeze, & S. Mthethwa-Sommers (Eds.), *Reprocessing race, language and ability: African-born educators and students in transnational America* (pp. 13–34). New York, NY: Peter Lang.

CHAPTER 11

Opening into Aletheia

Kate McCabe

We shall start from the standpoint of everyday life, from the world as it confronts us.

E. HUSSERL (2012, p. 3)

•••

Cancer, trauma, isolation, silence, bewilderment, rage.
Ugly?
Sometimes, and.
Sometimes it opens more than flesh. Aletheia. Openings into truth expansive spaces of possible beauty.

> No guarantees.
> Opportunities for layered, multi-vocal, interpretations imbued with the flux of salt air, rushing waves, pebbles and Grandmother's breath, warmed by tea.
> "How am I not yet dead?" "How am I not yet dead?"
> "How am I living?"

:.

This hermeneutic research began on a wild, windswept beach, with a plaster bust made in my likeness, the night before my breast cancer surgery. The incision, a cut into flesh, memories, and imagination, opens opportunities for courage to tell the stories. To let them go. The skin cells that cling to the bust's cavity call me to understand myself and to inquire into what is revealed and what is concealed.

The Bust's Story

The body I am is my most intimate point of entry into the world. (Kohák, 1985, p. 105)

I step into the tub letting its cool whiteness push against my feet. I steady myself with one hand on the edge of the tub before standing to notice the ornate edges of the dull silver paint of the mirror's frame. I reach for it with my index finger and slowly trace the curling surface. I turn my head, first right and then left, to take in the fullness of the large rectangular surface. It is about 10 p.m. The moonlight from the ceiling window mingles with the dimmed lights that glow above the sink. Shadows have begun to collect when I look up and see myself. I know the reflection is me but, at the same time, I am a stranger to myself. I am awkward. Naked. A sense of urgency makes its way up my legs but I am struck into stillness, looking at the face and the shoulders. I do not look below this line of sight for a long while. I am afraid. I know that in a few hours I will be in an operating room, on a table, and a surgeon will perform the procedure to remove the tumour from my breast. It feels odd, this looking. This makes me laugh a little. I laugh when I am nervous. How is it, after 54 years, I can't remember ever looking at myself in this way? What have I forgotten that these eyes and this skin still remember?

I coat my shoulders, chest, and belly with petroleum jelly to make the removal of the plaster cast easier. I dislike the smell of this oily substance. It clings to my nostrils like distasteful memories. I pull the thick, greasy mass across my skin and feel the tiny hairs stand at attention only to be quickly laid flat. Bound. My skin recoils. I grab a towel and wipe the residue from my hands. I grimace.

I take a breath and then exhale but I am impatient. I begin layering the wet, pre-cut, plaster strips upon my chest. It is awkward. I begin with my left shoulder. As I move across my collar bone the plaster cools and, if I use too much water, slips and crumples beneath my fingers. Every movement of my arm shifts the plaster already in place. I am forced to move more quickly and soon realize I cannot manage this task standing up. I gingerly get out of the tub and pause to think about abandoning this project. But I am steadfast and lying down makes the task easier. The memory of myself in the mirror quickly fades as I work to get the cast complete. The plaster gets hot as it hardens. The weight and the heat are uncomfortable, and I start to feel at odds with this cast. I want none of it. I finish with the strips to my waist and then, deciding the layers are thick enough, lift it from my body first raising the edges at the waist, then my rib cage, and finally my collar bone. My hands push the cast away from me and upward. I look for a moment at its underside. I am dizzy seeing the two cavities that have been formed by my breasts. Empty.

The Observer and the Observable

How am I not yet dead?

I can type this question, but I still have not vocalized it. It sits there, unspoken even as I read aloud the other sentences of this chapter. I try to keep these words at a distance, yet they continue to confront me. Touch me. There are worlds of events in those words. Cancer. Trauma. Running. Silence. Breath. Grandmother.

The winter sunshine had gathered in the small room where my friend and I sat to talk about hermeneutics, lived experience, memory, and ways of knowing. I shared how the performances I do in academic settings had begun almost two years ago when I wrote and performed a story of my cancer experience but kept it at a distance by telling it from my grandmother's perspective. I am named after her so the writing and telling seemed fluid. The story showcased my cancer diagnosis and therapy. It detailed the making of a plaster bust, surgery, radiation, and medication. The story whispered childhood memories into the air, unsticking them from their hiding places. In those moments of radiation treatment as the machine swayed and emitted its achingly long single tone first one side of my body, and then the other, memories of the wild sea crashed against Ireland's Cliffs of Moher. The sound of the sea was welcome. It combatted the sights and smells that flooded my mind. Memories of the wall of books, dusty and glaring, and the stale smells of cheap wine, seemed to have penetrated even the lead lined walls of the radiation room and continued to follow me into the academic settings where I read the story.

I continued to tell my friend how the plaster bust had been made and then banged about in the trunk of a car, as it was carried to beaches, forests, and to city cafés. I shared how I hated it and how I ripped at its ragged shoulder and then, full of remorse, added more plaster to repair it. Through the weeks and months, I layered the bust over with more plaster, smoothed it, tried to make it perfect. But like life, it would not oblige my expectations no matter how determined I had become.

At the end of my outpouring to my friend, I spoke a question: "How did I make it to this point in my life?" In the telling I was emptied of the story and in that moment of spaciousness I was ready for her rephrasing of my awkward and not wholly truthful question. She rephrased: "You mean, 'How am I not yet dead?'"

There, in the directness of her question, I am read back to myself. Her question offered a space of stillness that allowed an interpretation of myself to arise. This moment left room for a memory of my first radiation treatment when I remembered the large poster above my head. Tacked to one of the ceiling tiles was an image of cherry blossoms in full, riotous bloom. In order to escape the fear of the treatment and the flooding of childhood memories, I stepped into the beauty of those cherry blossoms. The imagined afternoon breezes had not the strength nor the desire to blow the petals from the thin branches. I remembered taking a slow, meandering breath before hearing the technician tell me the procedure was over and that they would see me the next day. Life, like the cherry blossom, is fleeting and precarious. Impermanent. Beautiful. Each breath gives rise to the opportunity to be in life afresh and to practice wholeheartedness knowing that I am dying beneath the tumbling, air filled petals and that I am not yet dead and that this is what matters for now.

During radiation therapy it is important to lie very still so that the beams of radiation hit the areas marked by permanent tattoos injected on the skin. A tumour had been removed eight weeks earlier but the radiation was meant to kill any stray cancer cells that might be huddling in my breast tissue. As a patient of the cancer clinic I performed my role well. I listened to and followed directions and smiled and looked at the technicians to give them a sense that I was at ease with the procedures. I showed curiosity about the numbers as they were reviewed and read aloud while my skin was being marked with the black pen. My only irregular request was that they not play any of the prescribed music selections meant to distract me from the procedure. I wanted the quiet to protect me. I wanted to hear my own breath and heartbeat.

In the cancer diagnosis and treatment processes patients are identified in terms of personal details such as name, birthdate, ID numbers, and diagnosis, which are repeated often at each appointment. This identity bound me like the hospital band on my wrist that dug into my skin.

Once the doctors feel they have successfully removed the tumour and applied the right course of treatment, I, a *patient*, become known as a *survivor*. I have carried the identity of survivor, like a troll on my back. I know I am supposed to be happy about this new identity; the expression is meant to note that the worst is over. But it lays itself over me and is never truly gone from view and continues to constrain fuller understandings and expressions of self. Sometimes there is downright alienation. These identities bind and limit feelings of spaciousness. It is difficult to see and hear or generate newness when my body is pushed into these forms.

"[T]he body is not merely matter but a continual and incessant materializing of possibilities" (Butler, 1988, p. 521). My reflection on and dialogue with others about cancer and its related processes helps me attend to the nature of these possibilities which are co-inspired by machines, texts, pounding shores, and friends. Recognizing these personal opportunities for self-understanding is a process of spirals among and between the particulars of cancer within a larger discussion of life lived wholeheartedly.

> Fundamentally, understanding is always a movement in this kind of circle, which is why the repeated return from the whole to the parts, and vice versa, is essential. Moreover, this circle is constantly expanding, since the concept of the whole is relative, and being integrated in ever larger contexts always affects the understanding of the individual part. (Gadamer, 2004, p. 189)

I began to disrupt the larger collective narrative of *patient* and *survivor* with personal narratives that arose in performance, reflection, and conversation. When I explored the encounter with machines and identities, I also tested the binaries of healthy/ill, patient/survivor, past/future in terms of my own self-knowing. Further, I learn how the self is formed and reformed in the company of others. This process has a steadying effect and makes it possible to act with more caring attention to the world.

Self as Performance

As a teacher of young children, I am no longer sure that what I have learned to do well is indeed the right thing. The more I study and listen to friends, colleagues, and mentors, the more I notice the materializing of possibilities. Like Annie Dillard (2016), "I myself [am] both observer and observable, and so a possible object of my own humming awareness" (p. xx). This observer stance began to take shape in my first performance at a Canadian curriculum conference. The story I had written from my grandmothers's perspective of cancer and cancer therapy was the script for that performance. My friend read the part of the narrator, and I read the phrases attributed to my grandmother. We spent time arranging the classroom to help the audience feel the environment in which the story unfolds. Strands of cherry blossoms hung from the ceiling. Chairs were positioned back-to-back to represent a waiting room in a medical setting. The participants, with a little sideways glance, could view the plaster bust I had made the night before the surgery. It sat on a chair in front of a transparent fabric curtain of cherry blossoms. The performance included a sound-scape of the beach and the radiation machine and ended with a recording of a soprano who had sung a poem I had written.

We had rehearsed the 22-minute performance. We modulated our voices and kept as tightly to the schedule as possible. During the performance, some participants didn't move until their shoulders rose at the sound of the radiation machine. Looking up from my script, I feared they would bolt from the room. Other participants seemed more relaxed and looked around at the objects and at my friend and me as we spoke. When the performance ended, there was silence in the room – a long, breath-holding silence. Then someone broke the heaviness saying that she was unable to speak about the impact of the work but that she would write to us later. This opened the way for others to say how frightened they had been and how they focused on the cherry blossoms in order to feel less unsettled. Others remained completely silent. Upon reflection, I realized that I, too, during the performance, held myself stiff against the onslaught my emotions. Reflecting on my experiences in this performance and on the comments I received put my understanding of the story in flight, pushing it beyond the static confines of the script.

> [Storytelling] is a fluid tradition that is as migratory as a winter bird, feeding as it goes from place to place and leaving something of itself behind. Those of us with gardens can attest to the hardiness of "volunteers" that spring up from seeds that have been carried in a bird's body over countless miles. (Yolen, 1988, p. 3)

With each performance, parts of the script shifted, fell away, or were amplified. Some changes were planned in advance based on my reflection of how I felt during specific parts of a previous performance. For instance, there is a line in the script where the radiation technician, through her light, Scottish accent, says, "Would you like a warm blanket?" This line was meant to help build audience awareness of the coldness of the radiation room. I didn't know how much this line held until, in one performance, I felt a shiver run along my spine as I spoke it. Through that performance I learned that I had been seen not just as patient, but as person by the technician. I began to understand that the offering of a warm blanket was an opening into another truth: I was not completely bound by the identities of *patient*, or *survivor*. I was human, being cared for by another human who saw me as a woman – a woman of flesh and blood. She offered the gift of connection in the way she offered the warm blanket.

> A gift comes to you through no action of your own, free, having moved toward you without your beckoning. It is not a reward; you cannot earn it, or call it to you, or even deserve it. And yet it appears. Your only role is to be open-eyed and present. Gifts exist in the realm of humility and mystery – as with random acts of kindness, we do not know their source. (Kimmerer, 2013, pp. 23–24)

I am beginning to know the performances, alive with their own direction at times, as gifts in themselves. With each retelling, understanding of my fears, insecurities, joys, and questions grows. The more I put the story into play, the more I realize I am being formed by the practice as much as, if not more than, forming it. The performances allow for a place to be and become. When I free the stories through performance, they become gifts. The stories and the performance of them are neither tool nor technique. Further, the performances turn me into a gift to myself and to others when I stay present to what arises in them.

> Interpretive research "... begins (and remains) with the evocative, living familiarity that this [or that] tale evokes. The task of interpretation is to bring out this evocative given in all its tangled ambiguity, to follow its evocations and the entrails of sense and significance that are wound up with it. Interpretive research, too, suggests that these striking incidents make a claim on us and open up and reveal something to us about our lives together and what it is that is going on, often unvoiced, in the ever-so commonplace and day-to-day act of becoming a teacher. (Jardine, 2016, p. 2)

Each performance offers an opportunity for me to be read back to myself "... as the breath-blood that dances possibility and interstanding into being" (Fels, 1999, p. 58). I learn about myself through the glances of the viewers, the comments they make after the performance, and the silence of the bust that still sits with me during the telling. A dramatic moment of knowing myself happened one afternoon in the summer of 2017. I had been taking a course with Professor David Abram that focused on oral traditions. We were allowed one prop for our final presentation, and we were asked to focus on our connection to "place." The final class also happened to coincide with another surgery that could not be postponed. I spoke to Professor Abram and let him know that I would be arriving to class after surgery, likely feeling the effects of the sedative. His response was warm, humorous, and inviting. I had a small outline for the presentation, but it is not what came forth. When it was my turn to present I carried the weighty plaster bust to the floor and we sat.

Still.

I began, after what seemed like a long silence, to speak to her. I started with an apology. In that moment of rawness, the script fell away and the space created by the letting go of the scripted words made room for other words. Feelings of sadness, loss, anger, and hope surfaced and were voiced as I sat on the floor and shared the making of the bust and the way I had carried it with me for several weeks before arriving on a rough and gusty beach in Tofino, before learning that the bust was really not *it* but *she*. She was her own subject *and* me at the same time. In that performance I understood what it means to listen to my own experiences and to the silence.

> Philosophy is not a making of a home for the mind out of reality. It is more like learning to leave things be; restoration in the wilderness, here and now ... By "leaving things be" I do not mean inaction; I mean respecting things, being still in the presence of things, letting them speak. (Bugbee, 1975, p. 155)

In this encounter, the bust offered a different view and, as she sat silently, I learned that silence is also a form of telling. The bust, in its material mixture of plaster and cotton, became a way of understanding my understanding. The bust is part of my history. It is also my real grandmother's history as it is carried within the very cells that come from my skin and still cling her to the cavity.

As I begin to understand the claim that the words and events of the performances make upon me, I realize the importance of living my history into my future with care and thoughtfulness and of knowing that my history is determined "from a position within it" (Warnke, 1987, p. 39). As the performances grow in number, they take on an increasingly visceral quality. As I focus less on the props and techniques of the performance I become more aware of making acquaintance with my body, not just becoming aware of it. I feel myself growing in relation to the idea of impermanence and the cycles of life the more I embody it. Further, I become more awake to the responsibility I have not to force love or understanding onto the subjects of my study, such as self, identity, impermanence, continuity, but rather to invite myself and others into attending to their difficulties as well as its affirmations.

Performance as Witness

I return to the question, carefully spoken on that winter sun-imbued morning after I had wondered aloud how I had come to this point in my life. "You mean," she said, "'How am I not yet dead?'" There, through the open, iterative, re-performing, retelling, I am confronted, with the task of understanding of self, of beaches, of plaster busts, and of grandmothers, as it begins (again).

The question that my friend rephrased holds a kinship with the question, "How am I living?" With each performance and conversation, new and better questions like this arise. The questions, and the performances that are shaped by them, become witness. I am coming to understand the performances as a weave of interpretations that include layers of traditions and prejudices. By learning to experience the performances as an ongoing and open process, I am more ready to attend to what is exerting itself and what is receding.

I used to think that a study of self in relation to worlds of memories was about finding an "it," an end-point with everything neatly categorized and arranged on a shelf. However, my cancer diagnosis put everything into play. Cancer opened up my past, present, and future all at once, and opens a way of learning what I know and what I may have forgotten. Understanding of myself and my connection to the world is reached through dialogue with others, with my body, and with the plaster bust. In my performances and in my writing, language is "something I and others find ourselves in, not something we find in us and at our beck and call. It is not an internal possession. It is an eco-poetic habitat in which we live, contested, multivocal, obscured and obscuring, clarifying, articulate, foolish. It is the soil of the world of our thinking (Jardine, February 2018, personal communication). Language reveals and it conceals. What I think I might say in performances sometimes gets pushed aside by other words that come along, often to my surprise, shock, delight, bewilderment, revelation, or wonder. This is my study of myself with others and apart from others.

The performances act as an open container for a variety of emotions, mine and those of the members of the audience. It takes time, and repeated exploration, and openness, and breath to learn to understand. "This, then, is a kind of progress – not the progress proper to research but rather a progress that always must be renewed in the effort of our living" (Gadamer, 2007, p. 244).

In this self-study, I am learning to write of the readiness to let go, of the understanding of self and memory in relation to cancer, of how cancer offers a place for the practice of interpretive inquiry, and of making sense of being in the world. The impact of the experience of the performance, the comments and silences of friends, the multi-vocal interpretations, all help me realize that my horizon of understanding is not permanently fixed. In each encounter, traditions, prejudices, doubt, playfulness, and imagination are brought forth and the possibility to interpret anew arises. Bernstein (1986) explains: "There can never be … finality in understanding or complete self-transparency of the knower. We always find ourselves in an open dialogical or conversational situation with the very tradition and history that effectively shaping us" (p. 63).

My commitment to the work of performance allows me to become more attuned to the possible answers to the questions: What does this performance open up to myself and to others? What does it close?

> "[R]emaining with the object of meditation, this gathering, requires, then, of me, a certain level of 'cultivation' (*Bildung*), but what is thus cultivated is not exactly my 'self' but my ability to forgo how myself persistently tries to foreground itself." It is a sort of "getting over myself" by giving myself over to detailing how things are (Dharma) with say, that species of bird, or this unseasonal warmth of clothes on the line, Jan 28, 2016 – both a pleasure and slightly nightmarish portent. Of course. Buddhism, ecology, hermeneutics: these are all lineages regarding how to come to understanding and intimately experience what is happening to us. Pedagogy. (Jardine, 2016, p. 80)

Cancer. Plaster busts. Beaches. Horizons.

All of these teachers help me put myself into question so that I might carry myself wholeheartedly into the world. Through the performances, I am learning to stay open to the arrival of the world into my life. This makes it possible to see how the world and I are not quite so separate as I once thought.

The title of this chapter, *Opening into Aletheia,* suggests more than I understand at present but I know that I am opening to new ways of understanding myself and the world. The image of the bust is reminiscent of the remnants of ancient Greek sculptures. Torsos without heads, arms and legs, are always only part of the story.

> Aletheia is a word that is about unconcealment. The word is the opposite of Lethal (dead) – aletheia then means to enliven. It is also connected to the mythical River of Lethe in Hades: the River of Forgetfulness – a river that, if crossed, erased memory. Aletheia is the antithesis of this: it is about remembering. In its unconcealment, enlivening, and remembering, aletheia brings home what may have been lost, forgotten, deadened, or concealed in our "simply getting by." The work of hermeneutics is the work of Aletheia. (Moules, 2015, p. 1)

Moules calls me to open to myself so that the fullness of life, and how it is lived, can be remembered, suffered, and let go.

References

Bernstein, R. J. (1986). *Philosophical profiles: Essays in a pragmatic mode*. Cambridge: Polity Press.

Bugbee, H. G. (1976). *The inward morning*. New York, NY: Harper & Row.

Butler, J. (1988). Performative acts and gender constitution: An essay in phenomenology and feminist theory. *Theatre Journal, 40*(4), 519–531.

Caputo, J. D. (1987). *Radical hermeneutics: Repetition, deconstruction and the hermeneutic project*. Bloomington, IN: Indiana University Press.

Dillard, A. (2016). *The abundance: Narrative essays old and new*. New York, NY: Harper & Row.

Fells, L. (1999). *In the wind clothes dance on a line–performative inquiry as a research methodology* (Unpublished doctoral dissertation). University of British Columbia, Vancouver.

Gadamer, H. G. (2004). *Truth and method*. London: Continuum.

Gadamer, H. G. (2007). *The Gadamer reader: A bouquet of the later writings* (R. E. Palmer, Ed.). Evanston, IL: Northwestern University Press.

Hanh, T. N. (2014). *No mud, no lotus*. Berkeley, CA: Parallax Press.

Husserl, E. (2012). *Ideas: General introduction to a pure phenomenology* (W. R. Boyce-Gibson, Trans.). London: Routledge. (Original work published in 1931)

Jardine, D. (2013). Time is [not] always running out. *Journal of American Association for the Advancement of Curriculum Studies, 9*, 1–32.

Jardine, D. (2016). *In praise of radiant beings: A retrospective path through education, Buddhism and ecology*. Charlotte, NC: Information Age Publishing.

Kimmerer, R. W. (2013). *Braiding sweetgrass: Indigenous wisdom, scientific knowledge, and the teachings of plants*. Minneapolis, MN: Milkweed Press.

Kohák, E. (1984). *The embers and the stars*. Chicago, IL: University of Chicago Press.

Moules, N. (2015). Editorial. Aletheia: Remembering and enlivening. *Journal of Applied Hermeneutics*. Retrieved from http://hdl.handle.net/10515/sy5qr4p68

Warnke, G. (1987). *Gadamer: Hermeneutics, tradition and reason*. New York, NY: Coward-McCann.

Yolen, J. (1988). *Favorite folktales from around the world*. New York, NY: Pantheon Books.

CHAPTER 12

Navigating a Narrative Path: A Self-Study on Using Stories to Deepen Learning in Pre-Service Teaching

Deborah Graham

Beginning with a Story – The Printing Lesson: How Children Remember

My most vivid memory from my first year in school is of a morning when we were doing a daily printing activity. The teacher would print verses on the chalkboard and we were supposed to copy down these verses into our lined notebooks. The purpose was to improve our formation of letters. This was a long and arduous task for me, as my hands were very small and I wanted each letter to be made to perfection. Therefore, I worked very slowly. The teacher moved up and down the rows of wooden desks monitoring our work that morning. As I attempted to complete this task she stopped beside my desk and commented on the limited progress I had made. The next words that escaped from her left me in a state of shock. She said that by the time she returned to my desk, my work had better be completed or I would receive the "strap." I knew what this meant, as I had witnessed other children get the strap, and I put my pencil down and froze. By the time this teacher had returned to my desk I had completely shut down. She took the strap out from the top drawer of her desk, and asked me to stand and stretch out my hands. I did not move. At this, she grabbed one of my arms and attempted to strap me, but could not peel open my tiny fingers; I was so frightened that they were locked shut, and no matter how hard she tried, she could not untangle them to strap me properly. In frustration she went next door to get the other teacher to assist her. One teacher held out my arm and the other attempted to untwine my small fingers. She also did not meet with success. Finally, in sheer frustration, my teacher threw down the strap, lifted up my dress and turned me over her knee. In a rage she spanked me over and over ....

Buchmann (1992) once wrote, in regard to memories, "looking back will impart a higher character, more refined perceptions, or nobler intentions to teachers" (p. 17). They can also be "retained and restored for successive viewings" (p. 17). It is my contention that the same can be said of stories. In my own life, such stories have become valuable sources of information that I have drawn from repeatedly to inform my teaching. Recalling such events and sharing such stories have served to give life to learning – my own and others. Some of these stories are derived from my teaching life while others are rooted in my own schooling or other personal experiences. Including stories in my teaching over the years has evolved and become an even more thoughtful and intentional process. Throughout my work with pre-service teachers, such stories were disseminated: personal narratives that highlighted the importance of forging connections; accounts of challenging moments that spoke to the need to become resilient in the face of adversity; anecdotes of loss that prompted me to realize the need to make every day in teaching count; experiences that demonstrated how stepping outside the box expanded learning; and mistakes that, when recounted, served to transform my practice. Sharing and reflecting on these stories has brought teaching and learning to new levels for me. The above story of the printing lesson, taken from my own schooling, was shared to help my students realize that they must be vigilant and thoughtful in their treatment of children, that how what they say and do can be retained by them for a long time, possibly even a lifetime.

Looking back at this particular memory, for a brief span of time I am once again that tiny, six-year-old child, sitting in that small wooden desk. I vividly remember the blackboards, one of which had "The 23rd Psalm" written on it, and the other, the words to the children's song "Puff the Magic Dragon" (Lipton & Yarrow, 1963). I can also still see the chart filled with different coloured stars, a testimony to the number of clean hands and fingernails in each row. In reflecting on this classroom and incident, I am struck by the paradoxes that existed. Reality stood in stark contrast to the promises of prayer that echoed in the refrain, "The Lord is my shepherd," a song that resounded the magic of "frolicking in the autumn mist," and rewards offered for effort. Instead, there was fear and oppression. Bolman and Deal (2001) say that, "Human history is full of stories of common people who do extraordinary things. In surmounting anguish and pain they kindle their spirits and give strength to others" (p. 66). Holding on to this memory has served to remind me that I now have an obligation. In knowing how difficult it is to surmount such anguish, as a teacher it is my duty to ensure that such pain is never inflicted on other students.

Teaching with Intention: An Evolving Practice

On the day that I shared the story of the printing lesson with a class of elementary pre-service teachers, I noted that many of them were deeply touched by it. In sharing this experience from my own schooling, I was striving to impart to them the importance of being thoughtful and caring with children. Furthermore, I suggested to them that, years later when meeting their former students, those students might not necessarily remember the well-constructed lessons that they planned as well as they would remember how they were treated. Conveying this lesson in a way that would reach these prospective teachers was very important to me. Since I view teaching as largely relational, I wanted them to realize that they must always be mindful of their words and actions when working with children. In addition to this, the course that I taught these students was rooted in particular *principles and practices of teaching* and emphasized that "competent teaching requires the formation of positive, caring relationships rooted in a vision of meaningful and inclusive education" (course outline, September, 2016). Helping pre-service teachers understand that the student "is more important, more valuable, than the subject" (Noddings, 1984, p. 74) was a lesson that I never wanted them to forget, and it was my contention that the most effective way that I could ensure meaningful learning and impart this information so that it would become data for their future teaching was through the sharing of stories. As Drake (2010) points out "For me, relevance is the key to meaningful learning. (Story is one way to ensure meaningful learning)" (p. 6). Additionally, through this particular story, I honoured one of the premises of the courses: teaching involves forging caring and meaningful relationships with students.

While I agree with Drake that stories hold significance and lead to deeper knowing, I also relate to Golombek and Johnson (2017) who suggest that, if we are to use stories as a means to enhance the development of teachers, we need to realize that this cannot be a mindless practice. They insist that narrative activity should entail three interrelated functions: narrative as externalization (teachers developing awareness of what they are experiencing, thinking and feeling resulting in change in their teaching activity); narrative as verbalization (being able to make sense of teaching experiences and beginning to regulate both their thinking and teaching practices); and narrative as systemic examination (procedures for how teachers engage in narrative activity). I agree with Golembek & Johnson that using stories in one's teaching must be a very thoughtful and reflective process that moves teachers beyond the mere telling of a story to transformation of practice through awareness, reflection, and examination. In my own circumstances, such awareness and transformation has been achieved through deep excavation to uncover such stories and realize the layers of significance and meaning that exists within them. It is critical to engage in this process because passing on such stories to pre-service teachers means that they might indeed become, as Buchmann (1992) suggested earlier of memories, "retained and restored for successive viewings" (p. 17). Like a book with a corner bent down to mark a special page, they might be retrieved and influence future action. Therefore, we must "move beyond the current genre of the 'personal-confessional' to ensure that our stories are 'ethically sensitive' and principled" (Lyons & LaBoskey, 2002, p. 196) as teacher educators. This is something that I came to realize more fully as I considered such stories in light of my teaching goals.

In my own excavation process of the above story, I considered the many years since I sat in that particular Grade 1 classroom and how long I had held on to this unhappy memory. Upon reflection, I realized that, in many ways, I might never know for sure the full impact that this experience had had on me. In hindsight, I could only speculate that other incidences that followed in my schooling may have been impacted by this single event. However, I grew quite certain that my pedagogic understanding of what it means to be punished in such a manner and for such a reason became "a form of deep learning, leading to a transformation of consciousness, heightened perceptiveness, increased thoughtfulness and tact ... " (van Manen, 1997, p. 163). In deconstructing this experience and unearthing what it meant for me as a teacher, there were lessons to be learned. For example, beyond realizing the importance of having a caring attitude towards children, I also understood more fully that another main purpose in teaching is to promote justice. To this end I acknowledged that "not everyone believes that freedom or emancipation is a leading purpose of education ... " (Cooper & White, 2004, p. 20). However, through deeper reflection I agreed with Griffiths (1998) who stated that "educational research is for improvements in education, with all its personal and political implications" (p. 92). In fact, she strongly advocated for research on injustices imposed upon particular groups, including wrongs against children who could not defend themselves (Griffiths, 1998). (Pinar, Slattery, & Taubman, 1995) also promoted research regarding oppression experienced by children and lamented that this was not addressed more. Perhaps one of the strongest advocates against oppression of children and others was Freire (1970) who deeply expressed the need to act in the face of such injustices. In my own teaching with pre-service teachers, sharing such stories has been one way for me to take up a similar cause as other aforementioned researchers in order to address such unfairness and discrimination, so that it does not continue to happen.

Methodology

This chapter is an initiated self-study that examines my evolving practice of using stories as a way to reflect upon and improve my teaching practice with pre-service teachers in a small Canadian university. In this study, I draw from stories that were scripted as part of a final assignment in my doctoral program. At that time, I endeavored to write an in-depth paper (unpublished) that examined significant stories from my teaching life that influenced my belief system as an educator. Along with writing these stories, I reflected on them and identified fundamental principles of teacher education contained within them. In summation, I further examined how such stories helped me to become a more resilient, efficacious, and compassionate teacher.

During my first two years as a teacher educator I often shared stories in the courses that I taught. Like slipping on a shoe that fits, such stories were fit unintentionally and naturally as various themes and discussions arose during classes. I was just completing my doctoral work, when I began to consider the infusion of stories into my practice in a new light: I wondered how might the stories I shared be reflected on more deeply and aligned with specific outcomes or goals in particular courses. It was not that I believed that stories should always be premeditated in my teaching. Nor did I fail to realize the power of stories verbatim to inform and expand knowledge, but rather that I recognized them as a way to see the full expanse of how stories fulfilled the goals that I outlined and sought to achieve in my teaching. In this way, stories became data to draw from in a much more intentional and fuller way.

This examination of my teaching practice through exploration of stories is chiefly anchored in self-study methodology, as recommended by Bullough and Pinnegar (2001) who insist that self-studies that draw from narrative or autobiographical forms must meet particular criteria including: promoting insight and interpretation; taking an honest stand; being concerned with problems or issues that make one an educator; seeking to improve the learning situation not only for the self but for the other; ringing true; and inspiring others. They expound upon the need to expose and examine any biases that we might have. They suggest that by throwing light on oneself in an authentic and honest way, it allows for reinterpretation of the lives of both the writer and the reader. Self-study is a process of delving deeply into the personal or, as Drake (2010) points out, "the way I have interpreted a lifetime of experiences" (p. 3). Hamilton, Smith, and Worthington (2008) further distinguish that narrative can be used as a *research strategy* in a self-study with a "focus on practice and improvement of practice, closely attending to self and others in and through their practice" (p. 25). Using narrative as a research strategy in this study was a three-fold process of scripting stories, reflecting on stories, and aligning stories to course requirements.

Scripting Stories

In this study, I draw from stories that were scripted over a period of several years, a process that began on one level with the writing of my M.Ed. thesis in 2000, and continued on in 2011 as part of a final assignment in my doctoral program. The paper, entitled *"Composing a Teaching Life"* comprised five different stories, including the story of *The Printing Lesson*. These stories portrayed events and incidences that significantly contributed to my formation as a teacher; defining moments were written in such a way that they might be read by others who could make connections of their own to the particulars of each story. Bullough and Pinnegar (2001) claim that, in quality autobiography, in some ways our life story interconnects and illuminates others; nodal moments written with such raw honesty may be read and lived vicariously by others. To write with any less intensity in their summation "would not be worth reading by teacher educators" (p. 17). It is in this way that I attempted to write, providing a voice for the many questions that had gone unanswered, the many feelings that had shriveled in neglect, and the many silent pleas that had gone unheeded in my own schooling, and in my life as a teacher.

In the years following completion of my doctoral work, as I continued to work with pre-service teachers, more and more stories began to surface. In addition to the five stories: *The Printing Lesson; The Student Who Stuttered; Memories of My Third Grade Teacher; Laments of Accepting a Teaching Award; and A New Era Begins,* I wrote six new stories: *The Teachable Moment; Show Don't Tell; An Elementary Version of Macbeth; The Story of Carly, Jesse and the Fish; and The Dance (which I am currently shaping into a children's book)*. Slattery (2000) once said, "As I wrote, I was able to get in touch with myself, as well as with my teaching practice. The more I reflected through my writing, the more my teaching and knowledge of myself was transformed" (Slattery, 2000, p. 117). Through the process of scripting stories, I experienced writing my way into knowing more about my teaching and my life. Writing in this way continues to shape my identity as a teacher educator, parent, grandmother, and citizen in the world.

Reflecting on Stories

Beyond writing stories, I deeply reflected on them. In my doctoral course this took on the pattern of scripting stories, writing about the lessons gleaned through such stories and uncovering principles for teacher education contained within each story. Bullough and Pinnegar (2001) discuss how through such stories others need to gain new understanding of fundamental issues in teaching and how these stories must reveal something important about the profession. Such narratives must clearly show evidence of why the experience or event was a defining moment; certain truths must be uncovered through the process. As I reflected on each story I asked essential questions of myself: Why is this story so significant to me? What was the context for this story? Who was involved? Am I being fully honest in my recounting of this story to the best of my ability? What is my purpose in sharing this story? What have I learned through this process? For example, in reflecting on *The Printing Lesson,* I came to a much deeper realization of the need to treat children with nothing less than the deepest respect. Furthermore, in revealing a principle of teacher education connected to this story, I wrote at length about the role of social justice in teacher education and how it must be a thread that connects all principles taught. In this regard I expressed that it must be understood that teaching demands more than simply standing in front of students and instructing them. It is in essence a humanitarian profession which must have as one dimension the purpose of constructing caring communities for children. This means creating environments that are compassionate and sensitive to the needs of others and ensuring that injustices of any kind are not inflicted on students. I further insisted that teacher education programs can play a very significant role in inviting teachers to begin to explore this notion. Furthermore, I contended that institutions which train teachers hold responsibility to extend this invitation to pre-service teachers. Beyond this, I proceeded to delve into ways that this was addressed in our particular institution. Through this process, I contend that fundamental issues were indeed addressed and truths uncovered.

Aligning Stories

It is most recently that I began to consider the need to align the stories I share with pre-service teachers with my teaching goals. As indicated earlier, such congruence would allow me to see how stories fit into my overall teaching. As I began to do this, it evolved into a meaningful process whereby I took each story and considered it in light of various general and specific outcomes. For example, the story of the printing lesson opened up a process of exploring critical learnings for teacher education contained within several general and specific curriculum outcomes including: learning environment, professional literacy, pedagogical relationships and formation of teacher identities as indicated in Table 12.1.

In gaining further perspective on this process it should be noted that sharing this story does not necessarily ensure meeting such outcomes. However, it does begin a process of exploring teacher education through a variety of

TABLE 12.1   Chart demonstrating the link between general and specific course outcomes in
              my EDUC 469 course to a narrative on my own schooling

Narrative title	General outcome	Specific outcome (s)
The Printing Lesson: How Children Remember (S=Schooling Experience)	Pre-service teachers will show evidence of the emergent knowledge, skills, and attitudes associated with classroom environment	2.2 Establishing a culture for learning (creating safe places for students, maintaining an open learning environment, setting respectful expectations of students; communicating fair and challenging expectations for all learners) 2.5 Developing strategies to manage disruptive behavior
The Printing Lesson: How Children Remember (S)	Pre-service teachers will show evidence of the emergent knowledge, skills, and attitudes associated with professional literacy	4.1 Reflecting on teaching for use in future instruction and in the moment 4.6 Acting professionally by adhering to a code of ethics
The Printing Lesson: How Children Remember (S)	Pre-service teachers will show evidence of the emergent knowledge, skills, and attitudes associated with pedagogy relational connections.	5.1 Acknowledging that teaching is a pedagogical act (the learner is the entry point for teacher decisions) 5.3 Developing awareness of tacit knowing – informing your decisions to act in ways that are appropriate for each student
The Printing Lesson: How Children Remember (S)	Pre-service teachers will show evidence of the emergent knowledge, skills, and attitudes associated with teaching identity–knowing self.	6.7 Examining beliefs as a teacher regarding factors in and beyond the school context that will/can affect the students' social, political, cultural, and educational awareness

lenses: the necessary learning environment; being professional; building peda-gogical relationships; and forming teacher identities.

Narratives as Vehicles for Teacher Knowledge

Reflecting on the role of stories as vehicles for gaining teacher knowledge began with the writing of my M.Ed. thesis (2000) that explored the phenomenon of professional isolation in teaching. Over the course of these years and through other academic writing, including my doctoral dissertation, I have drawn insights from many scholars regarding the role of stories to gain personal and professional knowledge (Atkinson, 1995; Clandinin, 1986; Clandinin & Connelly, 1991, 1992, 1995, 1999; Jalongo & Isenberg, 1995; Cole & Knowles, 2000; Lyons & Laboskey, 2002; Bryman, 2004; Craig, 2007; Orr & Olson, 2007; Drake, 2010; Lyle, 2013; Golombek & Johnson, 2017). While this list is not exhaustive, inquiring into stories consistently as a way to acquire meaning from experience and to open up possibilities for learning has been supported extensively in research.

> *The Relevance of Sharing Stories*
> Stories …
>   diverse
>   complex
>   retained
>   restored
> Hold power for …
>   guiding
>   connecting
>   understanding
>   transforming
> Emotionally charged they …
>   ignite
>   internalize
>   evoke
>   remain
> They are a path to …
>   learning
>   agency
>   healing
>   voice
> Stories …
>   (Graham, 2018)

Future teachers need to acquire "the ability to reflect upon the complex peda-gogical, psychological, and sociological processes occurring in the classroom and to develop professional judgment (course outline, fall 2017). To this end, engaging in professional reading, self-reflection, case studies, learning logs, and a myriad of other meaningful activities certainly help them to gain insights into a teaching life. Having eleven weeks in the field over the course of this time also gives them opportunity to experience first-hand the daily joys and challenges that teaching brings. Despite this, I never feel completely satisfied that these activities alone will remain with pre-service teachers and be fodder for their future teaching. Conversely, when I share stories, I feel more satisfied that what I have attempted to teach has the potential to remain with them. This is so for all pre-service teach-ers and in a profound way for those who have not yet had a practicum experience. I also concur with Golembek and Johnson (2017) who state that "engagement in narrative activity ... assists teachers as they attempt to internalize the academic concepts that they are exposed to in their teacher education programs" (p. 18). It is my belief that the stories I share, in a sense, become their stories.

Undoubtedly, in teacher education programs there must be room for stories. While this chapter has focused on the significance of stories being shared by a teacher educator, spaces also must be created for pre-service teachers to share their own stories. Cooper and White (2004) contend that "encouraging student teachers to begin with their own lived experiences, to listen and learn from their own and each other's narratives ... to reflect on these and share them, are nec-essary practices in developing respectful ways toward the children we teach in order to become 'good' teachers" (p. 41). In my work with pre-service teachers, one way that I encourage sharing of personal stories is through the keeping of learning logs. As they construct and share stories through this process these nar-ratives are interpreted and, as a result, teachers often reconstruct their stories and expand their understanding. Lyons and LaBoskey (2002) expound on this more when they say that "we came to see that narrative was fundamentally an activity of mind, a way of knowing, and a way of knowing that one knew" (p. 3). Perhaps one of the greatest benefits of sharing stories is the fact that "it is impossible not to become storytellers and story livers with those we are involved with ... the stories ... merged with our own to create new stories ... collaborative stories" (Connelly & Clandinin, 1991, p. 12). As I continue to teach pre-service teachers, I will persist in considering the role of stories in the education.

References

Atkinson, R. (1995). *The gift of narratives: Practical and spiritual applications of auto-biography, life narratives, and personal mythmaking*. Westport, CT: Bergin & Garvey.

Bolman, L., & Deal, T. (2001). *Leading with soul: An uncommon journey of spirit.* San Francisco, CA: Jossey-Bass.

Buchmann, M. (1992, April). *Figuring in the past: Thinking about teacher memories.* Paper presented at the American Research Association, San Francisco, CA.

Bullough, R., & Pinnegar, S. (2001). Guidelines for quality in autobiographical forms of self-learning research. *Educational Researcher, 30,* 13–21.

Clandinin, D. J. (1986). *Classroom practice: Teacher images in action.* London: Falmer Press.

Clandinin, D. J., & Connelly, F. M. (1991). Narrative and story in practice and research. In D. Schon (Ed.), *The reflective turn: Case studies in and on educational practice.* New York, NY: Teachers College Press.

Clandinin, D. J., & Connelly, F. M. (1992). Teacher as curriculum maker. In P. Jackson (Ed.), *Handbook of research on curriculum* (pp. 363–401). New York, NY: Macmillan.

Clandinin, D. J., & Connelly, F. M. (1995). Teachers' professional knowledge landscapes: Secret, sacred, and cover stories. In D. J. Clandinin & F. M. Connelly (Eds.), *Teachers' professional knowledge landscapes* (pp. 3–15). New York, NY: Teachers College Press.

Clandinin, D. J., & Connelly, F. M. (1999). *Shaping a professional identity: Stories of educational practice.* New York, NY: Teachers College Press.

Cole, A., & Knowles, J. (2000). *Researching teaching: Exploring teacher development through reflexive inquiry.* Needham Heights, MA: Allyn & Bacon.

Cooper, K., & White, R. (2004). *Burning issues: Foundations of education.* Lanham, MD: Scarecrow Education.

Craig, C. (2007). Dilemmas in crossing the boundaries: From K-12 to higher education and back again. *Teaching and Teacher Education, 23,* 1165–1176.

Drake, S. M. (2010). Enhancing Canadian teacher education using a story framework. *The Canadian Journal for the Scholarship of Teaching and Learning, 1*(2), Article 2.

Freire, P. (1970). *Pedagogy of the oppressed.* New York, NY: Herder & Herder.

Graham, D. (2000). *Weaving the voices: Breaking the silence of isolation* (Unpublished master's thesis). St. Francis Xavier University, Antigonish.

Griffiths, M. (1998). *Educational research for social justice: Getting off the fence.* Buckingham: Open University Press.

Golombek, P. R., & Johnson, K. E. (2017). Re-conceptualizing teachers' narrative inquiry as professional development. *PROFILE Issues in Teachers' Professional Development, 19*(2), 15–28.

Hamilton, M., Smith, L., & Worthington, K. (2008). Fitting the methodology with the research: An exploration of narrative, self-study and auto-ethnography. *Studying Teacher Education, 4*(1), 17–28.

Jalongo, M., & Isenberg, J. (1995). *Teachers' stories: From personal narrative to professional insight.* New York, NY: The Jossey-Bass Education Series.

Lipton, L., & Yarrow, P. (1963). *Puff the magic dragon* [Recorded by Peter, Paul and Mary]. New York, NY: Warner Music Group.

Lyle, E. (2013). From method to methodology: Reflexive narrative inquiry as perspective, process, and representation in an adult education context. *The Canadian Journal for the Study of Adult Education, 25*(2), 17–34.

Lyons, N., & Laboskey, V. (2002). *Narrative inquiry in practice: Advancing the knowledge of teaching.* New York, NY: Teachers College Press.

Murray Orr, A. M., & Olson, M. (2007). Transforming narrative encounters. *The Canadian Journal of Higher Education, 30*(3), 819–838.

Noddings, N. (1984). *Caring: A feminine approach to ethics and moral education.* Berkeley, CA: University of California Press.

Pinar, W., Reynolds, W., Slattery, P., & Taubman, P. (1995). *Understanding curriculum.* New York, NY: Peter Lang.

Slattery, P. (1995). *Curriculum development in the postmodern era.* New York, NY: Garland Publishing.

CHAPTER 13

International Novice Teacher Educators Navigating Transitional Sel(f)ves in Multicultural Education Teaching

Vy Dao and Yue Bian

Introduction

Multicultural education courses (MECs) are usually required in pre-service teacher education curriculum (June, 2016; Sleeter, 2001). The courses play an important role in shaping pre-service teachers' orientations and practices towards the increasing cultural and linguistic diversities in the U.S. classrooms (Ukpokodu, 2007). Teacher education communities acknowledge that MECs are critical to the development of pre-service teachers' understanding of structural and systemic challenges that minoritized students face in schooling (Gorski, 2012). However, there has been little done to understand how teacher educators, especially international novice teacher educators (INTEs), coming from multicultural and multilingual backgrounds with diverse life and professional experiences, learn to teach the courses in the U.S. (Foot, Crowe, Tollafield, & Allan, 2014). One way of understanding how INTEs learn to teach MECs in the U.S. is through the self-study of narratives of INTEs as they reflect on their teaching experiences and identity development across time, cultures, and places (Huang, 2010; Wang, 2005).

Researchers in self-study communities agree that novice teacher educators' identities can be understood through examining stories told by them about the struggles they encounter in new teaching places and the ways they confront struggles in the transition process from one working place to another (Hamilton & Pinnegar, 2015). Many of these studies focus on U.S. contexts but, in so doing, fail to account for non-American novice teacher educators who pursue doctoral studies in the U.S. By using collaborative self-study approaches and investigating our identities as INTEs teaching MECs, we address this gap. As we examine how our identities as INTEs inform our teaching experiences, we wonder how we, as INTEs, construct and negotiate our identities while we move from teaching practices in non-U.S. contexts to teaching MECs in the U.S. By investigating INTEs' identity development, we look for understanding the nature of this learning, the trajectories of INTEs teaching MECs, and how they might inform further research about INTEs' development as future faculty teaching MECs in the U.S.

© KONINKLIJKE BRILL NV, LEIDEN, 2019 | DOI:10.1163/9789004388864_013

Theoretical Perspectives

Identity and Learning

We rely on the notion that identities are dynamic, fluid, and ongoing (Lave & Wenger, 1991). According to Lave & Wenger's theory of situated learning, identity construction is connected to learning from and with others in a social setting. To learn means to become "a different person with respect to the possibilities enabled by the systems of social relations" (p. 53) through which identities take shape as one engages in the practices of making sense of others' talking, doing, and knowing. Novice teacher educators, including INTES, embody such learning. Even though they may be experienced teachers in their previous teaching, INTES are novices to the teaching practices in the U.S. universities. Thus, the experiences they gain through learning with and from others help them grow as they transit to the new teaching contexts. They are constantly learning to teach in order to become experienced teacher educators (Zeichner, 2005).

Novice teacher educators learning to teach is not just about their coming to know content and pedagogical matter knowledge, but also constructing an identity (Palmer, 2007). Thus, identities that INTES develop through learning to teach MECs depends on how INTES exercise their agency through establishing *beings* – a kind of thing one tells others about who one is and wants to be and do (Hamilton & Pinnegar, 2015). In this study, we focus on one dimension of those beings –*the cultural and temporal-spatial* relations.

The cultural and temporal-spatial relations, according to He and Phillion (2001), reflect the complexities of the tensions that encompass teachers' lived experiences as they "shifted between past, present, and future, from place to place, language to language, educational system to educational system" (p. 51). These relations become particularly important for the identity construction of those whose work is situated in cross-cultural contexts because they "provide specific types of plots for adoption by their members in their configuration of self" (Phelan, 2000, p. 290). That is, they help describe how the continuous reinterpretation of ones' lived experiences with a framework of meanings, which have previously been self-ascribed, takes place. When new lived experiences do not align with existing lived experiences, a negotiation of identity may occur. Akkerman and Meijer (2011) refer to this process as the ways in which individuals involve continual development of their living and working experiences "in such a way that a more or less coherent and consistent sense of self is maintained throughout various participations" (p. 315).

For INTES teaching in the U.S., their everyday adherence to the cross-cultural struggles and the societal, institutional, and classroom constraints they experience as they move between the teaching practices in their home countries to those in a new country results in the emergence of their new identities. This involves potential for change since it enhances "[our] understanding of who [we] are being and becoming as a teacher educator" and "the contexts that constrain [us]" and "opens possibilities for [our] individual and collective acting, and doing," and ultimately "bring[s] new ideas to the practice [we are] working on" (Hamilton & Pinnegar, 2015, p. 68).

Identity and Positioning

The MECs teaching practice is a social activity (Wang, 2005). The different ways in which this practice is set up and carried out (e.g., how teachers lead class discussions or interact with colleagues) create multiple social worlds (Foot et al., 2014). In this regard, when INTEs teach MECs, they might involve working with different social worlds that may be parallel or competing with one another (Trent, 2013). This often causes frustration, particularly for a novice struggling to construct an identity with which they are comfortable within the framework of others' acceptance and support (Newberry, 2014). However, it can be fulfilled if the novices can look beyond their challenges to understand what they have learned, ought to learn, and will be learning, in order to *become* a particular person in the new contexts (Foot et al., 2014; Dao, Farver, & Jackson, 2018).

In this becoming process, there is a close relationship between ones' identity formation and discursive positioning. Research found that while encountering social practices as one moves from one setting to another, individuals tend to involve various modes of positioning to express their personal agency and achieve a particular goal in their work (Harré & Lagenhove, 1999). They may *be positioned* by others, *self-position* in ways they think make sense to them, or they may *reposition* or adopt a new position to challenge the social world, in order to transform themselves and their practices. From this entry point, we argue that INTEs might choose to accept, engage, change, or even ignore new ideas, positions, and roles as they interact in their new teaching contexts; this, in turn, informs the development of their identities and teaching practices.

Context of the Study

Who We Are as People and as Teacher Educators

We became interested in this self-study because of our similar background as international doctoral students from Asian countries, and shared professional experience as teacher educators teaching MECs in the U.S. Yue was born in a middle-class family in a large city in China. She got her bachelor's degree in English literature and was a high school English teacher for two years.

Yue views Buddhism impacting her ways of being and doing in the world, and she considers the pursuit of inner peace as an important life goal. She hopes to create a peaceful environment for people around her, including her students in the classroom, which could be challenging when teaching MECs. Vy identifies herself as heterosexual, cis-gendered female and mother from Vietnam. Vy taught psychology and sociology for eight years for pre-service elementary school teachers in Vietnam. Despite this experience, Vy sees herself as a novice in teaching multicultural education for American pre-service teachers.

Both Vy and Yue taught courses at the university level in the U.S. focused on multicultural education. Vy taught a social foundation course that was required by all freshmen and sophomores who intended to join the teacher education program in their senior year. The course discussed the ways in which social inequality affects schooling and vice versa, and how socially constructed categories such as social class, race, language, and gender are used to privilege some and marginalize others. Yue taught a required course for students who joined a cohort program with a specific focus on global education. Three inter-related topics were addressed in the course: globalization in the 21st century; the hidden stories of immigrant families; and language ideology and its implications on the education of immigrant children. Mentoring support, in the form of informal and formal meeting with faculty course leaders, was provided to both Vy and Yue when they were teaching their courses.

How We Got Where We Are

Yue reached out to Vy for some self-study readings to help her reflect on her practices of teaching MECs. Vy then invited Yue to work on a self-study together, where they could both refine their teaching. We engaged in the discussion and reflection on our learning and teaching through four media. First, we used a semi-structured prompt in which we each constructed an autobiography about our life and professional experiences in our home countries and the U.S. that influenced our perspectives and practices of teaching. Second, over the course of the Spring and Fall semesters of 2017, we each kept memos of significant moments/incidents/people in our teaching and thoughts on how they impacted us as INTEs. Third, in the Spring of 2018, we shared our autobiographies and memos and commented on each others' writing, engaging in a recursive collaborative co-writing process. Fourth, we scheduled three debriefing meetings which each lasted for approximately two hours. During the meetings, we asked clarifying questions about our writing, talked about memorable events in teaching the two courses, and took notes on ideas that emerged through our conversations and writings.

Who We Are as INTES Teaching MECS

As noted earlier, the focus on cultural and temporal-spatial dimension of our teaching underscores the differences that exist between the teaching practice in our home countries and those in the U.S. As we made sense of the differences and developed our teaching over time, we were both challenged and rewarded for the need of understanding and managing our teaching intentions and our fluid positioning, thus, negotiating our identities. Below we present three themes emerging from our reflection: grappling with multiple forces; seeking and shifting selves; and shaping the vision.

"I Felt Captive" – Grappling with Multiple Forces

In Spring 2017, we each reflected in our memos upon how we self-positioned in certain teaching moments and considered our teaching intentions. We tend to position ourselves as teacher educators. Yet, this self-positioning was intertwined with our international identities and our previous perceptions about teaching. For example, Vy considered the ways she envisioned her teaching as an Vietnamese teacher educator when thinking about ways she wanted to engage with students. She wrote:

> I think that being a teacher educator means bringing my Vietnamese nuance to my teaching. I like the Confucian ideal that a teacher needs to be a part of class community who can create comfort, honesty, mindfulness, and mutual understanding with students, no matter if we [teacher and students] come from different cultural backgrounds.

Similarly, Yue shared about her intentions in teaching:

> As a high school English teacher in China, and a Buddhist, I like to be present in my class as a teacher educator who possesses multilinguistic experiences and who likes to encourage students' inner peace as a core of human being.

At the same time, however, we each seemed to be caught between the dual selves – a teacher educator and an international. As teacher educators, assigned by the institution to teach, we felt we had power in our teaching. However, because we each came from non-U.S. cultures, we felt we had little cultural power in the classroom. Huang (2010) named this situation a "paradox" (p. 99), referring to the specific power relations between Asian teacher educators' and U.S. students in an MEC. We reflected on the internal conflict as we realized that this paradox had significant impact on the way we saw who we were in the teaching.

Yue: Like other Chinese teachers in the U.S., I was, at least one time, asked: "what do you know about cultures HERE (in the U.S.)?" I am aware that I am from an Asian country and American living and teaching cultures are complicated. When teaching in China, I can't teach in a way to attend to the needs of all students, such as assigning group work, circulating around and facilitating. But, when I am teaching in here [US], I need to circulate and facilitate small group discussion. I know I was asked by the department to teach this course but it seems hard to position myself as an authoritative figure in the class due to my Chinese identity and my unfamiliarity with U.S. teaching cultures.

Vy: A student gave comments in the mid-term feedback that s/he saw my hesitant attitudes "at-odds," referring to my international background, and s/he felt uncomfortable about it. That made me feel captive. Although I have institutional authority (as a teacher), I carry international identities; thus, I am in a minority position in my teaching. As a minority, I possess a thin line of cultural knowledge about Americans while my students, who are mostly Caucasian Americans, have had long history immersed in American cultures. How can I be productive in a teacher educator position when I feel hard to make this limited knowing through my teaching so that my student learning can be authentic?

By portraying ourselves as a "captive" and not as an "authoritative figure," we were uncertain if others would see us as competent teachers. We wanted to embrace our international identities and infuse them with the teaching through our assumed positions as teacher educators. However, we each encountered the challenge of being positioned by others as "at-odds" or cultural outsiders. Our past experiences in international contexts as teachers somehow disrupted our current teaching intentions. In other words, there were dilemmas between the expectations set in our positions and the expectations derived from others (Akkerman & Meijer, 2011). Our teaching seemed to be driven by the intention that might not have met what others thought about what our teaching should be.

Reflecting on the dilemmas, we also wondered if somehow our presence in MECs might not be respected by our students, and whether that would lead to pedagogical gaps. Wang (2005) stated U.S. students often doubt the pedagogical abilities of international teacher educators in the first minutes of entering an MEC classroom. We asked: if we wanted to construct a classroom of intercultural interactions and mutual understanding based on our position as international teacher educators, would our students engage in our ideals, or would they remain in their own spaces, leaving the notion of interculturality and mutuality behind?

"Seeking and Shifting" – Authoring Selves as Co-Leaders and Intercultural Learners

By wrestling with this question, we agreed that we needed to find ways to reconcile the dilemma because, as Wang (2005) stated, "how the teacher deals with the issues of authority and agency has an important impact on how multicultural education is received by students" (p. 53). In looking for ways to reconcile this, we were reminded by Lave and Wenger (1991) of the notion that we are both learners and teachers in our MEC teaching process. We linked this to a Chinese metaphor, "stand higher, see farther." This motivated us to reach out to our course leaders – Dr. K and Dr. D – to seek help dealing with these challenges.

In the Fall 2017, through conversation with our course leaders, we both learned to shift our reflection from focusing on our internal dilemmas to thinking about ways to turn the challenges into pedagogical resources. From this point, we were able to reposition ourselves in the classroom as ones who can use our international identities as an asset in our teaching, while not losing our institutional roles as teacher educators. For example, beyond the discussion with Dr. K, Yue was able to engage multiple social acts, leading to her reposition as a "co-leader" and experience a pedagogical shift in her teaching. She reflected in her memos:

> Dr. K's discussion about the local-global connection framework encouraged me to think about how my living and teaching in the U.S. has changed my perception about multiculturalism in China and vice versa ... That also suggested that I can do something to help my minority aspects be in the teaching. I began to wonder ... how I would use my immigrant experiences to inform my students about language diversity issues in the U.S. In this Fall, I selected my immigrant stories and deliberately integrated them into teaching materials, then intentionally invited students to co-lead when those stories were discussed. One student approached me after class and shared that he felt he need to think out of his living experiences in his local places to find out what it means to be a native English speaker outside the U.S. contexts. This was a completely different experience from what I had from my teaching in the last Spring."

Similarly, after talking with Dr. D, Vy was able to engage in dynamic acts of repositioning. That is, she saw herself as an "intercultural learner" (Kim, 2007) who used her autobiography as curriculum materials to make connections with students. She reflected that, through her positioning switch, she felt released from the feeling of being a "captive." In her memos, Vy wrote:

> One time, I organized an intimate circle in which I shared with my students a poem I wrote about how my biographies related to my hope, love, and trust to people in both the U.S. and my home country where my life inhabited. I noticed that, at first, students only concerned personal accounts embedded in my poem. But, later, by mindfully working with students to go beyond the personal accounts and helping them to deepen thought about historical, social, and political constructs of those countries/places, I felt more autonomous in my ways to challenge my students' preconceived perceptions about the diversity and social justice issues rooted in their local places.

Emerging from our reflection is our identity development as "becoming" co-leaders and intercultural learners teaching MECs, rather than merely "being" teacher educators. We embraced the learning-to-teach process that reflected our willingness to make adaptations in our teaching. Such willingness came out of the conversations we had with our course leaders, who served as mentors. Those conversations pushed us to strive towards making "reflective turns" – the re-adjustment of our beliefs and positions as we made sense of new teaching contexts and social relationships (Russell & Munby, 1991, p. 164). Erikson (1980) named this kind of conversation a "psychosocial moratorium" (p. 156), referring to a time and a place given to the novices to experiment with different positions, social roles, and acts before making permanent commitment to new ideas, relationships, and a new scope of work. Indeed, the conversations with the course leaders encouraged each of us to engage in the discursive practice of positioning, which helped us reconcile the dilemmas through confronting cultural gaps that existed in our teaching. Our progressive leaning and repositioning made our identity development visible. But, this might not have happened without us each engaging in a psychosocial moratorium stemming from our conversations with our faculty mentors.

In so becoming, we began to blend our U.S. teaching experiences with our teaching experiences rooted at home into a resource for our learning, and thus, our teaching. By inviting students to an intimate circle of co-teaching, we each envisioned our classes as joyful and autonomous oriented. At the same time, we intended to handle tensions in class discussion in a mindful and personal manner. These pedagogical strategies combined the traits of student autonomy and freedom of expression – which we had learned to value in the U.S. – and the attentiveness and caring that we had each acquired from our home country cultures.

Indeed, the practice of repositioning helped us establish mutuality in the classroom in which we attend to our students' diverse cultural backgrounds, while opening a space for students to better understand our own cultures. In other words, we harmonized our presupposed institutional authority (as teacher educators) and internationals (as a Chinese and a Vietnamese) by creating reciprocal learning environment in MEC classrooms with students as co-learners, in which our identities as internationals became tools for our teaching and our students' sense of others were respected and included.

"Shaping the Vision" – Toward Adaptive Agents of Changes

Our reflection on the switch and turn of our positioning as teacher educators not only impacted the ways we made a shift in leading activities in the classroom space, but also helped us readjust our positions as learners. In coming together during the Spring of 2018, we reflected on what learning to teach MECs meant to us as INTES – a question we were reluctant to ask ourselves when we started teaching the course. Collectively, we wrote in our reflective essay:

> It [teaching MECs] is to acknowledge that the paradoxical notions toward the terms, such as norms and differences, self and other, and mainstream and minority have existed due to multiple social, cultural, and political forces. Teaching MECs in this context is to shape "cultures" in a fluid term and take it as a means to unsettle such paradox, rather than secure it. As INTES, we want to create a pedagogical space in which both teachers and students are open to embody one another cultural diversity. At the same time, we see learning to teach MECs in the U.S. does not mean that we need to give up the values of our own culture, in order to accept the new ones. When we live our stories as internationals alongside other people's stories in a new culture, our learning experience becomes a constant one. We learn through our openness to both criticism and opportunities over our own cultures without overruling students' perception about other cultures.

Our reflection indicates that while we constantly move back and forth between our past and present experiences, we switched between various positions – as teacher educators in the U.S., as learners, as cultural outsiders – and made, sense of the meaning of teaching and learning to teach MECs through these various positions. It is noteworthy that such fluid (re)positioning is intrinsically linked to the shift in our way of thinking about teaching and learning. Harré and Langenhove (1999) note that an individual continuously readjusts their position of self to adapt to a macro context associated with the evolution of new identities. In our journey over time and across cultural places, it is possible that we embraced our repositioning as adaptive agents whose work is likely to be engaged in transforming pedagogic practices (Tran & Nguyen, 2015). This potential adaptive agent position is a nice addition to our "becoming" as intercultural learners and co-leaders in our MEC classrooms.

Conclusion and Implications for Research, Teaching, and Self-Studies

Our self-study concurs with previous narratives about the ongoing learning process of becoming a teacher educator (see, for example, Williams & Berry, 2016), as well as the indispensable connections between teacher educators' identity formation across time, space, and various positioning. Like other novice teacher educators, our identities are seen through the ways we see ourselves in the midst of various challenges happening as doctoral student instructors teaching MECs and our learning to adjust our pedagogy through our positioning switch, noticing, analyzing, and dealing with challenges. In other words, our identities are formed in the triad between our elastic and evolving learning process over which our teaching progresses, making meaning of our relationships with students, and the classroom spaces where our teaching takes place. This connection is an important element for novices like us to become better teacher educators because "in the process of becoming [teacher educators] we have multiplicities and assemblages of ideas that fold into the rhizomatic development of connections in the past, present, and future of our evolving experiences" (Hamilton & Pinnegar, 2015, p. 4).

However, as INTEs, we also experience additional challenges and opportunities as we learn about who we are as teacher educators. By reflecting on challenges and opportunities, we add to existing literature about novice teacher educators' identities the nuance of doing this work as INTEs with East Asian cultural backgrounds. We highlight our many selves woven into the teaching, the hybrid nature of identity development and, ultimately, the reconstitution of those who are shifting in-between cultures (He & Phillion, 2001). Our identities have both continuous (and possibly fragmented) aspects, depending on time, place, the perspectives we take, and the particular focus of teaching MECs we are interested in.

Current research has done little to look at the particularities of in-betweenness and the temporal-spatial aspects of teacher identity development as a constitutive element of teacher educators' identities – especially with INTES (Huang, 2010). Our study indicates that, along with our individual endeavours (e.g., positioning switch and interactive learning with and from others) and institutional support (e.g., psychosocial moratorium), we were able to turn the challenge of cultural in-betweenness into teaching opportunities as we intentionally brought our experiences across cultures, time, and places into discussion with students. Theoretically, our study connects conversation across teaching MECs and research on agency and cultural and temporal-spatial dimensions with teacher educators' identity development. Practically, as international doctoral students teaching towards multiculturalism and social justice, we ask, what can we a learn from the complex teaching practices that international doctoral students are a part of? How do these practices help professional development in academic settings to support international doctoral students to be successful in academia and teaching, while engaging in social justice work in the U.S. and other parts of the globes?

Finally, this study is important for INTES like us as we develop as doctoral students, teacher educators, and researchers. Our use of self-study supports our teaching because our methodological approaches promote our teaching, and vice versa (Kitchen, 2005). Engaging in self-reflective inquiries and our explicit and intentional uses of our teaching experiences helped us analyze and better understand our identities. This, in turn, led us to more reflections on our teaching, creating an iterative cycle. Continuing throughout our research, this cycle generated important resources for our teaching both individually and collaboratively. In short, self-study sustained us while teaching, while our teaching sustained our self-study – we were both researchers and teachers throughout the process (LaBoskey, 2004). In this way, the complex issues of cultural and linguistic diversity, social justice, and equity in our teaching and learning contexts were better understood, and the students learning experiences about multicultural education was enhanced.

References

Akkerman, S. F., & Bakker, A. (2011). Boundary crossing and boundary objects. *Review of Educational Research, 81*(2), 132–169.

Akkerman, S. F., & Meijer, P. C. (2011). A dialogical approach to conceptualizing teacher identity. *Teaching and Teacher Education, 27*(2), 308–319.

Brown, E. (2004). The significance of race and social class for self-study and the professional knowledge base of teacher education. In J. J. Loughran, M. L. Hamilton, V. K. LaBoskey, & T. L. Russell (Eds.), *International handbook of self-study of teaching and teacher education practices* (Vol. 2, pp. 517–574). Dordrecht: Kluwer.

Dao, V., Farver, S., & Jackson, D. (2018). Getting down to identities to trace a new career path: Understanding novice teacher educator identities in multicultural education teaching. In J. Sharkey & M. M. Peercy (Eds.), *Self-study of language and literacy teacher education practices across culturally and linguistically diverse contexts* (pp. 55–72). Bingley: Emerald Publishing Group.

Erikson, E. H. (1980). *Identity and the life cycle*. New York, NY: Norton.

Foot, R., Crowe, A. R., Tollafield, K. A., & Allan, C. E. (2014). Exploring doctoral student identity development using a self-study approach. *Teaching and Learning Inquiry, 2*(1), 103–118.

Gorski, P. C. (2012). Instructional, institutional, and sociopolitical challenges of teaching multicultural teacher education courses. *The Teacher Educator, 47*(3), 216–235.

Hamilton, M. L., & Pinnegar, S. (Eds.). (2015). *Knowing, becoming, doing as teacher educators: Identity, intimate scholarship, inquiry* (Vol. 26). Bingley: Emerald Publishing Group.

Harré, R., & Lagenhove, L. (1999). *Positioning theory: Moral contexts of intentional action*. Malden: Blackwell.

He, M., & Phillion, J. (2001). Trapped in-between: A narrative exploration of race, gender, and class. *Race, Gender & Class, 8*(1), 47–56.

Huang, Y. P. (2010). International teachers' cross-cultural teaching stories: A tragic comedy. *Curriculum and Teaching Dialogue, 12*, 1–2.

Jun, E. J. (2016). Multicultural education course put into practice. *Multicultural Education Review, 8*(2), 83.

Kim, Y. Y. (2007). Ideology, identity, and intercultural communication: An analysis of differing academic conceptions of cultural identity. *Journal of Intercultural Communication Research, 36*(3), 237–253.

Kitchen, J. (2005). Looking backwards, moving forward: Understanding my narrative as a teacher educator. *Studying Teacher Education, 1*(1), 17–30.

LaBoskey, V. K. (2004). The methodology of self-study and its theoretical underpinnings. In M. L. Hamilton, J. J. Loughran, V. K. LaBoskey, & T. L. Russell (Eds.), *International handbook of self-study of teaching and teacher education practices* (Vol. 2, pp. 817–869). Dordrecht: Kluwer.

Lave, J., & Wenger, E. (1991). *Situated learning: Legitimate peripheral participation*. Cambridge: Cambridge University Press.

Miles, M. B., & Huberman, M. A. (1994). *Qualitative data analysis: An expanded sourcebook*. Thousand Oaks, CA: Sage Publications.

Newberry, M. (2014). Teacher educator identity development of the nontraditional teacher educator. *Studying Teacher Education, 10*(2), 163–178.

Palmer, P. J. (2007). *The courage to teach: Exploring the inner landscape of a teacher's life*. San Francisco, CA: Jossey-Bass.

Phelan, A. M. (2000). A knot to unfurl [Review of the book shaping a professional identity: Stories of education practice]. *Alberta Journal of Educational Research, 46*, 288–290.

Russell, T., & Munby, H. (1991). Reframing: The role of experience in developing teachers' professional knowledge. In D. A. Schön (Ed.), *The reflective turn: Case studies in and on educational practice* (pp. 164–187). New York, NY: Teachers College Press.

Tran, L. T., & Nguyen, N. T. (2015). Re-imagining teachers' identity and professionalism under the condition of international education. *Teachers and Teaching, 21*(8), 958–973.

Trent, J. (2013). Becoming a teacher educator: The multiple boundary-crossing experiences of beginning teacher educators. *Journal of Teacher Education, 64*(3), 262–275.

Ukpokodu, O. N. (2007). Preparing socially conscious teachers: A social justice-oriented teacher education. *Multicultural Education, 15*(1), 8–28.

Wang, H. (2005). Aporias, responsibility, and the im/possibility of teaching multicultural education. *Educational Theory, 55*, 45–60.

Williams., J., & Berry., A. (2016). Boundary crossing and the professional learning of teacher educators in new international contexts. *Studying Teacher Education, 12*(2), 324–334.

Williams, J., & Ritter, J. (2013). Constructing new professional identities through self-study: From teacher to teacher educator. *Professional Development in Education, 36*(1), 77–92.

Zeichner, K. (2005). Becoming a teacher educator: A personal perspective. *Teaching and Teacher Education, 21*(2), 117–124.

CHAPTER 14

Finding Layers in Our Stories: Using Collective Memory Work as Transformative Praxis

Sara K. Sterner, Amanda C. Shopa, Lee C. Fisher
and Abby Boehm-Turner

Stories are at once personal and social, about the individual and the collective. Coming out of feminist epistemologies, collective memory work (Haug, 1987) values stories as a space of self-study in order to explore the making and remaking of identities. Haug (1987) acknowledges this when she writes, "[f]rom a state of modest insignificance we enter a space in which we can take ourselves seriously" (p. 36). Use of collective memory work in teacher education and development (e.g. Beals et al., 2013; Goodson & Choi, 2008; Ovens & Tinning, 2009) accomplishes this aim by doing research *with* teachers, focusing on their stories of lived experiences, shifting their position from object to subject (Freire, 1972), and opening up a new avenue for collective self-study.

Collective memory work draws on the knowledge and experiences of its members, and the line between the personal and the professional is erased. We, the four authors, began our journey with collective memory work over a year ago as we bonded over conversations about our shifting identities as former K-12 teachers, now doctoral students and teacher educators, and we believe this experience with collective memory work has helped us grow in our professional pursuits. Collective memory work as a method of reflexive inquiry serves self-study and transformative praxis as teachers examine their own storied experiences of teaching and teacherness.

In this chapter, we begin by situating collective memory work in its traditions and history, and position it as a form of self-study. Then we describe how we came together as a collective. Next, we give an overview of Haug's (1999) collective memory work process and describe how we expanded it to better suit our collective's focus on identities within education. Finally, we conclude with suggestions of how collective memory work could be used by practicing teachers and students of education. In this way, we take the reader through our journey of writing and analysing memories in order to explore how this process invokes philosophies of teaching and learning while allowing us to constantly (re)negotiate our identities as teachers and teacher educators in the academy. We believe that this same process would benefit many stakeholders in education, particularly teachers, who seek out opportunities for self-study and transformational praxis.

Centering Theory: Collective Memory Work and Self-Study

Grounded in feminist epistemologies, collective memory work acknowledges that the collective is just as important as an individual within it. The methodology centers individual memories and collective analysis as theoretical truths in and of themselves. In 1982, Haug published the developing methodology, which evolved from the women's editorial board of *Das Argument*, a long-standing and highly valued journal of Marxist theory. Within this group, the collective members strove to bring together two aspects of their lives that had previously existed as separate entities: their work in *Das Argument;* and their commitment to the women's movement in the 1970s and early 1980s. The group eventually asserted the importance of collective work in which all the members of a collective participate in discussions of general themes while still exploring particular areas of focus. This response to the original division of labour that characterized the first volume of *Frauenformen* (Women's Forms) exemplifies the theoretical interests in disrupting mind/body and head/hand dualisms. Haug (1987) affirms that the inability for dualisms, along with the conceptual separation they create to explain the world, provided great potential to seek out new relationships and interventions.

Common association around *Das Argument* provided Haug's all-female editorial board a theoretical foundation in Marxism, critical psychology, and theories of culture and ideology. By focusing on gender in particular, they ultimately chose to reconstruct their theoretical foundations, and the seeds of collective memory work as a formal research methodology were born. Their debate with Foucault's conception of sexuality took special prominence. Representative of their contestation, they wrote, "[Foucault's] theoretical premises foreclose human self-determinism as a potential form of socialization. Yet the concepts of self-determination and heteronomy are central to our present investigations" (Haug, 1987, p. 206). This opened up a space in research that intertwined theory and experience which, at the same time, disrupted the Cartesian dualities that have long been central to academic research.

In ways that felt analogous to Haug's, we each entered a new professional space within the academy excited to explore issues related to our work and experiences with students within the K-12 setting. And yet our conversations in graduate classes led us to believe that our teacher-selves had little value compared to published researchers and those who could effectively utilize research to articulate a theoretical construct. We struggled at the crossroads of identities that we wanted to take up simultaneously. We wished to see ourselves as teacher/scholars, with a synthetic combination of our multiple identities, yet, while living through the socialization process of the academy, it felt as if only one identity was possible. In this midst we turned to collective memory work as a form of self-study, not to discover how we could become both teachers and researchers, but to understand ourselves as already being that which we desired.

It is in this state of taking ourselves seriously that we acknowledge self-study, embodied ways of knowing, and collectivity as a combination of critical literacy (Coffey, 2010; Luke, 2012) and creative methodologies that investigate the ways in which identity (Holland, Lachicotte, Skinner, & Cain, 1998), social discourses (Bakhtin, 1984), and an agentic consideration of voice as project (Lensmire, 2000) intersect in the memories we tell. As Lewis, Enciso, and Moje (2007) note, "Autobiographies, we argue, are not just personal. They are situated socioculturally, historically, and institutionally in ways that shape what, how, and for whom knowledge gets produced in research relationships" (p. 10). Collective memory work, with an explicit eye towards the socio-historically constituted discourses that instruct and construct, pushes us to not only take seriously ourselves, but also our study of the ways we narrate our past and, through the identity work it does, our futures.

There are multiple forms of self-study that can be used by teachers, including lesson plan study (Fernandez, 2002), video study (van Es, Tunney, Goldsmith, & Seago, 2014), case methods (Sato & Rogers, 2010), studying patterns in student work to improve teaching (McDonald, 2001), and action research (Forbes, Ross, & Chesser, 2011). We believe that collective memory work as a form of self-study is one way that teachers can examine teaching practice, teacher identity, and how other identities (such as race, class, gender, and sexuality) impact work in schools. It's also a way that teachers can work collectively to gain insight into their practices. We recognize the work of Milner (2007) who argues that teacher educators must do the same self-study and identity work that they ask of their education students.

Theory in Practice: Building Praxis through the LASA[1] Collective

A Gathering of Educators: Our Exploration of Identity and Methodology Begins

As doctoral students in the same program but in different stages of our studies, our paths had informally crossed through shared coursework, similar research interests, and graduate assistantships in common. Eventually we came together to formally create the LASA collective because we were interested in teacher education, and we also deeply missed the K-12 classrooms that had shaped our lives for so long. We were forming new identities in a new context and, as doctoral students, we felt slightly adrift in the world of academia. This recognition of multiple identities resonated from within the mixed messages we encountered from the community around us. Still connected to colleagues and friends working as K-12 teachers, the number of years we spent in our own classrooms were both valuable social capital in particular professional circles as well as foundational to our reasons for engaging in our current professional pursuits. New discourses introduced to us by our new community in the academy that seemed to devalue our experiences as educators outside of academia challenged these components of our identity. We felt knowledgeable while recognizing our inexperience within the figured world (Holland et al., 1998) of academia we desired to join. We were trying to navigate our roles as graduate students who still held their teacher identities with high regard. Collective memory work and the creation of our collective provided a framework in which we could embody all of these roles. Instead of seeing ourselves as only teachers or scholars, we could see ourselves as both. Additionally, we began to understand the process of developing new professional identities and practices as an important component of our professional lives.

Collective memory work comes out of an explicit recognition of and engagement with identities that might otherwise be left at the margins. As such, we find it important to name aspects of our identities that inform our orientation to the methodology's history and our use of it. Our collective includes three people who identify as cisgender female and one who identifies as cisgender male, with one identifying as bisexual and three identifying as heterosexual. Our experience as classroom teachers ranges from seven to seventeen years, and two of us come from elementary education while two come from secondary education. Two of us are enrolled in a program that focuses on critical literacy, one is a children's literature scholar, and one studies culture and teaching. At the time of this writing, we have been out of the K-12 classroom between two and four years. As scholars and teacher educators, we ground our work in social justice and equity and have worked to develop our own transformative praxis around race, class, gender, and power. We seek to develop K-12 teachers whose educational practices are steeped in the same consciousness raising we continue to work on ourselves.

Finding the Voice of LASA Collective

As scholars and teacher educators who center stories as essential to the epistemological underpinnings of our research, engage with feminist and post-structuralist philosophies, and value the embodied ways of knowing that are often overlooked in research, we sought out collective memory work (Haug, 1987; Davies & Gannon, 2006) as a foundational underpinning for our scholarly efforts. At our first meeting, the group, at that time numbering five, brainstormed a list of what we might want to write about using Haug's (1999) prompt "What are you afraid of?" We framed this question around the tension of being K-12 teachers in academia where we felt practical knowledge from classroom experience was not respected in the same way as theoretical knowledge. Sitting in one of our living rooms, we talked about the intersections between our professional and personal trajectories, trying to figure out if self-study was a good use of our time or a mistake, while grappling with the difficulty of navigating our changing identities. Key ideas and questions were listed on poster paper, first one sheet, then two, and eventually several covering the wall. Some themes were: that we would be seen as frauds in the academy or by K-12 teachers; that we wouldn't ever understand theory (really getting it, not faking it); that going back to graduate school and leaving the classroom might be a selfish choice; that loss of income and independence would be too big of a sacrifice (especially for our families); and that we were no longer *real* teachers. Though our conversation was based in sharing fears, we did not feel defeated. On the contrary, this moment in time felt rejuvenating and deeply connected to moments that had gone unvoiced along our professional journey. The conversation facilitated a process through which we were able to shed light on feelings and experiences where we had felt darkness. We laughed. We yelled. We quietly questioned and *mmm*ed as previously unrealized or unnamed realities took shape in our discussion. The seeds of our collective were built in that moment of previously unknown, but hinted at, solidarity. Our group talked through the lists of ideas created over that half hour, discussed the possibility of committing to the collective memory work process, and eventually crafted a prompt for our first set of memories.

It Begins with Individual Stories: Prompt Development

It became clear at our first meeting that we had a synergy of thought and a deep wealth of experiences that would benefit from the collective memory work methodology. Four of us decided to move forward as a group and see where the process would take us, using a prompt that we developed at our first brainstorming session: *Write about a time when you felt like you were not enough.* We agreed that we could write about any experience related to our teaching or academic careers. This required us to trust a practice with which we had little experience as well as ourselves, and that any aspect of our experiences (be they mundane or extraordinary) could hold meaning for us as individuals and as a collective. We individually wrote our memories using this prompt and collectively worked directly through the process that Haug (1999) set forth, analysing each memory over the course of multiple two hour sessions (see Figure 14.1).

The memory work that Haug had started with her colleagues at *Das Argument* centered the collective members but was always meant to live in a broader, public sphere. When we started our collective, the primary goal was the development and maintenance of our collective community. This space of professional and personal support centered around the core understanding that knowledge exists within our lived experiences and can be developed by us. Thus, while we wrote and analysed memories around the concept of 'not enough,' we did not build a platform to formally share those memories outside of our collective. However, as we moved to the next prompt, we explicitly considered ways in which we might share our writing with other audiences. We wanted our work to contribute to a larger professional community. In this way, we wished to recognize the role that agency serves as a set of strategic moves to make and remake the self "within relations of power" (Lewis et. al, p. 18). Collective memory work thus exists as distinct from, yet participating in, a broader community. This participation engages as an agentic critique of hierarchical structures of power that control and produce particular forms of knowledge. By continuing to contribute to these communities in a way that resists traditional ways of knowing, we affirm our commitment to our colleagues without restricting ourselves to the epistemologies and ontologies that collective memory work seeks to push against.

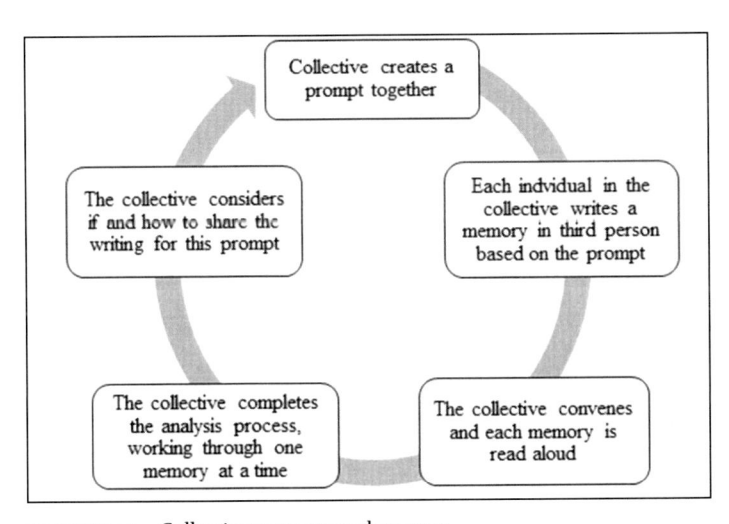

FIGURE 14.1   Collective memory work process

In this spirit, the next prompt we developed considered our teacher/teacher educator/doctoral student identities in educational spaces that either explicitly or implicitly take up the guise of a perceived neutrality. We recognized the way systemic emphasis on neutrality flowed in and out of our professional lives as teachers and wanted to explore moments when we attempted a stance of 'not neutral' in our work. As we started working through this concept, we defined neutrality as the disembodied moment when the teacherbot (Fisher & Sterner, 2017) takes over with a socially policed stance of perceived neutrality. This pre-programmed teacher enacts a pedagogy and curriculum recognized by schools and stakeholders invested in maintaining systems of power within schools. As such, the teacherbot gets labelled as good, professional, compliant, and unemotional. We acknowledge and affirm that educational spaces are never neutral and that the systems of education are infused with white supremacy, patriarchy, and racism that often reproduce hegemonic power structures. This does not mean that the label of perceived neutrality is not invoked within teacher education programs, staff meetings, and political discourse. In fact, we recognized moments in our own lives when the dominant discourses of education – to be apolitical, unemotional, and unembodied – were in very deep tension with the day to day realities of our classroom experiences.

Collective Analysis Process: Bringing Collective Memory Work to Life

As scholars who were relatively new to collective memory work, while working with our first shared memories, we found it crucial to follow strictly the original process that Haug set forth in her 1999 guide to the methodology. This process, as overviewed in Figure 14.1, flows from collective prompt development, to individual memory writing and sharing, and into a collective analysis process. In Figure 14.2 we build onto the visual representation of the memory work cycle in Figure 14.1 to include the analysis process in more detail. Each of these analytic steps is outlined and thoroughly explained in Haug's guide. In fact, we always have a physical copy of the guide at our meetings and, as we worked through our first memories of a time when we had felt 'not enough' during our teaching and/or academic careers, we routinely returned to the source for inspiration and clarification; gradually we began to grow more comfortable with the analysis process. It is in this analysis that the stories we share in third person, the remembered moments of 'not enough' or 'not neutral,' transform and become valued knowledges. Through our meetings, we not only were learning how to take up memory work as a form of self-study and transformative praxis, we were also beginning to settle in to our collective identity as the LASA collective.

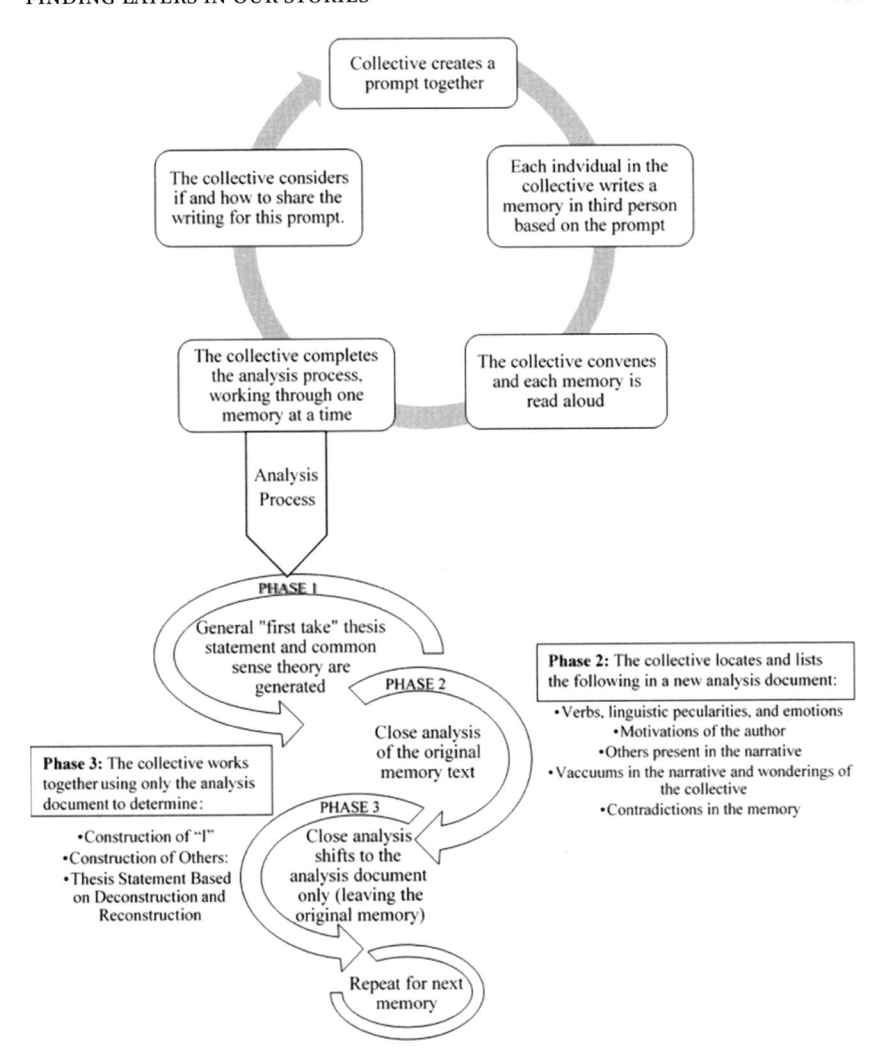

FIGURE 14.2   Collective memory work with analysis process

As our writing group became more connected and began to transform into a cohesive and interdependent collective, we found the need to fine-tune our memory work process, taking Haug's (1999) invitation "for individuals attempting to do memory work to change the method for themselves, remaining within – or critically expanding – the theoretical framework for the process" (p. 2). Our collective's memory work process has evolved to include expanded prompt development, utilization of digital tools for memory sharing and analysis, additional categories for analysis, and a recognition that our connectedness should be embraced in the analysis process and not bracketed.

As we started to prepare for writing and analysing our second memory and settled on the general topic of 'not neutral,' the use of trigger words (Crawford et al., 1990, 1992; Ovens & Tinning, 2009) felt like a logical shift in our prompt development process. This process is "typically done by using a particular phrase or word to help trigger each memory" (Ovens & Tinning, 2009, p. 1126), opening up opportunities for us as writers. Our word list for this prompt came from a larger conversation of what it meant to be a teacher within a particularly tumultuous political climate in the United States. Each of us wrote a memory on the concept of 'not neutral' as the umbrella topic and then considered trigger words from a larger list as a deeper focus of our work. Some of these triggers included *success, balance, performance, exclusion, resistance, advocacy,* and *legitimacy.*

For us, the use of trigger words to enhance the prompt expands the interstitial space in our work and allows multiple entry points for our identities, self-study, and praxis to emerge in the memories we write, share, and analyse. There were times for the members of our collective that one single question or a specific emotionally centered prompt didn't create a clear opening into a memory. Instead, it stifled our writing. Having a generalized topic and then a list of trigger words pushed us explore a prompt from multiple perspectives. Through our analysis of this set of memories, we have found that this change in prompt development has opened up a wider range of memories that are strongly connected, but vastly different from the method Haug outlines.

The second expansion we take up with collective memory work is reflected in two changes we made to the sharing of memories and the analytic process. Relying on technology, we put copies of our memories in a digital folder and followed along with a single text when the memory was read aloud to the group, instead of relying on Haug's suggested chart paper or chalkboard. We continued to follow Haug's model and used her memory work analysis matrix to begin looking more deeply at the original memory text. With the text digitally available to each member of the collective, we were able to easily transition between the written memory and the analysis matrix to collectively capture our thinking and take up the memories. We appreciate the cohesive process that has organically evolved through this shift from paper to virtual documents.

In addition to shifting to a shared digital platform, we have enhanced Haug's original analysis matrix by adjusting what counts as "emotion," as well as including three additional categories for analysis (these changes are bolded in Figure 14.3). Each member of our collective seeks for our work to be productively disruptive of the hegemonic forces in education and sees themselves as social justice oriented teacher educators, thus we thought it was important to

Initial Thesis Statement of the Author's Meaning:								
Common Sense Theory:								
Author's List of verbs as Activity	Author's Linguistic Peculiarities	Other's List of verbs as Activity	Other's Linguistic Peculiarities	Emotion (feelings through language, named emotions)	Motivation (interests, desires)	Others Present in the Narrative	Vacuums or wonderings	Contradictions
Race, Gender, Class, and Power:								
Writerly Moves:								
Construction of "I"/Author:								
Construction of Others:								
Thesis Statement Based on Deconstruction and Reconstruction:								
Analytic Bird Walks:								

FIGURE 14.3 Analysis Matrix (LASA collective changes noted in bold)

specifically name the manner in which we see (or don't see) race, class, gender, and power at work in the memories we share. We also found that, for our praxis as writers and researchers, it was important to consider the writerly moves that were made by each author. This diverges from Haug's work in two ways. In Haug's original process, only directly named emotions were included in the analysis matrix. By opening up this category to include vividly suggested emotion, we acknowledged and included the writerly moves (i.e. turns of phrase, embodied descriptions, etc.) that authors make to suggest powerful feelings. We also recognized that there was a difference between not explicitly naming emotions as a way to hide from or ignore them, and doing so because they could be shown instead of told. Secondly, we began to notice that each of us had a writing style that utilized different writerly moves to convey information. For example, in one memory, the author called an assistant principal by their last name in all of the dialogue, but used their first name in all of the narration. We noted that the author used these naming conventions in order to privately assert power in a situation which had made them feel powerless. By pinpointing these writerly moves, we have another entry point for analysis that recognizes the power that story craft has in the construction of memories. As academics who value the collective nature of storytelling, and the interwoven discussions that are central to memory analysis, we think it is important to capture that process. We have found that the conversations, disagreements, and analytic pathways that come from this work have been powerful moments of insight and have highlighted the transformative aspects of this methodology. Because this component of the work is rarely linear, and often takes unexpected pathways, we have entitled the section of the analysis chart *Analytic Bird Walks*.

The final change we have made in the analysis process is a recognition that our relationships extend outside of the collective. We often have insider knowledge about each other and each other's memories. Haug encourages distance, suggesting the collective honour the fidelity of the written text. While we respect that the text is a representation of self and usually follow her suggestion, we have occasionally chosen the opposite and opted to recognize the presence of our background knowledge of each other. After working closely together for over a year, we have heard many of the others' stories, and have even walked alongside each other as certain stories have unfolded. This does not mean that we use our knowledge of each other to amend the text, shifting the written construction of identity and experience. However, we acknowledge that attempting to ignore shared knowledges feels unnatural and negates the commitment to incorporating lived experiences, including those with each other, with our analytic process.

It has been essential for our own self-study to make these changes and build a collective memory work framework that reflects the nature of our collective. As we work across four separate memories written for the same prompt, this personalization has more effectively revealed commonalities in our experiences, moments where our identities as teachers and teacher educators are in development or tension, and has allowed us to explore what it means to work and learn as a collective. This not only expands the collective memory work repertoire, it also allows us to focus on our own identity development and recentre self-study as a means to build praxis.

Collective Memory Work as Transformative Praxis

Because of our collective memory work, we feel more at ease as our teacher selves, student selves, and scholar selves. While we were friendly acquaintances before coming together as a collective, it is the act of being in a collective that has made our relationships stronger. Although we have occasionally met on-site at the university, we have met most frequently in our homes, where we bridge our multiple identities by talking about our teacher lives and academic lives in our personal spaces.

In educational institutions, it can feel as if we are frequently surveilled by power structures that regulate behaviour and foster isolation. Memory collectives are spaces in which honesty and openness regarding successes and struggles can exist. Teaching is often positioned as a selfless vocation where self-care is set aside in the name of professionalism and practice. Memory collectives are spaces where members support and celebrate one another as they navigate personal and professional experiences; our collective has provided us with multiple perspectives through which to see ourselves and our practice.

We believe that collective memory groups, given the time to develop trust and build a collective cohesiveness, would be beneficial to teachers, both new and experienced.

We have talked extensively about how we wish we had such a supportive group at previous stages of our teaching careers. This is not to say that schools don't provide teachers with professional groups to talk through practice. However, implementation of such things as Professional Learning Communities (PLCs) or mentorship programs are often mandated as required practices with partnerships assigned externally and are focused on student outcomes. While we have experienced the benefits of mentorship and PLCs, we believe that the work does not provide the depth of self-study that comes from centering personal experiences as data along with deliberately and repeatedly choosing the collective over the individual. The interplay of story-telling, relationships, and thoughtful analysis that is central to collective memory work opens up spaces for deeply transformative praxis.

Note

1   The name of our collective, LASA, was created from the initials of our first names. It is also a formal rendering of our collective's nickname, Lasagna Collective, which alludes to both the multiple layers of our identities interacting in concert and a common shared meal during memory work sessions.

References

Bakhtin, M. M. (1984). *Problems of Dostoevsky's poetics* (C. Emerson, Ed. & Trans.). Minneapolis, MN: University of Minnesota Press.

Beals, F. M., Braddock, C., Dye, A., McDonald, J., Milligan, A., & Strafford, E. (2013). The embodied experiences of emerging teachers: Exploring the potential of collective biographical memory work. *Cultural Studies <-> Critical Methodologies, 13*(5), 419–426.

Coffey, H. (2010). *LEARN NC.* Retrieved from http://www.learnnc.org/lp/pages/4437?style+print

Crawford, J., Kippax, S., Onyx, J., Gault, U., & Benton, P. (1990). Women theorizing their experiences of anger: A study using memory work. *Australian Psychologist, 25*(3), 333–350.

Crawford, J., Kippax, S., Onyx, J., Gault, U., & Benton, P. (1992). *Emotion and gender: Constructing meaning from memory.* London: Sage Publications.

Davies, B., & Gannon, S. (Eds.). (2006). *Doing collective biography*. Berkshire: Open University Press.

Fernandez, C. (2002). Learning from Japanese approaches to professional development: The case of lesson study. *Journal of Teacher Education, 53*(5), 393–405.

Fisher, L. C., & Sterner, S. K. (2017). Making sense of the now. *Anthropology & Education Quarterly, 48*, 362–370.

Forbes, S. A., Ross, M. E., & Chesser, S. S. (2011). Single-subject designs and action research in the K-12 setting. *Educational Research and Evaluation, 17*(3), 161–173.

Freire, P. (1972). *Pedagogy of the oppressed*. New York, NY: Herder & Herder.

Goodson, B. I., & Choi, P. L. (2008). Life history and collective memory as methodological strategies: Studying teacher professionalism. *Teacher Education Quarterly, 35*(2), 5–28.

Haug, F. (1987). *Female sexualization: A collective work of memory*. London: Verso Books.

Haug, F. (1999). *Memory-work as a method of social science research: A detailed rendering of memory-work method*. Retrieved from http://www.friggahaug.inkrit.de/documents/memorywork-researchguidei7.pdf

Holland, D., Lachicotte, W., Skinner, D., & Cain, C. (1998). *Identity and agency in cultural worlds*. Cambridge, MA: Harvard University Press.

Lensmire, T. (2000). *Powerful writing, responsible teaching*. New York, NY: Teachers College Press.

Lewis, C., Enciso, P., & Moje, E. (Eds.). (2007). *Reframing sociocultural research on literacy: Identity, agency, and power*. New York, NY: Routledge.

Luke, A. (2012). Critical literacy: Foundational notes. *Theory into Practice, 51*(1), 4–11.

McDonald, J. P. (2001). Students' work and teachers' learning. In A. Lieberman & L. Miller (Eds.), *Teachers caught in the action: Professional development that matters* (pp. 209–235). New York, NY: Teachers College Press.

Milner, H. R. (2007). Race, narrative inquiry, and self-study in curriculum and teacher education. *Education and Urban Society, 39*(4), 584–609.

Ovens, A., & Tinning, R. (2009). Reflection as situated practice: A memory-work study of lived experience in teacher education. *Teaching and Teacher Education, 25*(8), 1125–1131.

Sato, M., & Rogers, C. (2010). Case methods in teacher education. In P. Peterson, E. Baker, & B. McGraw (Eds.), *International encyclopedia of education* (pp. 592–597). Oxford: Elsevier.

van Es, E. A., Tunney, J., Goldsmith, L. T., & Seago, N. (2014). A framework for the facilitation of teachers' analysis of video. *Journal of Teacher Education, 65*(4), 340–356.

CHAPTER 15

Eavesdropping on a Conversation: Thinking through Critical Self-Reflexivity, Whiteness, and Gender

Teresa Anne Fowler and Willow S. Allen

As two White[1] female educational researchers, we both came to awareness of Whiteness through different experiences that have culminated in us questioning ourselves and the impact our research may have on either decolonizing/colonizing or destabilizing/reinforcing a status quo (Breault, 2016; Cunliff, 2016; Norris & Sawyer, 2016). After meeting at an educational conference in spring 2017, we realized we were confronting similar issues and, through informal conversations, it became clear we were both critically examining Whiteness as part of our scholarly work and personal lives. We wondered how we, as White racialized[2] educators, could participate in research that does not perpetuate colonial relationships and research paradigms? How do we conduct research within anti-colonial and antiracist frameworks? We valued our open dialogue because we each struggled to find scholarship, as well as spaces in our lives and practice, in which to interrogate Whiteness and White masculinities and femininities.

We chose to engage in a critical examination of how Whiteness has been framed through our historical selves (Breault, 2016; May & Perry, 2017; Norris & Sawyer, 2016), and the emergence of Whiteness in our respective work. To do this, we utilize duoethnography as our methodology and take a critically reflexive stance. Duoethnography, as a dialogical exchange, allowed us to reveal that we were both focusing on self-identity and Whiteness in different educational environments: Teresa as part of her mother-educator-researcher identity exploring Whiteness and masculinities in public and postsecondary spaces; and Willow as part of her mother-educator-researcher identity investigating antiracism in home and community-based spaces. Our interaction helped us better understand our relationship with Whiteness and the potential implications of whiteness in our respective research (Breault, 2016; Nabavi & Lund, 2012).

We will first address duoethnography and then present our duoethnographic data, which is our dialogue with each other. Next, we share our current understandings of the meanings we have taken from our conversations, and conclude with the significance and need for a critically reflexive stance on Whiteness in research.

Duoethnography

Established in 2003 by Joe Norris and Richard D. Sawyer, duoethnography is a unique qualitative research method in which "two or more researchers of difference juxtapose their life histories to provide multiple understandings of the world" (Norris & Sawyer, 2012, p. 9). Through dialogical storytelling each author reveals herself and her life experiences as a site of critical inquiry, inviting the other author and readers into discussion and reflection. Through dialogue, the authors of a duoethnography create a *third space* (Bhabha, 1994; Norris & Sawyer, 2012) meant to foster a transformative learning process in which new connections can be made.

Meeting virtually in our private homes fostered an increased level of intimacy between us as we conversed in the non-institutional spaces of our lives. Our interactions included interruptions by children, partners, and pets, not unlike the moments that penetrated our research studies. Thus, our duoethnography reflects our embodied curriculum in its content, and how our process itself was integrated into our intimate personal worlds and differing research studies.

Dialogue

On Our Selves

Willow: When I reflect on my process of coming to think about colonialism and White supremacy, and my research on White women and race, I think of the notion of "embodied curriculum." In my case, what profoundly shaped me was my history growing up in a Jewish Socialist Zionist Youth Movement, my early understandings of what oppression and justice were, and learning in time that I was taught a "single story" (Adichie, 2009) of the world. I later understood social justice and anti-racism/anti oppression are not necessarily conceptualized or practiced in the same ways, and we, as educators and researchers, must face the deep contradictions that exist within our own selves (as learned through the landscapes, discourses, and relationships of our lives) and within our convictions.

Teresa: What shaped my entrance into my research with white male youth was my history of witnessing the ways in which privilege had an impact on my own schooling experience and how the white male athlete dominated the culture of our town. There was not much racial diversity in my town growing up (I remember one Black teacher), so I did not come to understand social justice until having biracial children and then working in the education system with marginalized groups of children. That, with the awareness of working in a system that ought to empower, really means selective empowerment. When I think of "embodied curriculum," it reminds me of Bourdieu's (1990) habitus and how we encompass ourselves within our work.

Do you think that your upbringing influenced your research and in what ways? In chapter eight of the text we are reading Nabavi and Lund (2012) state that "duoethnographers are not the topics but the sites of their studies" (p. 177), so then as a site of your study how did you, being White and Jewish and in a transracial/cultural family, taint your Whiteness? Is this still Whiteness? Is Whiteness inherently pure?

Willow: I do think that my Whiteness is no longer the same and never will be. It can't. Principally because I feel like White supremacy is sustained by the inability of White people to see their Whiteness and how their lives and actions are situated within broader historical relations. I do not have a "double consciousness" (Du Bois, 1903), but I see and move through the social world differently being White and Jewish and being in my family. My Whiteness has never been so-called "pure" (clearly a construction) because I am Jewish – and Jewish people seem to be White and non-White at the same time – and because I am associated with blackness through my partner and daughter. Ruth Frankenberg (1993) writes that White women who enter into multiracial partnerships become "unWhitened" when they permanently cross "colour-lines" (p. 104). Of course I am still White and, when I am by myself and no one knows my association to blackness (Luke, 1994), I continue to have White privilege and power. In this way, I will never know nor can I experience racism in a White settler society. It remains Whiteness because it is still linked to power within broader White supremacist systems.

Teresa: Are White supremacists then the pure form of Whiteness?
           We are witnessing the ideology of White supremacy revealed
           through the Trumpian times and becoming dismantled
           through the #MeToo movement. Perhaps the timing of
           Whiteness research is even more needed for these contexts,
           but do we risk identifying what White supremacy needs to
           be empowered? How does our own socialization or how we
           socialize others impact this as we watch the layers open? But
           back to us – I feel that our intersectionality as females and
           our class/religious backgrounds inform our differences within
           Whiteness and our (different) mixed-race children also
           inhabit that space.

Willow: While we are both White racialized women socialized
           into Whiteness in Canada, it appears that our differing
           backgrounds and locations have mediated our relationship to
           and embodiment of Whiteness and discourses of difference.
           We were socialized in different spaces; you grew up in small
           communities in Ontario and Alberta, while I was raised in
           large and medium urban centres in British Columbia and
           Ontario. We hold divergent familial histories, and different
           ethnic, cultural and religious identities, wherein I identify
           as a white settler of Ashkenazi Jewish and Irish descent and,
           you, a White settler with a history of Indigenous heritage
           through your grandfather. We also have dissimilar educational
           backgrounds with you in curriculum and education and me in
           East Asian studies, political sciences, and education. Moreover,
           our families shape our positionalities and perspectives; you
           now have four adult boys and I have one young daughter.

Teresa: My children are older, we have gender differences (male/
           female) and for me – researching within masculinities also
           came from living with boys and my history of men in my
           life coming and going because they struggle(d) with what it
           means/t to be a man. Geographically – I grew up in a town
           of contradictions (Stratford) when viewed through the lens of
           masculinities: you are either stereotypically manly and play
           hockey or are gay and an actor in the theatre. Our current
           geographies are different as well as are our educational
           backgrounds/institutional spaces. Another difference is how
           we arrived at Whiteness – your tainted experience and my
           purebred toxic masculinity ideology growing up in Stratford

and witnessing the experiences of privilege that comes with and raising boys that are/have been involved in athletics and art.

Willow: I would love to hear more about your experience with "purebred toxic masculinity ideology." Can you explain what "purebred" means and how you see it linking to toxic masculinitist ideology? How did you experience living with it and how does it impact your trajectory and understanding of yourself, your practice, and your whiteness?

Teresa: I think it resides in life in a contradictory town. It is a fascinating place really. On one side you have hockey players who were all White and identified as the "cultural symbols" (Messner, 2008, p. 51) that embody sports. They were rough, aggressive, privileged, and not known for being academically inclined, but they fueled our community. Friday nights the people in town spent their time watching the hockey players perform on ice and, when there was a known rival team in town, the stands were filled as we knew there would be more fights than usual. This could be considered toxic or hegemonic masculine ideology (Connell & Messerschmidt, 2005; Kehler, 2010; Martino & Kehler, 2007). On the other side, our town was also home to the Stratford Festival, which is a world-renowned theatre with Shakespearian plays performed every summer. This brought with it a strong arts and culture mix, including a vibrant LGBTQ+ community. There were gay bars and a general acceptance of genderism. While there were racist undertones and experiences, as teenagers we came to know both identities as normal. Interesting how my own family mirrors these cultural differences; I had not thought of this before.

On Whiteness

Willow: Can a different kind of Whiteness and White femininity exist?

Teresa: What do you mean by different femininity? Maybe this is like the difference between masculinity and masculinities – masculinities speaks to the various masculine identities (Connell, 2005) rather than just one. Maybe this is the idea of tainted Whiteness we can grapple with ...

Willow: Yes, I think the notion of tainted Whiteness could be something
           for us both to unpack. The question emerged from my research
           study on White women in transracial/cultural families, which
           I approached as "an insider" for I share experiential and
           embodied knowledge of the research subject. As I researched
           how the participants conceptualized dominant discourses
           of difference, I realized I had to gain deeper insight into who
           White women are as central figures in histories of White
           domination, in part because colonial histories and ideologies
           continue to inform how White women and White femininity
           are imagined today (Ware, 1992). As I moved through my
           study, I began to reflect critically on my own Whiteness and
           White femininity. How am I embodying Whiteness and White
           femininity in ways that reproduce oppressive discourses
           and relations? What alternative forms of Whiteness could I,
           and other White women, more broadly, embody? I think of
           bell hooks (1990) who writes, "one change in direction that
           would be really cool would be the production of a discourse
           on race that interrogates Whiteness" (p. 54). To even imagine
           producing such a discourse, there must be a willingness and
           a desire to be vulnerable and to reflect critically on oneself in
           relation to constructed 'Others.'

Teresa: I do love that now there is a shift in talking about Whiteness as
           a race – acknowledging that we/White people can no longer
           be the "human norm" (Frideres, 2015, p. 43) and everyone
           else is othered or "raced" (p. 43). Maybe this is part of what
           it means to decolonize race? Is this an act of decolonization?
           Naming Whiteness?

Willow: I love your question. I think naming Whiteness is a beginning
           and it really depends on if or where one goes from there in
           terms of what it could mean for decolonization, which is
           a contested concept in and of itself (Tuck & Yang, 2012). As
           critical Whiteness studies make evident, the examination of
           Whiteness is not new and scholars of colour have long been
           exposing the invisibility of White supremacy and racism
           (e.g., Allen, 1994; Omi & Winant, 1994; Morrison, 1992). The
           increasing visibility of Whiteness relates to what some identify
           as a growing "crisis of Whiteness" (Doane, 2003) or "White
           angst" (Andersen, 2003). It seems like it is becoming harder to
           ignore Whiteness ... but where does this lead? If this historical

period is indeed characterized by "outing" Whiteness, then White people can respond by acknowledging their White privilege, or they can search for new means to maintain White supremacy. As educators I really wonder how we link Whiteness to understanding White supremacy and connect awareness to action for ourselves and others.

Teresa: Interesting – I think socially we can see this assertion of a renewed call for White supremacy through the rise of Donald Trump, Robert Moore, Arthur Jones, etc. very publicly claiming positions of power. They are 'outing' themselves amid this culture of safety for White supremacy. What this perhaps gives us is the opportunity to be a catalyst in this crisis of exposing Whiteness as a race. For educators catalyzing this crisis, we can begin to question "issues related to our own privilege and Whiteness working within the reality of systemic racism and bias" (Donsky & Champion, 2015, p. 242). But not only challenge and question the role Whiteness – our Whiteness has/had/is having on our experiences with/in schools and society – we need to step back and engage in "an examination of the foundations of frameworks of thought themselves" (May & Perry, 2017, p. 3). This involves examining our own reflexivity and how this has been informed by the structural and social institutions surrounding us.

On Critical Reflexivity

Teresa: So, then, I think about the work I do in mental health. I have never claimed to be a mental health educator, but I feel my emerging identity as an anti-racist educator opened the door for me to become an ally in this work. And every day I witness the structural and social barriers young people must work around, and the barriers they put up themselves. The structural institution supports these students with laws and legislation; however, a social change is needed for them to feel more included. In examining the role of White supremacy, then, these students who don't fit neatly in schools are also "cultural Others" (Comeau, 2017, p. 185). What I find interesting, although not surprising, is that most students left behind to be cared for are female. Male students with mental health needs are often engaged in the discipline cycle and excluded from school. What role, then, does White supremacy have when structural laws and legislations enacted to support inclusion are not abided by if a child does not identify with the cultural/heteronormative norms in their school?

Willow: I want to pick up on your reference to "a culture of safety for White supremacy" and our roles in exposing Whiteness, and in interrogating our own positionalities and the Western knowledge systems that (re)produce a White supremacist order. I struggle to figure out the most effective and realistic ways to not participate in maintaining a White culture of safety. Is disrupting White supremacist discourses, which are so often masked in White liberal multiculturalism, enough? No. As a researcher, educator, and partner/parent in a multiracial/cultural family, critical reflexivity must be part of my life at all times, and in all interactions I have. I know I continue to reproduce hegemonic forms of Whiteness, and I will always fight that. The purpose of critical reflexivity for me, with respect to Whiteness and White femininity, is driven by the notion of praxis – of working towards structural change. I think we can achieve that in so many seemingly small acts in everyday practices as educators and researchers (Calliste & Dei, 2000).

Conducting my study moved me into scholarship that no longer only addressed racism, from which "good White people" can claim to distance themselves, but explicitly confronted Whiteness and White supremacy. Through that and my family I began to experience in real, tangible, and ongoing ways how my life as a White Euro-Canadian woman and my partner's as a black Zimbabwean new immigrant to Canada, were fundamentally different; this was particularly evident throughout his long immigration process. I began to understand that he read the world and others in multilayered ways that I had been socialized not to see. As I began to form a greater level of awareness of how White supremacist dynamics play out in our lives – at home, on the playground, at work, the grocery store – a culture of ceased to exist anymore because the violence of White supremacy was exposed and I could see how we actively participate in its reproduction. So again, what kinds of anti-colonial Whiteness can there be? What does that look like?

Teresa: This is tricky for me. I think perhaps as an agent/ally for detoxifying masculine identities and hierarchical cultural symbols (especially in sports and schooling) that elevate/ privilege Whiteness ... but then I worry if my work could be taken up as a means to reinforce White supremacy? Awareness needs to come before praxis. Being aware of the pluralism, rather than historical White heteronormative prescriptions of what it means to be a boy, could help approach boys with a different perspective and give them space to be who they are no matter what is being grafted onto them.

Willow: One of the big questions I struggle with is how do we get White boys invested in challenging White supremacy when it is a system that most benefits them. For instance, I think here of a White male teacher candidate in an antiracism education class I taught. His engagement with the course material demonstrated to me that he *got it*, yet I challenged him to examine himself instead of focus solely on how he was going to "help" his "other" students. In a candid response paper, he wrote that he understood how systems of inequity oppressed people other than himself. Then he stated that, as someone who benefits from that system, what was his investment (beyond supporting his students within the existing paradigm) to fight to change it? I imagine he was thinking what many White males must be thinking. What do you do with that? I do not think appeals to White benevolence, empathy, and kindness are enough for White males to want to dismantle a system that benefits them above all ... I think they need to be forced to.

Teresa: Maybe they are dismantling the system but we are not listening and, really, is the system working for them? Boys are often kicked out of school because of their behaviours and there is a collective need to protect the girls so they get referred to special programs and supports. In both my practice in mental health and my study, the "boys will be boys" narrative is hurting them. I am intentionally shifting to create this awareness with my colleagues, pre-service teachers, and those who may engage with my research. Related, there was a study in British Columbia on the role of Gay Straight Alliances (GSA) in schools and they found that when schools have a GSA, suicide rates for White boys drop (Saewyc, Kinishi, Rose, & Homma, 2014). This really speaks to the boy crisis in schools and indicates they need allies so that they can shift the cultural identities they see in sports, the media, and society that define what it means to be a boy/man.

Willow: Yes, especially during this period when we see the rise of the #MeToo movement as well as appeals to White supremacist discourses, it seems like a crucial moment to talk about new kinds of masculinities, especially White ones, away from domination and power. What does the socialization of White boys (or White girls) look like? How can this process be disrupted? I think examining White boys is important in part because the patriarchal discourse of "boys will be boys" you referenced is still pervasive in how issues of sexuality and sexual violence are rationalized. Moreover, we tend to focus on women's bodies and behaviours, but really we need to explore how we raise and teach boys to be different subjects.

Teresa: We cannot talk about gender based violence without inviting boys and men into the conversation and I think that the #MeToo movement is doing that – inviting men into the conversation within the public forum. At first I was quite skeptical about this movement; for one thing it took a white woman, Alyssa Milano, to tweet before traction was gained, totally ignoring the intersections/invisibility of oppression as a Black woman, Tarana Burke, who had founded this movement years before. Burke's movement is focused on Black bodies so why does it take White bodies being violated for the world pay attention? And what role does this leave open for our men?

Willow: There appears to be a fine line between centering Whiteness to interrogate White supremacy and engaging in self-indulgence. As critical Whiteness scholars caution, Whiteness studies should not be a place for White scholars to recenter themselves or become "entirely self-reflexive" (Najmi & Srikanth, 2002, p. 1). How do you conceptualize critical reflexivity? How do you think about it specifically as a White researcher doing research on Whiteness? I think of this notion of "radical reflexivity" (Gunaratnam, 2003) in which broader social, political, and economic conditions are reflected in the research process.

Teresa: Maton (2003) states there is little agreement to what it means to be a reflexive researcher, however this is reflected throughout this conversation here and within our own research. What critical reflexivity gives us is space to interrogate an "iterative and continuous characteristic of good social scientific practice" (May & Perry, 2017, p. 150). So, critical or radical or just reflexive, reflexivity allows you and I to question the ways in which we have come to our own understandings of Whiteness as we have been socialized to view Whiteness.

Willow: Critical reflexivity for me is a way of being and a lens through which I engage the world in all aspects of my life. As an educator-scholar I believe my role is to provide learning opportunities that nurture critical reflection and growth, enable students to expand beyond their boundaries of knowing, and encourage them to rethink their assumptions. I must necessarily create learning opportunities to do this myself and, also share my processes with students and other White people. When I think about this in the Canadian context, I feel like an ongoing critical self-reflexive practice is an integral part of demonstrating commitment to racial identity development and decolonization. At the same time, I remain aware that there are limits to my knowing and I always have more to learn ...

Discussion

Our dialogue brought forth our individual and collective responsibility as White educators, researchers, and parents to implicate ourselves as to how we perform our own racialized subjectivities, and how we teach and socialize children/pre-service teachers to be White racialized subjects (consciously and not). We both note that educational researchers need to interrogate Whiteness *with* our participants (Allen, 2016), and White researchers must analyze Whiteness as part of educational research and teaching practice. Together, we realize that critical reflexivity on Whiteness is about existing with the tension born of self-interrogation while not expecting/seeking the world to revolve around us.

As we reflect on our exchange, we agree that we have examined ourselves to better navigate and understand this "relation between thinking and doing" (May & Perry, 2017, p. 64) in a space between ourselves and the structures we research with/in. At the same time, we contend this is not about us; it is about our roles as White educational researchers accepting that Whiteness has found its way into our studies.

What Teresa noticed throughout this dialogue was that both of us were/are grappling with power dynamics within research relationships – with our participants, selves, and potential others. While this is not new in educational research, Teresa found that without an interrogation into our Whiteness, the power dynamics took on a different identity, one that entered us into a space to challenge Whiteness and its agential role with/in our lives (Barad, 2007). Before this exercise, Teresa had not considered Whiteness as agential but this has opened up space for her and others to consider the active role Whiteness has in either (de)colonizing or (de)framing static ideologies of power.

For Willow, our duoethnographic process made evident that, although we both identify as white Euro-Canadian women, we conceptualize and experience Whiteness in distinctly different ways. From our conversations, Willow understands Whiteness as an even more complex, multilayered construction that we not only embody and perform, but we can also feel, touch, hear, and sense in our interactions with each other, research participants, students, and family members. This engagement has also made Willow contemplate the gendered nature of Whiteness in relation to place and nation-state. Through Teresa's shared experiences about the diversity of White masculinities, Willow has begun to ponder more deeply how Whiteness is performed as, and entrenched in, regional and national identities. She has realized we cannot falsely separate White femininities and White masculinities, but must explicitly analyze how they continue to operate in tandem to reproduce a White supremacist order, a consideration this ongoing duoethnographic exchange will unpack further.

Conclusion

The intention of duoethnography is not to present a master narrative or to argue a key assertion, but to bring forth a shared *third space* (Bhabha, 1990; Norris & Sawyer, 2012) between the authors and readers to address contentious issues and to face ourselves as socially constituted subjects (Breault, 2016). We seek to create not only a place to have challenging and disruptive conversations with each other, but also to open this space for others to be part of our ongoing discussion. We do not have the answers, but we continue to ask the questions.

Acknowledgements

We would like to thank Dr. Michael D. Kehler and Dr. Darren E. Lund, Werklund School of Education, University of Calgary, for their eavesdropping/editing of this conversation/chapter and their support for our work.

Notes

1   We use capital letters for 'White' and 'Whiteness,' however the capitalization of these terms remains a discussion point in our ongoing conversation as we both have differing thoughts. For this chapter, we will use capital letters as we invited

Dr. Darren Lund into our dialogue and at this point will pick up Lund's (2018) suggestion to "write White and Whiteness (and Black) using upper case to differentiate it from the colour, and denote it as a socially constructed racialized category" (personal communication, March 18, 2018) until we can return to each other in conversation.

2   Kehler (2018) inquired into our reasoning for our naming ourselves as 'White racialized educators' as "white is identifying and acknowledging race but you tend to use 'White racialized' educators as though white as a term does not imply racialized" (Kehler, personal communication, March 22, 2018). We name ourselves as White racialized educators as in our experiences, Whiteness does not tend be regarded as a distinct race or even seen as a colour outside of academia or those involved in racial activism, despite the vast history of Whiteness research and scholarship.

References

Adichie, C. (2009). *The danger of a single story*. New York, NY: TED Global. Retrieved from http://www.ted.com/talks/chimamanda_adichie_the_danger_of_a_single_story.html

Allen, T. (1994). *The invention of the White race*. New York, NY: Verso Books.

Allen, W. (2016). *White Euro-Canadian women in transracial/cultural families: Lived experiences of race and difference* (Unpublished doctoral dissertation). Simon Fraser University, Burnaby.

Andersen, M. L. (2003). Whitewashing race: A critical perspective on whiteness. In R. A. Breault (Eds.), Emerging issues in duoethnography. *International Journal of Qualitative Studies in Education, 29*(6), 777–794.

Bourdieu, P. (1990). *The logic of practice* (R. Nice Trans). Stanford, CA: Stanford University Press.

Butler, J. (1988). Performative acts and gender constitution: An essay in phenomenology and feminist theory. *Theatre Journal, 40*(4), 519–531.

Calliste, A., & Dei, G. J. S. (Eds.). (2000). *Anti-racist feminism: Critical race and gender studies*. Halifax, NS: Fernwood.

Comeau, L. (2017). Re-inscribing Whiteness through progressive constructions of "the problem" in anti-racist education. In D. Lund & P. R. Carr (Eds.), *Revising the great White north?: Reframing Whiteness, privilege, and identity in education* (2nd ed., pp. 179–188). Rotterdam, The Netherlands: Sense Publishers.

Connell, R. W. (2005). *Masculinities* (2nd ed.). Berkeley, CA: University of California Press.

Connell, R. W., & Messerschmidt, J. W. (2005). Hegemonic masculinity rethinking the concept. *Gender & Society, 19*(6), 829–859.

Cunliff, A. (2016). "On becoming a critically reflexive practitioner" Redux: What does it mean to be reflexive? *Journal of Management Education, 40*(6), 740–746.

Doane, A. W. (2003). Rethinking Whiteness studies. In A. W. Doane & E. Bonilla-Silva (Eds.), *White out: The continuing significance of racism* (pp. 3–18). New York, NY: Routledge.

Doane, A. W., & Bonilla-Silva, E. (Eds.). (2003). *White out: The continuing significance of racism* (pp. 21–34). New York, NY: Routledge.

Donsky, D., & Champion, M. (2015). De-centering normal: Negotiating Whiteness as White school administrators in a diverse school community. In D. Lund & P. R. Carr (Eds.), *Revising the great White north?: Reframing Whiteness, privilege, and identity in education* (2nd ed., pp. 241–250). Rotterdam, The Netherlands: Sense Publishers.

Du Bois, W. E. B. (1903). *The souls of Black folk*. New York, NY: Dover Publications.

Frankenberg, R. (1993). *White women, race matters: The social construction of Whiteness*. Minneapolis, MN: University of Minnesota Press.

Frideres, J. (2015). Being White and being right: Critiquing individual and collective privilege. In D. Lund & P. R. Carr (Eds.), *Revising the great White north?: Reframing Whiteness, privilege, and identity in education* (2nd ed., pp. 43–54). Rotterdam, The Netherlands: Sense Publishers.

Gunaratnam, Y. (2003). *Researching race and ethnicity: Methods, knowledge, and power*. Thousand Oaks, CA: Sage Publications.

hooks, b. (1990). *Yearning: Race, gender, and cultural politics*. Boston, MA: South End Press.

Kehler, M. (2010). Boys, books and homophobia: Exploring the practices and policies of masculinities in school. *McGill Journal of Education* (Online), *45*(3), 351–370.

Luke, C. (1994). White women in interracial families: Reflections on hybridization, feminine identities, and racialized othering. *Gender Issues, 14*(2), 49–72.

Martino, W., & Kehler, M. (2007). Gender-based literacy reform: A question of challenging or recuperating gender binaries. *Canadian Journal of Education, 30*(2), 406–431.

Maton, K. (2003). Reflexivity, relationism, & research: Pierre Bourdieu and the epistemic conditions of social scientific knowledge. *Space and Culture, 6*(1), 52–65.

May, T., & Perry, P. (2017). *Reflexivity: The essential guide*. Los Angeles, CA: Sage Publications.

Messner, M. A. (2007). *Out of play: Critical essays on gender and sport*. Albany, NY: State University of New York Press.

Morrison, T. (1992). *Playing in the dark: Whiteness and the literary imagination*. Cambridge, Mass: Harvard University Press.

Nabavi, M., & Lund, D. E. (2012). Multicultural nation in an era of bounded identities. In J. Norris, R. D. Sawyer, & D. Lund (Eds.), *Duoethnography: Dialogic methods for social, health, and educational research* (pp. 177–197). Walnut Creek, CA: Wolf Creek Press.

Nader, L. (1972). *Up the anthropologist: Perspectives gained from studying up* (ERIC No. ED065375). Retrieved from http://www.eric.ed.gov/PDFS/ED065375.pdf

Najmi, S., & Srikanth, R. (2002). *White women in racialized spaces: Imaginative transformation and ethical action in literature.* Albany, NY: State University of New York Press.

Norris, J., & Sawyer, R. D. (2012). Toward a dialogic methodology. In J. Norris, R. D. Sawyer, & D. Lund (Eds.), *Duoethnography: Dialogic methods for social, health, and educational research* (pp. 9–38). Walnut Creek, CA: Wolf Creek Press.

Omi, M., & Winant, H. (1994). *Racial formation in the United States: From the 1960s to the 1990s.* New York, NY: Routledge.

Saewyc, E. M., Konishi, C., Rose, H. A., & Homma, Y. (2014). School-based strategies to reduce suicidal ideation, suicide attempts, and discrimination among sexual minority and heterosexual adolescents in Western Canada. *International Journal of Child, Youth, and Family Studies, 5*(1), 89–112.

Taylor, C., Peter, T., Edkins, T., Campbell, C., Émond, G., & Saewyc, E. (2016). *The national inventory of school district interventions in support of LGBTQ student wellbeing* (Final Report). Vancouver: Stigma and Resilience Among Vulnerable Youth Centre, University of British Columbia.

Tuck, E., & Yang, K. (2012). Decolonization is not a metaphor. *Decolonization, Indigeneity, Education and Society, 1*(1), 1–40.

Ware, V. (1992). *Beyond the pale: White women, racism, and history.* New York, NY & London: Verso Books.

CHAPTER 16

Illuminating Teacher Educators' Self-Understanding through the Study of Relationships in the Teacher Education Classroom

Aaron Zimmerman

The practice of classroom teaching is often presumed to be work that should come naturally or as second nature (Labaree, 2000; Murray, 2008), and, similarly, the practice of teacher education is often presumed to be work that does not require any preparation or professional development (Ben-Peretz, 2001; Korthagen, Loughran, & Lunenberg, 2005). Many presume that if someone has served as a classroom teacher, then teaching teachers should be little more than a "commonsense activity" (Zeichner, 2005, p. 123). Yet, being a teacher educator – like being a teacher – requires assuming a professional role fraught with ambiguity, uncertainty, and dilemmas, and teacher educators must reflect on their experiences in order to make sense of their complex roles (Berry, 2009; Bullough & Young, 2002; Freese, 2006; Kelchtermans, 2009; Shapira-Lishchinsky, 2011; Williams & Ritter, 2010). The purpose of this chapter is to explore how the practice of self-study can help to develop teacher educators' self-understanding.

The Self-Understanding of Teacher Educators

Because the aims of education can never be decisively settled (Carr, 2003; Hardarson, 2012, 2017), the aims of teacher education are equally indeterminate (Britzman, 2007; Correa Gorospe, Martínez-Arbelaiz, & Fernández-Olaskoaga, 2018; Sachs, 2001; van Rijswijk, Bronkhorst, Akkerman, & van Tartwijk, 2018). While equipping preservice teachers with the requisite knowledge and skills for teaching is, unquestionably, an essential task of teacher education, teacher educators are also forced to wrestle perpetually with questions of meaning (Berry & van Driel, 2013; Vagle, 2011; Williams & Power, 2010; Wood & Borg, 2010). For example, what is the proper role of a teacher educator? What should the aims of teacher education be? How can a teacher educator best contribute to the professional development of a preservice teacher? In addition to these questions, teacher educators must also ask themselves more subjective questions: Am I someone who can adequately serve as a teacher educator? What are the most significant ways in which I can serve the preservice teachers in my classroom? What do I find to be the most meaningful components of my work? To answer all of these questions, teacher educators must possess "professional self-understanding" (Berry, 2009, p. 305).

To highlight one tension that requires negotiation through professional self-understanding, Berry (2004) explores the teacher educator's perpetual tension between confidence and uncertainty. While teacher educators are presumed to be experts on teaching (see Ball & Forzani, 2009; Grossman, Hammerness, & McDonald, 2009), teacher educators are also responsible for exposing preservice teachers to the inescapable uncertainty of teaching (Beeman-Cadwallader, Buck, & Trauth-Nare, 2014; Floden & Clark, 1988; Lampert, 2001). Thus, even as preservice teachers look to teacher educators for authoritative guidance, teacher educators must convey expert knowledge while simultaneously preserving preservice teachers' appreciation for the complexity of teaching. How a teacher educator finds a balance between these two essential requirements is rooted, in part, in the teacher educator's own professional self-understanding. A teacher educator's professional self-understanding is, therefore, a rich object for self-study.

In this chapter, I will present anecdotes that explore the professional self-understanding of four teacher educators. While teacher-student relationships are acknowledged as being a critical component of high-quality teaching in the K-12 context (den Brok, van der Want, Beijaard, & Wubbels, 2013; Newberry, 2013; Pianta, 2006; Raider-Roth, 2011), less attention has been paid to the way in which relationships shape the professional growth of both preservice teachers and teacher educators. While some self-studies have explored this important dimension of teacher educator practice (Butler & Diacopoulos, 2016; Dinkelman, 2011; McDonough & Brandenburg, 2012), the anecdotes presented in this chapter reveal how inviting teacher educators to reflect on relationships can illuminate particularly important dimensions of self-understanding.

Methodology

Self-study is a practice that invites teachers to reflect on meaningful experiences and to make adjustments to their practices accordingly (LaBoskey & Hamilton, 2010). Through the telling and interpreting of personal stories from the classroom, teachers can refine the tactful ways in which they respond to their students (Huber, Caine, Huber, & Steeves, 2013; van Manen, 2007). In this chapter, I present a study in which teacher educators used self-study to reflect on the ethical – and ontological – dimensions of their classroom interactions (see also Rosiek & Gleason, 2017).

I interviewed four teacher educators (each represented through a pseudonym) serving at a large university in the Midwestern United States. In each interview, the teacher educator was asked to describe, in rich detail, anecdotes of particularly memorable or meaningful lived experiences in the context of the teacher education classroom (Dahlberg, Dahlberg, & Nyström, 2008; van Manen, 2014). One conversational interview (lasting approximately two hours) was conducted with each participant. These interviews were transcribed, and I searched the transcriptions for anecdotes that illuminated moments in which the teacher educators were reflecting on and reevaluating their professional self-understanding in light of their interactions with their students. The data analysis was hermeneutic in nature (Gadamer, 1996; van Manen, 2014), and, as such, this chapter does not seek not to offer statements of verifiable knowledge but, rather, to present the participants' stories in an interpretive and evocative manner such that readers may experience a resonant sense of what it was like for these teacher educators to live through these experiences.

In this chapter, I will present two sets of anecdotes. The first set presents moments of personal and professional vulnerability, while the second set presents moments of personal and professional fulfilment.

Moments of Vulnerability

Charles described a memorable experience in which, while teaching a class of preservice teachers, he slowly became aware of two students who were off-task and, indeed, began mocking his questions:

> I was teaching the class. I was doing what I had always done ... There were two of these gentlemen that were kind of laughing ... I took this personally. I felt like they had betrayed ... my trust, or relationship ... [As a teacher] I try to get to know my students and have that type of relationship ... I certainly took [this incident] personally because they thought that [their misbehaviour] was okay .... I don't like that I took it that personally ... That's really easy to say ... but, in the moment, wow, I thought these guys were with me. I thought I was doing okay. I thought we were headed somewhere together. I thought I had this relationship, this learning environment ... and all of sudden, here's a reminder: Nope, it's not there. It's not where you thought it was. There's more work to do, and that was very unsettling. I thought that the rug had been pulled out from under me.

Charles, elsewhere in the interview, described himself as a high school teacher who was successful in building positive teacher-student relationships and productive learning environments. The incident described in the anecdote, however, caused him to question whether or not his teaching ability had transferred to the teacher education classroom. Dealing with off-task students is a professional problem of practice for any teacher; yet, Charles articulates feeling "betrayed" and is forced to reevaluate his competency both as a teacher educator and as a teacher. He interprets his students' misbehaviour as a deep affront. While Charles wants to interpret this moment as solely a professional challenge, he recognizes that he cannot help but to interpret the interaction in personal terms. For Charles, this classroom dilemma unearthed both professional and personal vulnerability.

Another example of vulnerability is found in an anecdote described by Catherine. Here, she recounts having to manage a particularly outspoken and argumentative preservice teacher:

> We were talking about literary devices ... I remember the thorn in my side, [this student], pushing back against the way I was defining [the concept of] "theme" ... He was very frustrated with this and he pointed that out to the class, and that was one moment where I kind of felt, okay, you are kind of undermining my expertise here, and so I went up to him ... and I said ... "I hear you on this critique. This is why I've chosen to stick with this [definition]" ... To the degree that he bought that [explanation], I don't know. But it is interesting that I have this need in that moment ... I really remember ... being like, "No, I *do* know what 'theme' means, you asshole. I *know*! I got a fucking 5 on my AP exam when I was 18, I know what it is! You little pipsqueak!"

Like Charles' two misbehaving students, Catherine's internal dialogue communicates that this particular preservice teacher was more than an inconvenient classroom annoyance; he was a clear and present threat to Catherine's entire professional (and personal) self-understanding. When her student challenged the definition of a fundamental literary construct, Catherine interpreted this objection as a direct threat to her self-esteemed status as expert. Her interaction with this student not only presented an immediate challenge in the context of her lesson, but also enraged Catherine as she felt her very identity was being assaulted. For Charles and Catherine, problems of practice were experienced as both professional challenges and personal affronts. Caught within interpersonal interactions, Charles and Catherine found it difficult to disentangle the professional and the personal dimensions of their identities.

Moments of Fulfillment

Andres described a memorable moment in which a preservice language teacher shared one of her professional accomplishments with him:

> I [had] told [this preservice teacher], I'm not going to let you finish your [student teaching] if you don't combine [music and Spanish], because ... she loves music and she loves Spanish. So, I said, you have to do something where you teach Spanish through music ... I just kept pushing ... And then [one day] she showed me a video ... She [had] developed this whole lesson ... She taught students a song in Spanish and then she had them rewrite it based on [their lives and their neighborhood], and then she had them perform it ... That's awesome ... That's what we need, and those are the ... moments that make me cry .... This is *my* teacher! ... [One day] she showed me an email from a [special education] teacher [at her school] ... cc'd to her mentor and to the principal ... [The email said] "Thank you. Thank you for allowing this experience to happen. I just want to tell you that my students were really overwhelmed by the experience of music ... You really changed our lives ... I'm really thankful to be part of this school because of teachers like you." ... I was just silent for a minute, I was just like, let me enjoy this ... Just let me read that email over and over and over. And I still have that email because that's just awesome.

Andres encouraged the preservice teacher to synthesize her interests in a meaningful way, and this resulted in an ambitious and impactful lesson. In this way, Andres' advice and encouragement contributed significantly to the preservice teacher's professional development. What is even more notable, however, is the manner in which Andres describes this moment as both professional and personally fulfilling: "those are the ... moments that make me cry ... This is *my* teacher!" Andres describes feeling overwhelmed, and still uses the email of gratitude as a way to remind himself of his commitment to his work. As Andres reflects on his interaction with preservice teachers, he highlights not only his successful teacher education pedagogy (e.g., push the preservice teachers to craft ambitious lessons that synthesize their multiple interests) but also his gratitude. Andres derived professional and personal meaning from the fact that *his* student was able to create a meaningful experience for *her* students.

Ian, during his interview, described a moment during which he created a shared experience for the preservice teachers in his classroom:

> [I had decided that we should] sing together ... I chose this song ["Build Me Up, Buttercup"], because [I think] it represents [their] experience

... It's kind of like you have this love-hate relationship with teaching ... We sang it, and the whole class sang it, and even those who claimed they didn't know the song sang, clapped their hands ... A couple students came up to me after that and said ... "That was great, I really appreciated that." One particular student said, "You might forget what people do to you, but you will never forget what they make you feel, and today you made me feel safe and comfortable." ... I was proud, I was proud of that moment ... [I think] she felt the acknowledgement of her struggle throughout the semester and to release that emotion and [to have that] tension to be acknowledged ... I think that was very powerful ... [and] I think it was just, for me, the validation from her appreciation, [it] just strengthened what I believe.

Like Andres, Ian made a curricular decision based on what he believed would serve preservice teachers' professional development. Specifically, Ian believed that the acknowledgement of the preservice teachers' struggles and tensions (their current "love-hate relationship with teaching") would contribute to their professional growth. Yet, like Andres, Ian also described feeling "proud" of the experience that he had created, noting that this shared moment "was very powerful." These reflections seem to transcend an assessment of this classroom activity's pedagogical effectiveness; rather, these words convey that this classroom experience generated a deep personal resonance shared between teacher educator and preservice teachers. The one preservice teacher's expressed gratitude provided Ian with "validation" for his commitments as a teacher educator. Interestingly, Ian's words and his student's words powerfully express how the experience made them *feel*. The experiences shared in the teacher education classroom, therefore, may not only serve preservice teachers' professional development but may also infuse the classroom with feelings of personal significance.

Implications for the Practice of Self-Study

Teacher educators can gain insight into their own professional and personal self-understanding by reflecting on the lived experience of relationship in the teacher education classroom. Based on the anecdotes presented in this chapter, I will discuss three potential implications for teacher educators' self-study practices.

First, the four anecdotes underscore the extent to which teacher education is a relational endeavour. Each of the four teacher educators reconsidered their professional self-understanding as a direct result of their interactions with their students (either after having been confronted by their students or after having their students express their gratitude). While the relational dimension of teacher education is, perhaps, self-evident, too often this dimension is overlooked in favour of emphasizing the knowledge, beliefs, and pedagogical expertise that teacher educators must possess (Ball & Forzani, 2009; Castro Superfine & Li, 2014; Goodwin et al., 2014; Grossman & McDonald, 2008; McDonald et al., 2013). Thus, I argue that self-study in the context of teacher education ought to begin by framing teacher education as a relational pedagogy. Indeed, all teaching can (and, perhaps, should) be understood as an experience rooted in relationships (Giles, 2010; King, 2015; Raider-Roth, 2011; Saevi, 2011; van Manen & Li, 2002).

Second, the four anecdotes illuminate the significance inherent within specific moments of lived experience. That is to say, while self-study approaches that utilize overarching life narratives and longitudinal autoethnographic approaches are valuable (Bullough & Pinnegar, 2001; Hamilton, Smith, & Worthington, 2008), these approaches should be complemented with studies of individual moments of meaningful interaction (Akinbode, 2013; Brandenburg & McDonough, 2017; Garcia & Lewis, 2014). Thus, I argue that inviting teacher educators to concentrate their self-studies on the nature of classroom experience as it unfolds may afford teacher educators the opportunity to obtain unique insight into the manner in which their professional self-understanding evolves through interpersonal interaction with preservice teachers.

Third, the four anecdotes illustrate how a teacher educator's self-understanding contains both professional (Goodwin et al., 2014; Loughran, 2014) and personal (Rice, Newberry, Whiting, Cutri, & Pinnegar, 2015; Williams & Power, 2010) components. In other words, teacher educators cannot address questions related to professional practice without also considering questions rooted in personal meaning. Because relationships formatively shape the nature of both professional and personal dimensions of being a teacher educator, engaging in self-study supports teacher educators in making central their interpersonal interactions with preservice teachers.

Conclusion

Relationships in the teacher education classroom create moments of vulnerability and frustration as well as moments of affirmation and fulfilment. Within these moments, teacher educators are compelled to reassess self-understanding. This process is fundamentally a process of making meaning of one's work and one's identity (Allard & Gallant, 2012; Hostetler, Macintyre Latta, & Sarroub, 2007; Williams & Power, 2010; Williams & Ritter, 2010). It is worth reminding ourselves of these claims, for, when teacher education is viewed only as an instrumental project concerned with training teachers, "skills supplant ideas, technique is confused with authority and responsibility, and know-how short circuits the existential question[s]" (Britzman, 2007, p. 10). Thus, it serves teacher education programs, as well as teacher educators engaged in self-study, to regard the work of teacher education as a practice that is concerned with constructing meaning in a dialogical process with others. For, at its root, teacher education is a relational experience, and a teacher educator's understanding of his or her own self continuously emerges through interactions with preservice teachers.

References

Akinbode, A. (2013). Teaching as lived experience: The value of exploring the hidden and emotional side of teaching through reflective narratives. *Studying Teacher Education, 9*(1), 62–73.

Allard, A. C., & Gallant, A. (2012). Is this a meaningful learning experience? Interactive critical self-inquiry as investigation. *Studying Teacher Education, 8*(3), 261–273.

Ball, D. L., & Forzani, F. M. (2009). The work of teaching and the challenge for teacher education. *Journal of Teacher Education, 60*(5), 497–511.

Beeman-Cadwallader, N., Buck, G., & Trauth-Nare, A. (2014). Tipping the balance from expert to facilitator: Examining myths about being a teacher educator. *Studying Teacher Education, 10*(1), 70–85.

Ben-Peretz, M. (2001). The impossible role of teacher educators in a changing world. *Journal of Teacher Education, 52*(1), 48–56.

Berry, A. (2004). Confidence and uncertainty in teaching about teaching. *Australian Journal of Education, 48*(2), 149–165.

Berry, A. (2009). Professional self-understanding as expertise in teaching about teaching. *Teachers and Teaching, 15*(2), 305–318.

Berry, A., & van Driel, J. H. (2013). Teaching about teaching science: Aims, strategies, and backgrounds of science teacher educators. *Journal of Teacher Education, 64*(2), 117–128.

Brandenburg, R., & McDonough, S. (2017). Using critical incidents to reflect on teacher educator practice. In R. Brandenburg, K. Glasswell, M. Jones, & J. Ryan (Eds.), *Reflective theory and practice in teacher education: Self-study of teaching and teacher education practices* (Vol. 17, pp. 223–236). Singapore: Springer.

Britzman, D. (2007). Teacher education as uneven development: Toward a psychology of uncertainty. *International Journal of Leadership in Education, 10*(1), 1–12.

Bullough, R. V., & Pinnegar, S. (2001). Guidelines for quality in autobiographical forms of self-study research. *Educational Researcher, 30*(3), 13–21.

Bullough, R. V., & Young, J. (2002). Learning to teach as an intern: The emotions and the self. *Teacher Development, 6*(3), 417–431.

Butler, B. M., & Diacopoulos, M. M. (2016). Re/learning student teaching supervision: A co/autoethnographic self-study. *Studying Teacher Education, 12*(2), 117–134.

Carr, D. (2003). Moral educational implications of rival conceptions of education and the role of the teacher. *Journal of Moral Education, 32*(3), 219–232.

Castro Superfine, A., & Li, W. (2014). Exploring the mathematical knowledge needed for teaching teachers. *Journal of Teacher Education, 65*(4), 303–314.

Correa Gorospe, J. M., Martínez-Arbelaiz, A., & Fernández-Olaskoaga, L. (2018). Professional identity and engagement among newly qualified teachers in times of uncertainty. *European Early Childhood Education Research Journal, 26*(1), 26–36.

Dahlberg, K., Dahlberg, H., & Nyström, M. (2008). *Reflective lifeworld research* (2nd ed.). Lund: Studentlitteratur.

den Brok, P., van der Want, A., Beijaard, D., & Wubbels, T. (2013). The interpersonal dimension in the classroom: A model of teachers' interpersonal role identity, appraisal and teacher-student relationships. *Advances in Research on Teaching, 18*, 141–159.

Dinkelman, T. (2011). Forming a teacher educator identity: Uncertain standards, practice and relationships. *Journal of Education for Teaching, 37*(3), 309–323.

Floden, R. E., & Clark, C. M. (1988). Preparing teachers for uncertainty. *Teachers College Record, 89*(4), 505–524.

Freese, A. R. (2006). Reframing one's teaching: Discovering our teacher selves through reflection and inquiry. *Teaching and Teacher Education, 22*(1), 100–119.

Gadamer, H. G. (1996). *Truth and method* (2nd ed.). New York, NY: Continuum Publishing Company.

Garcia, J. A., & Lewis, T. E. (2014). Getting a grip on the classroom: From psychological to phenomenological curriculum development in teacher education programs. *Curriculum Inquiry, 44*(2), 141–168.

Giles, D. (2010). Developing pathic sensibilities: A critical priority for teacher education programs. *Teaching and Teacher Education, 26*, 1511–1519.

Goodwin, A. L., Smith, L., Souto-Manning, M., Cheruvu, R., Tan, M. Y., Reed, R., & Taveras, L. (2014). What should teacher educators know and be able to do? Perspectives from practicing teacher educators. *Journal of Teacher Education, 65*(4), 284–302.

Grossman, P., Hammerness, K., & McDonald, M. (2009). Redefining teaching, reimagining teacher education. *Teachers and Teaching, 15*(2), 273–289.

Grossman, P., & McDonald, M. (2008). Back to the future: Directions for research in teaching and teacher education. *American Educational Research Journal, 45*(1), 184–205.

Hamilton, M. L., Smith, L., & Worthington, K. (2008). Fitting the methodology with the research: An exploration of narrative, self-study and auto-ethnography. *Studying Teacher Education, 4*(1), 17–28.

Hardarson, A. (2012). Why the aims of education cannot be settled. *Journal of Philosophy of Education, 46*(2), 223–235.

Hardarson, A. (2017). Aims of education: How to resist the temptation of technocratic models. *Journal of Philosophy of Education, 51*(1), 59–72.

Hostetler, K., Macintyre Latta, M. A., & Sarroub, L. K. (2007). Retrieving meaning in teacher education: The question of being. *Journal of Teacher Education, 58*(3), 231–244.

Huber, J., Caine, V., Huber, M., & Steeves, P. (2013). Narrative inquiry as pedagogy in education: The extraordinary potential of living, telling, retelling, and reliving stories of experience. *Review of Research in Education, 37*(1), 212–242.

Kelchtermans, G. (2009). Who I am in how I teach is the message: Self-understanding, vulnerability, and reflection. *Teachers and Teaching, 15*(2), 257–272.

King, J. (2015). Standing at the crossroads: The pedagogical intersection between standards and relationships. *Journal of Cases in Educational Leadership, 18*(1), 77–91.

Korthagen, F., Loughran, J., & Lunenberg, M. (2005). Teaching teachers – Studies into the expertise of teacher educators: An introduction to this theme issue. *Teaching and Teacher Education, 21*, 107–115.

Labaree, D. F. (2000). On the nature of teaching and teacher education: Difficult practices that look easy. *Journal of Teacher Education, 51*(3), 228–233.

LaBoskey, V. K., & Hamilton, M. L. (2010). "Do as I do": The role of teacher educator self-study in educating for reflective inquiry. In N. Lyons (Ed.), *Handbook of reflection and reflective inquiry* (pp. 333–350). Boston, MA: Springer.

Lampert, M. (2001). *Teaching problems and the problems of teaching*. New Haven, CT: Yale University Press.

Loughran, J. (2014). Professionally developing as a teacher educator. *Journal of Teacher Education, 65*(4), 271–283.

McDonald, M., Kazemi, E., & Kavanagh, S. S. (2013). Core practices and pedagogies of teacher education: A call for a common language and collective activity. *Journal of Teacher Education, 64*(5), 378–386.

McDonough, S., & Brandenburg, R. (2012). Examining assumptions about teacher educator identities by self-study of the role of mentor of pre-service teachers. *Studying Teacher Education, 8*(2), 169–182.

Murray, F. B. (2008). The role of teacher education courses in teaching by second nature. In M. Cochran-Smith, S. Feiman-Nemser, D. J. McIntyre, & K. E. Demers (Eds.), *Handbook of research on teacher education: Enduring questions in changing contexts* (3rd ed., pp. 1228–1246). New York, NY: Routledge.

Newberry, M. (2013). Reconsidering differential behaviors: Reflection and teacher judgment when forming classroom relationships. *Teacher Development, 17*(2), 195–213.

Pianta, R. C. (2006). Classroom management and relationships between children and teachers: Implications for research and practice. In C. M. Evertson & C. S. Weinstein (Eds.), *Handbook of classroom management: Research, practice, and contemporary issues* (pp. 685–709). Mahwah, NJ: Lawrence Erlbaum Associates.

Raider-Roth, M. B. (2011). The place of description in understanding and transforming classroom relationships. *The New Educator, 7*(3), 274–286.

Rice, M. F., Newberry, M., Whiting, E., Cutri, R., & Pinnegar, S. (2015). Learning from experiences of non-personhood: A self-study of teacher education identities. *Studying Teacher Education, 11*(1), 16–31.

Rosiek, J., & Gleason, T. (2017). Philosophy in research on teacher education: An onto-ethical turn. In D. J. Clandinin & J. Husu (Eds.), *The Sage handbook of research on teacher education* (pp. 29–48). Los Angeles, CA: Sage Publications.

Sachs, J. (2001). Teacher professional identity: Competing discourses, competing outcomes. *Journal of Education Policy, 16*(2), 149–161.

Saevi, T. (2011). Lived relationality as fulcrum for pedagogical-ethical practice. *Studies in Philosophy and Education, 30*, 455–461.

Shapira-Lishchinsky, O. (2011). Teachers' critical incidents: Ethical dilemmas in teaching practice. *Teaching and Teacher Education, 27*, 648–656.

Vagle, M. D. (2011). Critically-oriented pedagogical tact: Learning about and through our compulsions as teacher educators. *Teaching Education, 22*(4), 413–426.

van Manen, M. (2007). Phenomenology of practice. *Phenomenology & Practice, 1*(1), 11–30.

van Manen, M. (2014). *Phenomenology of practice: Meaning-giving methods in phenomenological research and writing*. Walnut Creek, CA: Left Coast Press.

van Manen, M., & Li, S. (2002). The pathic principle of pedagogical language. *Teaching and Teacher Education, 18*, 215–224.

van Rijswijk, M. M., Bronkhorst, L. H., Akkerman, S. F., & van Tartwijk, J. (2018). Changes in sensed dis/continuity in the development of student teachers throughout teacher education. *European Journal of Teacher Education,41*(3), 282–300. doi:10.1080/02619768.2018.1448782

Williams, J., & Power, K. (2010). Examining teacher educator practice and identity through core reflection. *Studying Teacher Education, 6*(2), 115–130.

Williams, J., & Ritter, J. K. (2010). Constructing new professional identities through self-study: From teacher to teacher educator. *Professional Development in Education, 36*(1–2), 77–92.

Wood, D., & Borg, T. (2010). The rocky road: The journey from classroom teacher to teacher educator. *Studying Teacher Education, 6*(1), 17–28.

Zeichner, K. M. (2005). Becoming a teacher educator: A personal perspective. *Teaching and Teacher Education, 21*, 117–124.

CHAPTER 17

Always Becoming: Life as Self-Study

Charity Becker

> To choose a teaching life, or to have a teaching life choose you, means
> entering into an intense and intimate act of relations.
>
> M. INGERSOLL (2014, p. 44)

∵

I had a tenth grade student a couple of years ago ask me, if I didn't have any
children of my own, how could I be such a good teacher. I told him that because
I don't have any children of my own, my students are my children and that's
why I take such good care of them. My children. Sadly, I did not always see my
students in this way.

Identity itself is a transient and fragile concept. (Badley, 2016, p. 377)

There Was Once

There was once a high school English teacher who worked very hard to be
good at her job. She had a BA with Honours in English, an MA in English, and a
BEd; she was an avid reader, and she had expertise in literature and grammar.
This teacher planned meticulous lessons and maintained control of her class
at all times. Her students all read the same texts at the same times, did the
same assessments at the same times, and were held to the same expectations.
She knew each of her students by name and their marks in the class and not
much else. Her students knew her by name and the subject she taught and not
much else. And they all existed separately in a common space in relative indif-
ference to one another.

Shift.

There was once a high school English teacher who became a student (again)
and who worked very hard to be better at her job. She expanded her expertise
in literacy. This teacher planned more thoughtful lessons and worked with her
students to maintain a disciplined class. Her students still read the same texts
at the same times, did the same assessments at the same times, and were held

to the same expectations. She knew each of her students by name and their marks in the class and knew some of the interests of some of her students. Her students knew her by name and the subject she taught and some of her interests. And sometimes the teacher and students existed together and sometimes they existed separately in comfortable respect for one another.

Shift.

There was once a high school English teacher who became a writer and became part of a community of writers and who worked very hard to become a better person. She gained expertise as a writer but she also became more vulnerable through her writing and became more open-minded and understanding of others through the sharing of writing. This teacher became more flexible in adapting lessons to meet the individual needs of her students and worked with her students to create a community of learners. Her students then sometimes read different texts at different times and had some choice in their assessments and were still held to high expectations. She knew each of her students by name and knew many of their stories and her students knew her by name and knew many of her stories. And the teacher and students learned together as a collaborative community.

Shift.

There is a human being with a passion for reading and writing and teaching who engages in learning with other human beings who are in the process of becoming adults. She continues to grow and develop as a human through courses and workshops and reading and writing and discussions and travel and mindfulness. She plans and re-plans and reflects on the teaching and learning that happens in her classroom and serves her students with an open and loving heart. She knows many of her students' fears and dreams and challenges and hopes, and her students know many of her passions and vulnerabilities. And they all work together at becoming better versions of themselves and bettering the world for all.

Shift.

There will be ...

Teacher identity is critical to successful teaching; connectedness spills over life into the classroom, into teaching and learning. (Sameshima, 2007, p. 16)

What does it mean to be a pedagogue? Max van Manen (1982) writes that "pedagogy is the most profound relationship that an adult can have with a child" (p. 290) and that "the teacher as pedagogue is oriented toward the child in a special way ... [the pedagogue] immediately [enters] a very personal relationship with the child" (van Manen, 1979, p. 14). The very notion of pedagogy, according to van Manen (1991), "always assumes that there exists a personal learning relationship between people, usually an adult and a child" (p. 30), and Sameshima (2007) reiterates that "transformational learning is influenced by a strong, even loving, teacher/learner relationship" (pp. 25–26). For years I taught without a personal relationship to my students. I taught the way I had been taught. I stood at the front of the room spilling forth knowledge which my students, sitting in rows of desks, were expected to drink in and pour back out on test days. I did not know my students. I did not have a personal relationship with them. I taught, but I was not a pedagogue. Wiebe and Yallop (2010) write: "In school, hearts need caring, hearts need our attention, our investment, our time" (p. 179). My being with my students was predicated on a sense of responsibility but not on a sense of care. I perpetuated the problems evident in many educational systems that place subject knowledge and classroom management above care of students.

But how was I to break free from these constraints, which my own educational experience had so ingrained within me? Mandated professional development for teachers, often disjointed and disconnected one-off sessions that sometimes were and sometimes were not relevant to my individual needs and that sometimes provided and sometimes did not provide an opportunity for professional growth, did not seem to instigate any significant change in who I was as a teacher. I often left a PD session with a new idea for an assessment or activity or a new way to teach a certain concept but rarely was there any significant transformation in my way of being with my students. So how does authentic pedagogical transformation occur? How was I to stop teaching, in the most basic definition of the word, and become a true pedagogue?

Mette Hauch, a teacher from Denmark, states: "I have to teach by being engaged and being human and involving [my students]. They need to know that I am a person who has a life [outside of teaching], and I need to come across as a human who they can identify with; and then it becomes real to them" (Fullan & Langworthy, 2014, p. 14). When I began teaching, I was not engaged in my students' lives. In the classroom, I assumed the persona of a teacher, or what I thought a teacher should be. I was concerned with maintaining control of what happened in the classroom. I had an objective view of my students, rather than seeing them individually and subjectively. van Manen (2015) writes: "As the teacher interacts with the students, he or she must maintain an authentic presence and personal relationship with them" (p. 92). In my life outside of the classroom, I was authentic in my relationships: I was caring, compassionate, vulnerable, loving. But within the classroom, with my students, I was acting a part, playing a character who differed significantly from who I was off the stage. When I began writing and engaging in stories and reflecting on my life as an educator, however, I was able to see the disjunction between my personal self and my professional self and I was able to begin the work to bring these two selves together.

Sameshima (2007) writes, "the sharing of stories encourages reflexive inquiries in ethical self-consciousness, enlarges paradigms of the 'normative,' and develops pedagogical practices of liberation and acceptance of diversity" (p. xi). I began to write my stories, in prose and poetry, and to listen to others' stories. I began to share my stories with a select group, tentatively and reluctantly at first. Eventually I found my voice and my narratives began to find their way into my classroom. I began to read my poems and stories to my students and, when the space was opened up, they reciprocated by sharing their stories with me. As Wiebe and Margolin (2012) write:

> What poetry does is to work outside the paradigms that stifle change. Poetry enlivens and invigorates my attention so that I'm attending to school in ways that are more likely to matter to students in their present circumstances ... Poetry offers a respectful rendering of care ... bringing sacredness to live beside and within heart-wrenching data. (p. 30)

Leggo (2005) also states that "teachers, both beginning and experienced, should learn to know themselves as poets in order to foster living creatively in the pedagogic contexts of classrooms and the larger pedagogic contexts outside classrooms" (p. 442). Through writing, I have come to view the world differently. I am more attentive to details, to colours, to patterns. I see beauty in brokenness and decay, in transitions and juxtapositions. And I see differently as a teacher as well. I see the student who is always alone in the hallway. I see the dark circles under the eyes of the student who has been crying over the lunch break. I notice when a usually talkative student is quiet or when someone is suddenly no longer sitting with their usual group of friends. I recognize loneliness and pain and fear in faces which, in another time, I would have passed over without notice. And because I see, I must act. In seeing and acting in service to my students rather than to my own teaching, I have become a pedagogue. I have learned to practice what van Manen (1991) calls "pedagogical thoughtfulness and tact" which are practiced through "exercising a certain perceptive sensitivity as well as by practicing an active and expressively caring concern for the child" (p. 172). I have continued to become a better pedagogue not through professional development but through the personal development that happens when I am reflective on my way of being with my students. van Manen (2002) writes that when "I experience this child's life as more important than my own," I must look more carefully and reflectively at my own life, I must "question and reshape it" because I must live a life I would want for my students; thus "the education of the child turns into self-education" (p. 14). In order to change on the outside, I had to change on the inside. As Fidyk (2012) notes: "inner work may be the most far-reaching ethical act in which one can engage" (p. 356). Through inner personal development, through becoming a better human, I become a better teacher and authentic pedagogical transformation occurs.

> *These stories in our lives are the work of our human becoming.* (MacDonald & Wiebe, 2011, p. 104)

Though I came to writing a decade into my career, becoming a writer has had the most significant transformational impact on my living and my teaching. Like Laurel Richardson (2001), writing became "the method through which I constituted the world and reconstituted myself ... writing was and is how I come to know" (p. 33). In order to write my stories, I had to dig deeper into myself. Nairne and Thren (2017) write, "stories are how a person knows who they were, who they are, and, potentially, who they will be" (p. 115). Writing has required me to look more closely at who I am and to recognize the disjunctions between my personal and professional selves and between who I was, who I am, and who I want to be. And so began the process of creating and recreating myself through words. Ted Aoki claims: "Whenever I write a story, I not only produce a narrative but I'm reproducing myself. The very narrating acts upon me, and I'm changing" (in Leggo, 2004, p. 99). For me, reflecting happens through writing. As I write my experience, I reflect on my experience; in the rewriting, I am able to change who and how I am and thus to change future experiences. van Manen (2003) also states, "the writer dwells in an inner space inside the self. Indeed this is a popular way of spatially envisioning the self: an inner and an outer self. But phenomenologically it is probably just as plausible to say that the writer dwells in the space that the words open up" (p. 2). Words cracked through to the places within that I had hidden even from myself and as I collected the fragments of my being I realized new ways of putting the pieces back together, new ways of being.

> *It is the word that makes us human.* (Arden, 2004, p. 119)

words
reach into my soul
each sound
each syllable
a single note
in a symphony
a stroke of colour

across a canvas
a sunset
an embrace
an electric shock
to wake me from myself
into myself
i am touched
by words

> *The writing was the net in which I tried to catch the intimate splinters of my*
> *experience.* (Barnes, 2014, p. 249)

"Words," writes Carl Leggo (2012), "are wild with insight, with ways for seeing
and knowing the world" (p. 147). Words are powerful. Words can change lives.
Words have changed my life. Not just my own words, but also the words of others. van Manen (1990) writes, "we gather other people's experiences because
they allow us to become more experienced ourselves" (p. 62); and "this is
where the listening to and witnessing of the life stories of others lies. You listen
because you do not know and you listen because you understand that each
person is the expert of his or her own life" (Norton, 2017, n.p.). My own experience expands when I am attentive to the stories of others. I come to know
things I could not have known on my own. I have become a gatherer of stories, particularly the stories of my students. As MacKenzie (2012) states, "I have
become, as a result of my encounters with the students and their writing"
(p. 213). Because of my students' stories, I have become more – more open,
more vulnerable, more understanding, more patient, more empathetic, more
tactful, more kind. Because of my students' stories, I have been transformed
from merely teaching to being a pedagogue, from playing a role to living as a
complete, embodied human being. Together, my students and I continue our
process of becoming and of making the world a better place. As Sameshima
writes, "when all stories can be heard, then we can be truly democratic, overcome privileging, and develop in ourselves and in our schools lives of peace,
happiness, and joy" (2007, p. 288).

> *We end up loving the people we serve.* (Durman, 2017)

Last spring I attended a workshop on archetypes with Newfoundland author,
Donna Morrissey. Prior to the workshop, participants completed a self-inven-
tory to determine which archetypes were their strongest. In the past, I had
always struggled with self-inventories of this type. I was never sure whether

to answer as my personal self or as my professional self, two sides which stood in contrast to one another. This time I did not have that struggle. My prevalent archetypes – the lover, whose aim is to build community and oneness; the caregiver, whose aim is to help and care for others; the creator, whose aim is to create a better world for others; and the innocent, whose aim is to be safe and to maintain hope – apply to both my personal and my professional selves. As my professional self has come into alignment with my personal self, I have become more comfortable in my classroom. I am no longer playing a role. I am authentic, and I am no longer afraid to let my students see who I am, to see my passions and my vulnerabilities.

Wiebe and Snowber (2012) write, "living my vulnerabilities in the classroom must not be excluded from a theory of practice. The continuous struggle with the complexities of living are the complex vulnerabilities that I ought to bring with me into the classroom" (p. 454). My students struggle every day with unimaginable challenges. I have taught students who live in extreme poverty and miss classes because they have no food or no shoes; students who live with chronic pain or who are battling depression or anxiety or addictions; students whose parents are addicts and who sometimes have no electricity because the money has gone for drugs; students who have been the victims of bullying, of sexual, physical, and emotional abuse; students who are lonely and can't understand why no one wants to be their friend; students who have never known how it feels to be successful or to be praised for anything. There are so many things about which I can do nothing. But I can, at the very least, let them know that they are not alone. I can make sure that they leave school knowing that someone cared about them, that someone appreciated them, that someone loved them. Shields and Reid-Patton (2009) write:

> Kindness has the power to restore dignity and extend grace even when it seems undeserved. Kindness can bring with it healing and restoration. It seems to call forth the best in the other. Kindness is a response to the perceived value of the other, an acknowledgement of the sanctity of life and the dignity of all humanity. In embracing kindness as the cornerstone for teacher and learning, we see that we can create situations that offer others the respect and consideration that is so essential for learning to occur. (p. 13)

I hope that all of my students experience this kindness in my classroom. I wish it had always been that way.

We are always becoming. (Ingersoll, 2014, p. 53)

I am ...
(in the style of Carl Leggo)

zealous zestful
youthful yearning
xenodochial (e)xpressive
wondering worrying
vocal vulnerable
understanding uplifting
trusting tenacious
sensitive seeking
researching renewing
questing questioning
open organized
natural nonconforming
mindful motherly
loving learning
kind kaleidoscopic
joyous journeying
inspired introspective
hopeful happy
guiding growing
friendly fierce
enthusiastic encouraging
dedicated determined
creative caring
brave blossoming
attentive aspiring

always becoming

> *In the doing, in the creating we are becoming. We are transforming ourselves.*
> (Irwin in Sameshima, 2007, p. xx)

References

Arden, J. (2004). *I'll tell you one damn thing, and that's all I know.* London: Insomniac Press.
Badley, G. F. (2016). Composing academic identities: Stories that matter? *Qualitative Inquiry, 22*(5), 377–385.

Barnes, L. G. (2014). Writing from the margins of myself. *International Journal of Qualitative Methods, 13*, 237–254.

Durman, T. (2017, October). *Save the cat – Making connections.* Presented at PEITF Annual Convention, Charlottetown, PE.

Fidyk, A. (2012). Visitor, host and chrysanthemum: Hosting the unconscious through poetic form. In S. Thomas, A. L. Cole, & S. Stewart (Eds.), *The art of poetic inquiry* (pp. 347–360). Big Tancook Island, NS: Backalong Books.

Fullan, M., & Langworthy, M. (2014). *A rich seam: How new pedagogies find deep learning.* London: Pearson.

Ingersoll, M. (2014). Curriculum windows: Frames of possibility. *Transnational Curriculum Inquiry, 1*, 44–54.

Leggo, C. (2004). Narrative inquiry: Honouring the complexity of the stories we live. *Brock Education, 14*(1), 97–111.

Leggo, C. (2005). The heart of pedagogy: On poetic knowing and living. *Teachers and Teaching, 11*(5), 439–455.

Leggo, C. (2012). Living language: What is a poem good for? *Journal of the Canadian Association for Curriculum Studies, 10*(1), 141–160.

MacDonald, C., & Wiebe, S. (2011). Attention to place: Learning to listen. *Journal of the Canadian Association for Curriculum Studies, 9*(2), 86–108.

MacKenzie, S. K. (2012). Sensing distance: A poetic exploration of touch. In S. Thomas, A. L. Cole, & S. Stewart (Eds.), *The art of poetic inquiry* (pp. 203–216). Big Tancook Island, NS: Backalong Books.

Nairne, D. C., & Thren, J. (2017). Storytelling: A unique approach to developing partnerships with students. *The Vermont Connection, 38*, 115–122.

Norton, L. (2017). Pathways of reflection: Creating voice through life story and dialogical poetry. *Forum: Qualitative Social Research, 18*(1), Article 9.

Richardson, L. (2001). Getting personal: Writing-stories. *International Journal of Qualitative Studies in Education, 14*(1), 33–38.

Sameshima, P. (2007). *Seeing red: A pedagogy of parallax.* Youngstown, NY: Cambria Press.

Shields, C., & Reid-Patton, V. (2009). A curriculum of kindness: (Re)creating and nurturing head and mind through teaching and learning. *Brock Education, 18*(2), 4–15.

van Manen, M. (1979). The phenomenology of pedagogic observation. *Canadian Journal of Education, 4*(1), 5–16.

van Manen, M. (1982). Phenomenological pedagogy. *Curriculum Inquiry, 12*(3), 283–299.

van Manen, M. (1990). *Researching lived experience: Human science for an action sensitive pedagogy.* London: The Althouse Press.

van Manen, M. (1991). *The tact of teaching: The meaning of pedagogical thoughtfulness.* London: The Althouse Press.

van Manen, M. (2002). *The tone of teaching: The language of pedagogy* (2nd ed.). London: Althouse Press.

van Manen, M. (2003). *Writing in the dark: Phenomenological studies in interpretive inquiry*. New York, NY: Routledge.

van Manen, M. (2015). *Pedagogical tact: Knowing what to do when you don't know what to do*. New York, NY: Routledge.

Wiebe, S., & Margolin, I. (2012). Poetic consciousness in pedagogy: An inquiry of contemplation and conversation. *In Education, 18*(1), 23–36.

Wiebe, S., & Snowber, C. (2012). En/lived vulnere: A poetic of im/possible pedagogies. In S. Thomas, A. L. Cole, & S. Stewart (Eds.), *The art of poetic inquiry* (pp. 446–461). Big Tancook Island, NS: Backalong Books.

Wiebe, S., & Yallop, J. J. G. (2010). Ways of being in teaching: Conversing paths to meaning. *Canadian Journal of Education, 33*(1), 177–198.

CHAPTER 18

Looking In – Leading Out

Diane Burt

I don't like change. There, I've said it. I know most people don't, but I thought I was different. I have spent years researching, studying, and teaching theories and models of personal and organizational change. I have led many organizational changes from simple restructuring to full-scale transformations. I understand what people go through during times of transition. I recognize the signs of resistance, when people worry about loss of control over their environment or aspects of their work. I can see how fear of the unknown affects people. While I have spent a great deal of time trying to help others build their resilience and increase their ability to successfully navigate through change, I have not made a conscious effort to look inward – to spend time examining and reflecting on my own beliefs, preferences, and actions within the context of my work as both an educator and educational leader.

This chapter is a self-study that is both an introspective and retrospective examination of who I am as an educational change leader. Koster and van den Berg (2014) describe self study as a part of the action research tradition in education in that it is a method that can be used to study and improve one's practice. The goal of my self-study is three-fold. First, drawing on the work of Louie, Drevdahl, Purdy, and Stackman (2003), I hope to develop greater awareness of my development as a change leader in a post-secondary educational institution. I am specifically interested in exploring my resilience levels and my resiliency skill development during times of organizational change. Second, and guided by the seminal work of Abt-Perkins, Dale, and Hauschildt (1998) and Candy (1991), I hope to uncover how a deepened understanding of values and biases embedded in practice can help me and others build on strengths to overcome leadership limitations. Third, I hope to discover whether this self-study might inform a collaborative self-study at the institutional level (Louie et al., 2003). This final goal relates to my interest in utilizing appreciative inquiry as a process for professional growth and positive organizational change (Cooperrider, 2017).

Praxiological Reflection

Periodic self-reflective learning exercises can help us explore past and current experiences, attempt to make sense of personal and professional change, and reflect upon how we and others cope with change. Asking questions can focus self-reflections on specific thoughts, actions, and interactions with others during a change. The concept of praxiological reflection (Vasilev, 2016), which connects reflection to action or applies knowledge to practice, provides a practical approach to questioning. It involves questions like: 'How can I use what I learned here? What do I need to do to apply my new knowledge?' In this chapter, I will use questions to connect my reflections to my practice. Scharmer (2013) suggests that creating change requires a new consciousness – one where self-awareness comes before we can encourage change in a group. He names this shift as moving from an ego-system to an eco-system, a process that has three dimensions: better relating to others; better relating to the system; and better relating to oneself (Scharmer & Kaufer, 2013). Drawing on his argument that the most important aspect of leadership is knowing yourself, I reorder his dimensions such that leadership begins with relating to the self, then relating to others, and finally relating to the whole system.

Looking In: Relating to Self

Although I currently have a leadership position in an educational institution, I think of myself as an educator first. I taught full-time for several years, and I continue to teach part-time now, within an instructor development program and a Master of Education program. My experience has taught me that we need to have the tools to navigate change ourselves before we can assist others through a change or transition. Thomson (2014) also suggests that, once we understand what a change means for us, we can think about what it means for others and for the organization. In this spirit, I proceed by exploring my own interiority. Drawing on Tager and Willard (2001), I examine my coping levels and skills during times of change though considerations of stress, importance/control, and resilience.

Stress
People often associate change with feelings of unhealthy stress. However, healthy stress associated with change can encourage growth and foster motivation. Tager and Willard (2001) argue that stress can make people stronger. Thinking through their argument led me to recall situations when stress

helped me to. I also recalled times when too much stress threatened to become overwhelming.

> *I recall a change I experienced when I was a relatively new college department head. The first couple of years in the role were stressful for me. But it was a good kind of stress because I was learning a lot about leadership and administration, and I was stretching myself, really building my leadership capacities. The following year, we went through an organizational change and my role shifted considerably. All of a sudden, I had less responsibility – six direct reports instead of thirty and fewer programs and projects to lead. My stress level dropped. However, instead of relief, I felt unmotivated and unchallenged. I started taking longer lunches and, instead of working late on projects that excited me, I left the office at 4:30 every day. I had little accountability, and I was bored. I realized then I needed some degree of stress to push me to excel in my work. So, I left that job and took another one that proved to be more challenging. Over time, I took on more and more responsibility in that organization, and I found myself reaching a level of stress that was beyond my challenge limit. It took a while for me to figure out the right balance of stress that I require to perform at my peak, where I am motivated, challenged, and able to meet my goals.*

Through this reflection, I realize I have learned to be conscious about maintaining a balanced level of stress in my work. I think the kind of stress I need is something Sen, Mert, and Aydin (2017) call *encouraging stress* as opposed to *inhibiting stress*. I need some degree of continuity and stability, but I like deadlines and pressures to push me forward in my work. I also thrive on dealing with urgent issues and achieving quick wins. But I need to have breaks in between, where I can think and plan and be more proactive and creative. While I can maneuver through change, I like to arrive at a destination where I can feel settled for a while.

Importance/Control

Tager and Willard (2001) suggest we can assess change based on the degree to which it is within our control and according to its level of importance. The higher the degree of importance to us, the more we tend to worry about it; however, if we have a lot of control over the change, we can take action. It is when we have little control over a highly important change that we feel most uncomfortable. But even fairly unimportant changes that we can control may cause discomfort.

I have a small team that is geographically dispersed. Next month, we will have a new member join the team and, the following month, another one. I think the current group works well together as a team, and we make effective use of technology to connect regularly. There is an opportunity for two of us to move to a different site when the new team members come on board. I currently work in a nice office with new furniture in a convenient location. If we move to the other site, we will be in an old building, with old furniture, and parking will be limited. But the team will be together in one place enabling us to simply walk across the room instead of using Skype, email, or phone to connect. If I view this change through the control/ importance lens, I recognize I do have control over this change. I can decide whether to leave things as they are or move us all to one location. In terms of importance, I realize that this is not really important because we can be an effective and productive team whether we move or not. Therefore, my change problem has high control and low importance and I should stop worrying about it. I should simply make a decision and implement it. Here's the thing; I have not made the decision. I circle round and round without decisiveness. How can I access some deeper learning here? Why am I not making the decision to move?

I went back to read Kotter (2008). He says to behave with urgency every day. "Without urgency, all sorts of needed action is not initiated ... " (Kotter, 2008, p. 96). I am now thinking about whether I need a sense of urgency to push me to change. Maybe I do; maybe it is the same thing as needing a little bit of encouraging stress to help me to move forward.

Resilience

I know myself to be quite resilient, but I have had experiences where I did not cope well. These were situations that were highly important to me, but I felt I had no control. Tager and Willard (2001) suggest we each function normally at a certain level of well-being. When a change occurs that we perceive to be a negative change or a loss of some kind, depending on our readiness or resilience, we might follow one of three different paths. If we lack resilience, we may become anxious and despondent and simply give up (resignation). The second option is that our level of functioning may decrease slightly while we adjust to the change, but then we bounce back to where we were (resilience). The third path is when we not only bounce back, but we incorporate our learning from the change and move to a higher level of functioning (thriving); that is, we use the challenge to make us stronger.

When I was working in the learning and organizational development division of a national corporation, I was involved in leading an organizational restructuring initiative that involved moving from a regional divisional structure to a functional structure. This meant changes in the responsibilities of many team members and changes in how our team would work with others across the organization. It also resulted in new reporting relationships. I recall meeting with people individually to communicate the changes and discuss the impacts to their position. Every person reacted to the changes in their own way. Some perceived it negatively, thinking they were losing control over their work domains or were being shifted from areas of established competency to new and unknown areas of the business. Others were concerned about reporting to a new manager at another site. The level of well-being and efficient functionality for most dipped and, for some, dropped quite significantly. Once the new structure was implemented and employees were given support and time to adjust, I observed particular team members begin to bounce back. Those employees who were more resilient returned to their former level of functioning quickly. Over time, two employees in particular began to embrace the opportunities the new structure provided and they thrived. They were both eventually promoted.

It was difficult for me to lead others through this situation, knowing the individuals involved and observing how their readiness and resiliency levels impacted their abilities to deal with the change. I realized that I had the opportunity and the responsibility to help my team members build effective resiliency and coping skills that would enable them to get through not only this change, but other changes in the future. Thinking about this challenging time reinforces for me the notion that we cannot lead others if we do not understand our own reactions to change. It also makes me want to explore the practice of change leadership with my current colleagues.

Leading Out: Relating to Others

The previous reflection has my thoughts quickly moving forward to how I relate to others during change. One story in particular comes to mind.

I had been teaching English in an academic upgrading program for a few years. Early one fall, my department head asked to meet with me. She asked if I would be willing to teach math that year. I explained it was not my area of strength; I had a degree in English, and I had actually failed math in high school. She said she was stuck; she really needed me to teach math. It was a big change for me, but I agreed and began preparing as best as I could. I was assigned to work in a class with another teacher who would be teaching science, but who had taught math previously. For a while, I was doing quite well, considering the short notice to prepare and my lack of expertise. In fact, students seemed to appreciate my approach; we would often sit and figure things out together. I could relate to their struggles with the more complicated concepts. One day, though, I came across a math problem that I could not figure out, so I approached my colleague for help. She helped me but, later that day, she went to the department head and said I should not be teaching math. The department head called me to her office and told me of the concern. My response to this was twofold. First, I was trying to help the department head by taking on something that was obviously outside my area of expertise. I thought she should have explained that to the other teacher and asked for her support. Second, the other teacher should have had a conversation with me, rather than with the department head, about her concern. I had candid conversations with both of them about the issue and their behaviour. In fact, it was more like a respectful confrontation. Using Scott's (2002) purposes of confrontation, I interrogated reality, provoked learning, tackled a tough challenge, and enriched relationships. As a result, we were able to put together a plan where they supported me in my learning and teaching, and our relationships were not damaged, but strengthened.

I think back on this experience with this question in mind: 'How can I apply what I learned here?' As Vasilev (2016) explains, a praxiological reflection is one that does not just think about the 'what' and the 'why,' but also asks 'for what' and 'how' (p. 213). He stresses the idea is to "analyze not only the object or the result, but the means by which it is achieved" (Vasilev, 2016, p. 211). The 'for what' in my case was a better teaching experience for me and a better learning experience for my students. I knew I had to make it through the year, and I wanted to be as effective as possible. To do this, I needed support from my leader and from my co-teacher. The 'how' leads me to consider the practice of what Scott (2002) calls fierce conversations. Although this story happened quite early in my teaching career, and I was still somewhat professionally naïve, I grew up in a family that regularly engaged in real or fierce conversations. My parents were my roles models as they taught me not just to speak my mind, but how to do it. Scott (2002) says, "there is something within us that responds deeply to people who level with us" (p. 18). I observed many times my father's direct, honest, and clear approach in communicating with others, even in the toughest conversations. Being able to describe reality in a simple and compelling way is both an art and a skill. I think I was able tell my story to my department head and my colleague in a compelling way, explaining how I was trying to succeed and what I needed from them to support our mutual goals. I respectfully called them out on their approach, but I involved them in my problem, and I asked for their help. *Perhaps my ability to communicate with others, in a way that interrogates reality and provokes learning while enriching relationships, is a strength. Through praxiological reflection, I identify this ability as something I need to consciously cultivate in both myself and those who look to me for leadership.*

Collegial Collaboration: Relating to the System

Having attempted to become more aware of my own strengths and limitations when dealing with change, and having reflected upon how I relate to others, I want to consider how I might develop and improve change leadership practices within my organization through a collaborative self-study. I would like to invite others in my organization to explore our shared leadership practice in a collegial way.

I am sitting in a meeting with a group of colleagues, all educational leaders who are involved in an organizational restructuring initiative. We are discussing alternative structures and different ways to accomplish the same work. Our goal is to create new positions that will focus on new strategic priorities and initiatives to lead the organization forward; however, much of the old work will not go away immediately, so the group in the room and their teams will likely have to do more for a while. I can see and feel the resistance in the room. A couple of people say they support a proposed structure, but then they tear it apart, finding reasons why it will not work. Everyone is trying to be professional and supportive, but I can see fear and worry on some faces as I scan the room. One person says we need more time to implement the change. I can tell our leader is frustrated. I feel fortunate that I am not directly impacted by the change, but I am in a position to help others. I do my best to engage people in thinking through the options, keeping the vision and end goal in mind without losing sight of our current needs that must still be met. When a decision is finally reached and the meeting ends, I wonder how each person is feeling about the change, whether their personal values and biases will impact how they adapt, and how their leadership of the change will appear to their respective teams. Will their teams see fear,

reluctance, resistance, or disagreement, or will they see support and enthu-
siasm for the possibilities of the new direction?

This reflection left me considering where we are going as a college and how we might get there. One benefit of working in an educational organization is that our mandate is clear: we identify as a collaborative, learner-centred college that is committed to advancement through applied learning. We have a strategic goal to welcome more learners, which means we have to be more flexible and accessible. I am part of the leadership team that will help us achieve this goal. We are going to become a transformed college, changing from a traditional bricks and mortar institution to something very different. Where we are going is difficult to picture right now. Our entire leadership group must be engaged in imagining and achieving our future. As Wheatley and Kellner-Rogers (1998) say

> Participation is not a choice. We have no choice but to invite people into the process of rethinking, redesigning, restructuring the organization. We ignore people's need to participate at our own peril. If they're involved, they will create a future that already has them in it. We won't have to involve in the impossible and exhausting tasks of "selling" them the solution, getting them "to enroll," or figuring out the incentives that might bribe them into compliant behaviors. For the past fifty years a great bit of wisdom has circulated in the field of organizational behavior: People support what they create. In observing how life organizes, we would restate this maxim as: People *only* support what they create. (para. 22)

During the course of this reflection, I realized that involving this group of leaders in collaborative learning can be a valuable exercise. We can help each other lead out, engaging others and our organizational eco-systems, in the changes we need to make. A structured collaboration will ensure we are engaged in the creation of our futures. How can I use the learning from this reflection? Through a combined strengths-based and appreciative inquiry (AI) approach, I would like to design and facilitate a community of practice where my colleagues and I can tell stories of our successes, share best practices, and highlight effective approaches to change leadership. Utilizing an AI methodology could augment this self-study to strengthen organizational trust and create a safe environment in which to share our reflections, experiences, and stories (Burt, 2011). Similarly, positioning AI as a collaborative self-study would also help us enhance our relationships with one another as we seek deeper understanding with the aim of developing personally, professionally, and institutionally. Like McArthur-Blair and Cockell (2018), I maintain that this type of leadership is "about having the courage to invite others to engage and co-create in the everyday and in the complex times" (p. 40).

Conclusion

Looking back at the questions that I aimed to address through this self-study, I realize I have more thinking to do about how I engage with change. I have developed resiliency skills over my career. I am resilient when changes happens to me but, when I am in control of making change happen, I may not take action as quickly as I should. I seem to need some degree of external stress to help me take action. One strength I intend to cultivate in my leadership practice is having conversations with others that interrogate reality and provoke learning (Scott, 2002). I sense this is an area of potential that I need to take with me into the future. Finally, I intend to develop a collaborative learning group or community of practice with colleagues who are also interested in exploring the potential of looking in and leading out.

References

Abt-Perkins, D., Dale, H., & Hauschildt, P. (1998). Letters of intent: Collaborative self-study as reform in teacher education. In A. L. Coles, R. Elijah, & J. G. Knowles (Eds.), *The heart of the matter: Teacher educators and teacher education reform* (pp. 81–100). San Francisco, CA: Caddo Gap Press.

Biswas-Diener, R., Kashdan, T., & Minhas, G. (2011). A dynamic approach to psychological strength development and intervention. *The Journal of Positive Psychology, 6*(2), 106–118.

Burt, D. (2011). *Exploring employee involvement in change: Appreciative conversations with community college leaders* (ProQuest dissertation). Fielding Graduate University, Santa Barbara, CA. Retrieved from https://search.proquest.com/docview/907104959/fulltextPDF/D4216002A7664E77PQ/1?accountid=142373

Candy, P. C. (1991). *Self-direction for lifelong learning: A comprehensive guide to theory and practice.* San Francisco, CA: Jossey-Bass.

Conner, D. (1992). *Managing at the speed of change.* New York, NY: Random House, Inc.

Cooperrider, D. (2017). The gift of new eyes: Personal reflections after 30 years of appreciative inquiry in organizational life. In A. Shani & D. Noumair (Eds.), *Research in organizational change and development* (Vol. 25, pp. 81–142). Bingley: Emerald Publishing.

Cooperrider, D., & Whitney, D. (2005). *Appreciative inquiry: A positive revolution in change*. San Francisco, CA: Berrett-Koehler Publishers, Inc.

French, J., & Raven, B. (1959). The bases of social power. In D. Cartwright (Ed.), *Studies in social power* (pp. 150–167). Ann Arbour, MI: University of Michigan.

Koster, B., & van den Berg, B. (2014). Increasing professional self-understanding: Self study research by teachers with the help of biography, core reflection and dialogue. *Studying Teacher Education, 10*(1), 86–100.

Kotter, J. (2008). *A sense of urgency*. Boston, MA: Harvard Business School Publishing.

Louie, B. Y., Drevdahl, D. J., Purdy, J. M., & Stackman, R. W. (2003). Advancing the scholarship of teaching through collaborative self-study. *The Journal of Higher Education, 74*(2), 150–171.

McArthur-Blair, J., & Cockell, J. (2018). *Building resilience with appreciative inquiry*. Oakland, CA: Berrett-Koehler Publishers, Inc.

NBCC. (2017). *Together we rise: New Brunswick Community College 2017–2022 strategic plan*. Retrieved from http://nbcc.ca/docs/default-source/default-document-library/strategic-plan-2017-2022.pdf?sfvrsn=4/

Scharmer, O. (2006). Commentary. *Reflections, 7*(1), 28–29.

Scharmer, O. (2013). *Addressing the blind spot of our time: Executive summary*. Retrieved from https://www.presencing.com/executivesummary

Scharmer, O., & Kaufer, K. (2013). *Leading from the emerging future: From ego-system to eco-system economics*. San Fransciso, CA: Berrett-Koehler Publishers, Inc.

Scott, S. (2002). *Fierce conversations*. London: Penguin Books Ltd.

Sen, C., Mert, I., & Aydin, O. (2017). The effects of positive psychological capital on employee's job satisfaction, organizational commitment, and ability coping with stress. *Journal of Academic Research in Economics, 9*(2), 164–184.

Tager, M., & Willard, S. (2001). *Powersource: How people and organizations can transform stress and manage change*. La Jolla, CA: Workskills-Lifeskills.

Thomson, B. (2014). Coping with and introducing change. In *Understanding yourself and others*. London: Sheldon Press.

Vasilev, V. (2016). Reflection as an applied problem in psychology. *Cultural-Historical Psychology, 12*(3), 208–225.

Volckmann, R. (2013). Otto Scharmer: Theory U – Leading from the future as it emerges. *Integral Leadership Review*. Retrieved from http://integralleadershipreview.com/10916-otto-scharmer-theory-u-leading-future-emerges/

Writing from the Heart-Mind: Cultivating Not-Knowing towards an "Earthly Pedagogy"

Jodi Latremouille

Families, practices, languages,
roles both inherited and resisted,
times, places, heartbreaks and joys,
geographies known through the body
and breath and the labor of hands,
and, too, great arcs
of reminiscence,
ancestry,
old ways barely recollected
or inscribed in practices
learned hand over hand,
face to face,
full of forgotten-ness.
　　　　DAVID W. JARDINE (2014, p. 1)

∵

I

Reflexive practice implies a constant uncovering and journeying forward, a quest towards knowledge of oneself, in the interests of mastering a profession, a problem, a relationship, a student, a life. When we use writing in this journey sometimes we deftly turn a phrase, play with synonyms, metaphor, and imagery. It can be thrilling for a writer to evoke tears, laughter, and gasps of recognition or insight from their audience. Yet, one of my dearest friends and mentors, David Jardine, ever reminds me that there is a difference between being *clever* and being *wise*. He points to a self-reflexive practice that "leads out" beyond mere self-referential cleverness towards a more earthly, relational wisdom. He whispers a soft aside, or utters a sharp injunction: "what is it *good* for?" (Jardine, personal communication, n.d.).

David Geoffrey Smith (2014) calls for educators to "reimagine new, wiser, human possibilities given the deep [ecological, economic, social, cultural ...] damage suffered at local domestic levels, both at home and abroad" (p. 1). This question of "what is it good for?" is relevant, too, in educational practice, where the allure of cleverness – in the languages of cutting-edge pedagogy, of excellence, of high-tech curriculum delivery – is often characterized by a low-grade buzz of exciting new developments, of endless, vacuous *innovation*. Teachers can pick and choose from an array of innovations to suit any classroom. We are relentlessly inspired by emails from our administrators encouraging us to attend one-off professional developments workshops, or by tips and tricks splashed all over educational websites. All of these innovations *could* be good but many come with a (false) stamp of approval and guarantee: evidence-based, "proven" methods for increasing efficiency, creativity, workplace skills, docility, critical thinking, and so on. And yet, a question remains. "Young people want to know if, under the cool and calm of efficient teaching and excellent time-on-task ratios, life itself has a chance, or whether the surface is all there is" (Smith, 1988, p. 27). All of these practices are *possible*, but not necessary or inevitable, in the grand smorgasbord of educational cleverness and efficient mastery.

Life itself *does* have a chance. It is *also* possible for pedagogy to be experienced as earthly: as a multiple, layered, and relational (Smith, 1999) *not-knowing*, with each un-covering insight implying a covering or re-covering of something else beyond my limited understanding. When I recognize the world, and my own conception of myself within it as *greater than my knowledge of it* (Berry, 1983), my self-recognition as a human being living in, depending on, and being responsible for particular places and communities requires a "healthy humility" (Smith, 1997, p. 1).

In these reflections on my journey as a teacher and instructor in faculties of education, I ask how I find myself identified by and accountable to these layered and composting relations in and with my earthly places and beings-in-relation (Haraway, 2016). "It is precisely the difficulty of living in a specific place, with specific people, under specific conditions, that inspires the need for reflection and a deepening of our understanding of what we truly need to live" (Smith, 1997, p. 1). This questioning includes even those – and perhaps especially those – beyond my realms of knowing. As I cultivate and compose more lively, generous, careful, incomplete, loving, and not-known understandings of self-in-relation, I seek an imperfect opening of my "heart-mind" (Macy, 2014, par. 6) towards a multiple, layered, and relational "earthly pedagogy."

In this chapter, I dwell in narrative, ecohermeneutic life writing, and poetic inquiry (Butler-Kisber, 2005, 2010; Derby, 2015; Brady, 2009; Hasebe-Ludt,

Chambers, & Leggo, 2009) as a form of not-knowing towards a relational earthly pedagogy. I compose, de-compose, and re-compose an unfinished understanding of myself as a being-in-relation who lives, loves, and suffers together-with-others in the midst of our collective earthly trouble (Haraway, 2016). In this ecological practice I seek to become "increasingly skilled in learning to read and understand [my] own childhood ... to understand [my] personal and collective pasts in a truly pedagogic way, that is, in a way that contributes positively and dialogically to a new understanding and appreciation for the world" (Smith, 1988, p. 27). This writing entails risks and possibilities, as it takes up self-reflexive poetic practice as a vulnerable act of conviviality and possibility. Through these writings, I explore how subtle shifts in educational language – away from the tenets of cleverness and mastery, and towards inklings of wisdom and mystery – may nourish a self-reflexive practice of richer, more evocative, more communal pedagogical possibilities. In these writings, I find myself accountable to those topics, languages, ancestors, children, more-than-human relations, and the questions of my seven-year-old daughter. In the spirit of possibility, I eschew a standardized literature review, I evade a methodical treatment of methodologies, and I shy away from clear-cut conclusions and precise practical advice. Rather, this work "meanders and wanders, ruminates and cogitates, interrogates and invites" (Leggo, 2018, p. 73).

II

Life writing and poetic inquiry, as creative and critical forms of discourse (Leggo, 2018), serve as sites of critique, both of one's own practice, and of the fields and boundaries opened up to the world. The work of writing that is conducive to playing in these fields comes with the recognition that our meanings can never be complete, whole, or defining. I notice that "[t]his 'worded world' never accurately, precisely, completely captures the studied world" (Richardson, 2001, p. 35). Self-reflexive writing as inquiry in a dialogical context allows meanings to emerge, crystallize, retreat, show up once again. In merging the horizons between method and art, I may play on boundaries that encourage me to reflect on the nature of knowledge. Poetry and life writing is "both a style of representation as well as a vehicle through which the academic/research community can engage in larger questions about the nature of social research, truth, and knowledge" (Leavy, 2009, p. 84). In developing my abilities to reflect upon and understand my own histories, I begin to read my "personal and collective pasts in a truly pedagogic way" (Smith, 1988, p. 27). Like bell hooks

(2003), I share my personal narratives "to remind folks that we are all struggling to raise our consciousness and figure out the best action to take" (p. 107). As I write through a relational earthly pedagogy, I write outwards to the infinite and constitutive relations with my students, our topics of study, our locales, our more-than-human relations. These openings allow me to then spiral back down to an intimate, sensuous understanding of myself-in-relation.

> There is an intimate reciprocity to the senses; as we touch the bark of a tree, we feel the tree *touching us;* as we lend our ears to the local sounds and ally our nose to the seasonal scents, the terrain gradually tunes us in in turn. The senses, that is, are the primary way that the earth has of informing our thoughts and of guiding our actions. Huge centralized programs, global initiatives, and other 'top down' solutions will never suffice to restore and protect the health of the animate earth. *For it is only at the scale of our direct, sensory interactions with the land around us that we can appropriately notice and respond to the immediate needs of the living world.* (Abram, 1997, p. 268)

With this sensory intimacy in mind, which brings to bear all of my embodied ways of knowing in and through the world, I seek to foster dialogical and transformative (Cole & Knowles, 2001, p. 213) conversations with students that tend to learning in its own right, that list and sway towards wisdom and mystery.

> *now, a question ...*

> *What might education be when it is seen as abundant, convivial, enmeshed in those whispers trailing back/from/into/within worlds of relations?*

> *and a question ...*

> *What happens when the stories we tell of education are grounded in rich histories, lived topics, real people, and earthly potentialities?*

On Being Smart

Please
Don't tell me that I'm smart.
I've heard it a million times and so have you
Thank you, but I am so done with the platitudes

If you can't say anything nice, don't say anything at all, young lady!

At one time, I held onto it so tightly
As if being smart could show me the way, protect me
Navigate me through the wondrous, terrifying uncertainty
To that silent bubble of pristine, calm, collected control

But the language is the control, oh my god, no
Me
My classmates
My relations
My babies
Setting up the dichotomy, knocked down by the judgment

Rank us

And set us on the right path
The one pre-determined for each of us
Ordained by the Ministry of Aptitude (insert heavenly music, maestro)
You are on the path to nowhere, young man
Oh no! I wail at the sheer hopelessness of my life!
But you, young lady, can do anything you want
Thank you, oh thank you sir! Bobbing head, backing out

Are you in or are you out?
Just work harder, and you can play on the margins for a while
But you will never be really in
The desired label eludes you
I, on the other hand,
Am in the club
But don't forget, with every next test, I could be thrown out
Without a second glance
Turn back, nose squashed on a slamming oak door
All it takes is one mis-step and
Teetering on the edge, I tumble into the vast out
Only to claw back, redeemed, I hope, in time
Keep working hard

I learned to wonder, oh yes
I learned to wonder about wondrous things

Like how I was being judged
And if I was cutting it
Cutting myself properly
Could my grand plan outlast my life?
A war of attrition
That can only be won looking back
From the future of my past
And what good is it to me then?

So don't tell me I'm smart
I might be
Today
Or once upon a time
Or forever
But that is not what I want to talk about

We, here, now
We have better language than that
Beautiful, functional, shifting language
And isn't that the wonder of it
It is time to start existing in that space
The space of the collective
Collective brilliance, oh yes, friend, give it to me!
Give me that moment when our sheer genius is so overwhelming
That it bursts out upon our glowing, nodding faces
Gasps out of us in unbidden exhalations

I am part of something
Oh yah, bring it on, something big like an ocean of grains of sand
Something so small it is like a tiny newborn chick in the palm of my hand
A bundle of peeping yellow fluff,
flopping around and hoping for strength to stand
stand and take up its space under the warm glow
I can no longer ignore it
Too big to bury myself in
Too small and precious to cover up and leave
Leave it in the future, frozen

I can no longer hide from us behind my smartness
I am being called to listen, to act, to speak,

to be tongue-tied and insistent
As we all are, in our ways and places and spaces of being

Finding my voice does not make me unique
It does not make me amazing or special or wonderful
To claim special is to despair of my entire life of relations
My voice and your silence makes us part of something
Yes, together in our variousness
Our gut reactions and compositions
Please don't single me out as a martyr to the machine

That is their language

To separate and annihilate

To hold up one is to push down another

That is their language

Not ours
Let us Other the obvious
We build
We build with words
We build with words these beautiful,
terrible,
common uncommon understandings
We build with love
We build with love our connected,
Yes connected,
Simple,
Strange and heartful interpretations
We are not broken-down, isolated, smart pathologies
We are broken, yes
Broken traditions in the making
But not broken-down
Let us love that
Let us love words and wonder and questions
Let us be grateful
And powerful
And humble

But not smart
Not me
And not you

III

As a writer and educator who is "willing to endure failure as the price of admission" (Berry, 2013, n.p.), I embrace a deep vulnerability that opens up spaces
for relational pedagogy, but I also open myself to the pain of "coming up short"
(n.p.). When I try to face my own layered imperfections and inconsistencies as
an educator, I recognize in my storytelling Okri's (1997) sense of "a fundamental human unease [that] hints at human imperfection" (p. 112). Because I can
never manage, control, or predict how others will respond (Hasebe-Ludt et al.,
2009, p. 7), self-reflexive life writing and relational teaching are, in many ways,
acts of faith (Hendry, 2007, p. 492). And here, precisely, is where the openings
arise: in these patchy sketches, these bumbling quarrels, these faithful writings.
Narrative and poetic inquiry, like ecological understandings and relational
pedagogies, are irreducible to clever methods and confident pre-conceived outcomes (Hendry, 2010). And yet, when I open myself to the potential risks and
ethical obligations of inquiry, I may also create openings for the possibility of
"transformation through education" (Hasebe-Ludt et al., 2009, p. 1). Not knowing the answers in advance *could* be understood in some educational languages
as a form of weakness or the lack of a particular brand of control-preparation.
But *that* story, too, is neither necessary nor inevitable. It is *also* possible to speak
in poetic languages of earthly possibilities, and in the languages of love. "The
new language we need in education is the language of love, which is always
committed to possibility and hope. This kind of language is always radical"
(Leggo, 2018, p. 74). Here, now, in writing in a language of love, a space is opened
whereby we may re-story this relational work as an undertaking of *courage*.

A call ... from Carl Leggo

... the academy is a speed dating service
where there is no romance, no seduction,
just reduction and a stupefying trance

we need textual intercourse full of pleasure,
instead of this coitus interruptus that leaves us

desiccated, depleted, dry like a dean's dirge
about branding, and random, never randy,
encounters with potential wealthy benefactors

we need to claim more, declaim more
exclaim more, proclaim more
we need to reclaim
the bold voices of poetry

our poetry needs to startle
our poetry needs to howl

... who wants cosmetic curriculum
when the cosmos calls, a cacophony

chaos is not wild & random, instead
inimitably orderly & complex

cosmos & chaos dance
an Argentinian tango

moment by moment in the momentous
composing of living wholeness

like a poem is never closed & controlled
curriculum is emergent & startling

we are not sentenced to linear expression
sitting meekly at desks in tight uniforms

curriculum attends to the spaces between
letters & words & lines where poetry grows

with spell-binding delight in wild possibilities
leaning into love with tantalizing hope for the other
        (Selections from Carl Leggo, 2018)

And a response ...

A confessional to the academy

I have a confession ...

I have been studying and working in universities for eleven years ...
Yes, count them, eleven years,

And

Shhhh ...

I still don't know what "epistemological" means.
No, not really.
I know it goes with "ontological" somehow
I know that because they told me
Over and over and over again
In every philosophy class I ever took

Oh, I have a vague intellectual sense
But I confess,

A good friend once even made me a cheat sheet,

and still,

"The way we know things" (hint: epistemology)

And "what things are" (hint: the other one)

Still feel fuzzy, woozy, swarmy to me ...
I get a hot little rush every time I read one of those words
Or hear someone else obviously much smarter than me
Casually tossing it around
Like they're playing a sport they are so good at they could do it with their
eyes closed
I have to pause and calm myself down, breathe
They're simple words, really
But all the world is in those two words
The responsibility to wield them well feels
Really heavy

I have another confession …

I am not good at drawing boundaries.
On anything.
Never have been, well, actually, I used to be better than I am now

Not on disciplines
(How can you have economics without philosophy and ecology? Math without art? Physical education without psychology?)

Not on rooms
(I study on my couch and exercise in my bedroom. I send students to the library to hang out and outside to read)

Not on relationships
(I can be a friend *and* a teacher, can't I? But just not at the same time? What? I don't get it)

Not on ecosystems
(I am most at home in the ecotone – yes, look it up, don't worry, I had to my first time too. I now confidently claim it as my epistemology – can I even *say* that and still have a real job in the academy?)

Not on my life
(Mother, scholar, wife, beekeeper, artist, singer, poet, sapiosexual, environmentalist, wonderer, feminist, traveler, pianist, cook – am I even allowed to claim things I am really, really bad at?)

Not on other lives
(How do I, a teacher, grade a life? Based on the size of the word-stones they hurl at others to impress me in class discussions? Based on the fact that just making it to class every day is a victory in their life? Based on a sterile, static rubric? Based on how many years they have been speaking and writing "my" English? Based on how much money their parents make? Based on how much they travel? Based on what they had for dinner last night? Based on "self-esteem?" Growth? Stagnation? Passion? Pride? How do I grade a life?)

I have a third confession …

I am very very bad at teaching

None of my answers ever *say* anything
that helps my students figure out
what to do!
I don't know the answers.
Ever.
I tell stories that don't make sense
Sometimes even to me
They don't get to the point
They wander and digress
And they're never clear
With no conclusions
They just peter out into silence

I have a final confession ...

This is what I believe it is to teach
                                            ... badly.

IV

Another way to evaluate a story is by its consequences when we live according to it. (Loy, 2010, p. 16)

The writing-work and our responses to this work, too, are never fully grasped in an end-game articulation, never extinguished in a final proclamation of all-encompassing knowledge, for "it is in fact an infinite process" (Gadamer, 2004, p. 298). Each time I return to a story, I am changed, too, and thus the work is never completely, neatly bound up and finished. "... living with children means living in the belly of a paradox wherein genuine life together is made possible only in the context of an ongoing conversation which is never over, yet *which must be sustained for life together to go on at all* (emphasis added)" (Smith, 1988, p. 27).

In the poem "Advice from the Geese" (Bly, 2018), the geese urge me to

"Hurry! The world is not going to get better!
Do what you want to do now! [...]
"Please don't expect that the next president will be better than this one"
(n.p.)
They remind me that, perhaps, no, everything is not going to be *all ... right.*
It isn't going to get better, not for sure.

And in the face of uncertainty and despair, in the face of climate change, and ever-narrowing boundaries of what counts as research, what counts as teaching, and in the face of young people who hope there is something more to life than the "surface," the geese advocate for one simple act: to study (Bly, 2018, n.p.).

This reflexive practice creates a space from which to respond to my children, my students, my earth-relations, as subject[s] not of mastery but "of mystery – producing wonder and awe in us" (Huebner, 2008, p. 8). I am called upon to respond to this wonder and awe with an earthly pedagogy of relational implicatedness. And when I approach life's curriculum offerings with wonder and awe, as a being-in-relation *implicated* in the stories of curriculum in the lives of young people and all of our more-than-human relations, my teaching life is – and becomes – more carefully, and more patiently, measured.

> The answers will come not from walking up to your farm and saying this is what I want and this is what I expect from you. You walk up and you say what do you need. And you commit yourself to say all right, I'm not going to do any extensive damage here until I know what it is that you are asking of me. And this can't be hurried. This is the dreadful situation that young people are in. I think of them and I say well, the situation you're in now is a situation that's going to call for a lot of patience. And to be patient in an emergency is a terrible trial. (Berry, 2013, n.p.)

Active Falling in Progress: Keep Out

the long arm of the excavator
bright orange mechanical industrial efficient
rises up above the roofline of the doomed bungalow
we know how it goes
drops down I hear the crunch snap squealing wheels
powersaw teeth roar
all morning, murder and loud voices strategizing
the next cracking splintering

fall ...

balsam

and fall ...

fir

and fall and fall again ...

cedar and spruce

fall ...

blackberries
brambles rising up to the roofline yes twenty feet high how marvelous we
picked our bellies full just last week
ripped out
I smell the crushed ripe berries from all the way back here
Where I sit
in the backyard
the backyard still intact
for now
a delicate rustling back here in the underbrush
a young black industrious squirrel
scrambling up the trunk of the towering cedar
that shades my afternoon work
I dreamed once of a way to dig them all up and bring them all home with me
impossible
too big too many too pricey too alive too crazy I know

I know ...

and all those people need
somewhere to live I know

I know ...

I can't stand to work for a moment not at this very moment
roaring crunching blackberry wafting moment

I know too much

I mourn
calmly resigned
at least on the outside

It's Life
no! not *life-*

Development

Building Futures

Progress

Active Falling in Progress:

Keep Out

V

As an educator I am compelled and challenged by the responsibilities of doing more, doing better, doing what works, doing what *they* are doing over *there*, gaining mastery over my practice. I tend to hamster-wheel in the *next best thing* excitement or alternatively, the weary, moribund *seen it all before* and *that didn't work last time* dismissals. Both of these spinning-out exhaustions arise from my suspicion that this *cleverness* lacks the earthy character of wisdom: a heart-mindful reckoning with the ecological questions of responsibility and renewal. "We don't have a right to ask whether we are going to succeed or not. We only have the right to ask Wendell Berry's (2013) enduring question, 'what's the right thing to do? What does this earth require of us if we want to continue to live on it?'" (n.p.). It takes the piercing, ushering reminders of my human and more-than-human teachers, to bring me up against myself, to loosen the grasp of confident and contented cleverness, to do something that is *good* for something, for someone, here, now, that (I hope) may more wisely honour the mystery of this place and these relations (Somerville, 2012). I thus propose that a self-reflexive practice of not-knowing towards an earthly pedagogy requires an "honest mutual consideration of problems held in common" (Smith, 2014, p. 9); a simultaneous uncovering what was forgotten, and a covering and re-covering of what has become too obvious. I am *held to account* by those topics, ancestors, children, more-than-human relations that I work, breathe, mourn, and play with – we, in not-knowing kinship with each other. In this narrative and poetic self-reflexive practice, I seek to cultivate a relational pedagogy of wisdom and abundant mystery. I ask of my work with children and young people: What might this writing/research/pedagogy be good for? Who might it serve? How does it nourish possibilities for freedom, peace, love, health, breath, soul, the continuation of life on earth? How are we held to account by the earthly consequences of the stories that we live by?

Now, a question ...

Now she stands in front of her classroom, reaching for this ineffable sense of kinship with things, pointing and hoping, not for explanations, but for the right kinds of questions, for what *calls for questions.* (Derby, 2015, p. 1)

and, a final question ...

mythological meditations of a seven-year-old
on a frigid, snowy day in February
Mom, I worry about all the other animals and plants and everything on
this planet
Sometimes I wonder, how did this happen?
Well, I wonder, because, you know
in maybe the last hundred years or so,
or maybe about two hundred years
humans came on this earth and started to expand,
to take over the world.
We just took over the world.
How did this happen, Mom?
    (K. Nyeste, personal communication, February 27, 2018)

References

Abram, D. (1997). *The spell of the sensuous: Perception and language in a more-than-human world.* New York, NY: Vintage Books.

Berry, W. (1983). *Standing by words.* San Francisco, CA: North Point Press.

Berry, W. (2013). *Wendell Berry: Poet and prophet* (Online interview with Bill Moyers). Retrieved from http://billmoyers.com/segment/wendell-berry-on-his-hopes-for-humanity/

Bly, R. (2018). *Advice from the geese* (Audiorecording). New York, NY: Academy of American Poets. Retrieved from http://www.poets.org/poetsorg/poem/advice-geese

Brady, I. (2009). Foreword. In M. Pendergrast, C. Leggo, & P. Sameshima (Eds.), *Poetic inquiry: Vibrant voices in the social sciences* (pp. xi–xvi). Rotterdam, The Netherlands: Sense Publishers.

Butler-Kisber, L. (2005). Poetic inquiry. In L. Butler-Kisber & A. Sullivan (Eds.), *Poetic inquiry in qualitative research. Journal of Critical Inquiry into Curriculum and Instruction, 5*(1), 1–4.

Butler-Kisber, L. (2010). *Qualitative inquiry: Thematic, narrative and arts-informed perspectives.* Thousand Oaks, CA: Sage Publications.

Cole, A., & Knowles, G. (2001). Qualities of inquiry: Process, form, and 'goodness.' In L. Neilsen, A. L. Cole, & J. G. Knowles (Eds.), *The art of writing inquiry* (pp. 211–219). Halifax, NS: Backalong Books.

Derby, M. (2015). *Place, being, resonance: A crtical ecohermeneutic approach to education.* New York, NY: Peter Lang.

Gadamer, H.-G. (2004). *Truth and method* (3rd ed., J. Weinsheimer & D. G. Marshall, Trans.). London: Continuum. (Original work published in 1975)

Haraway, D. (2016). *Staying with the trouble: Making kin in the chthulucene.* Durham, NC: Duke University Press.

Hasebe-Ludt, E., Chambers, C. M., & Leggo, C. (2009). *Life writing and literary métissage as an ethos for our times.* New York, NY: Peter Lang.

Hendry, P. M. (2010). Narrative as inquiry. *The Journal of Educational Research, 103,* 72–80.

Hendry, P. M. (2007). The future of narrative. *Qualitative Inquiry, 13,* 487–496.

hooks, b. (2003). *Teaching community: A pedagogy of hope.* New York, NY: Routledge.

Huebner, D. E. (2008). The capacity for wonder and education. In V. Hills (Ed.), *The lure of the transcendent: Collected essays by Dwayne E. Huebner* (pp. 1–9). New York, NY: Routledge. (Original work published in 1959)

Jardine, D. W. (2014). "You need accuracy": An appreciation of a modern hunting tradition. *In Education: Exploring our Connective Educational Landscape, 20*(2), 1–2.

Leavy, P. (2009). *Method meets art: Arts-based research practice.* New York, NY: The Guilford Press.

Leggo, C. (2018). Poetry in the academy: A language of possibility. *Canadian Journal of Education, (Teaching Creativity, Creatively Teaching), 41*(1), 70–97.

Loy, D. R. (2010). *The world is made of stories.* Somerville, MA: Wisdom Publications.

Macy, J. (2014). Joanna Macy on how to prepare internally for whatever comes next. *Ecobuddhism.* Retrieved from www.ecobuddhism.org/wisdom/interviews/jmacy

Matchar, E. (2015, June 5). Seven inspiring innovations in education from around the globe. *Smithsonian.* Retrieved from https://www.smithsonianmag.com/innovation/seven-inspiring-innovations-in-education-from-around-the-globe-180955484/

Okri, B. (1997). *A way of being free.* London: Phoenix House.

Richardson, L. (2001). Getting personal: Writing-stories. *International Journal of Qualitative Studies in Education, 14*(1), 33–38.

Smith, D. G. (1988). Children and the gods of war. *Phenomenology + Pedagogy, 6*(1), 25–29.

Smith, D. G. (1997). The geography of theory and the pedagogy of place. *The Journal of Curriculum Theorizing, 13*(3), 1–8.

Smith, D. G. (1999). *Pedagon: Interdisciplinary essays in the human sciences, pedagogy and culture*. New York, NY: Peter Lang.

Smith, D. G. (2014). *Teaching as the practice of wisdom*. New York, NY: Bloomsbury.

Somerville, M. (2012). The critical power of place. In S. R. Steinberg & G. S. Cannella (Eds.), *Critical qualitative research reader* (Vol. 2., pp. 67–81). New York, NY: Peter Lang.